CUT the CLUTTER DROP the POUNDS

The Six-Week Plan to
Shed Your Weight, Worries, and Stuff

PETER WALSH

This book is being published simultaneously in the trade by Rodale Inc. as *Lose the Clutter, Lose the Weight*.

© 2015 by Peter Walsh

All rights reserved. No part of this publication may be reproduced or transmitted in any form or by any means, electronic or mechanical, including photocopying, recording, or any other information storage and retrieval system, without the written permission of the publisher.

Printed in the United States of America

Rodale Inc. makes every effort to use acid-free ♾, recycled paper ♻.

Book design by Christina Gaugler

Photographs by Thomas MacDonald / Rodale Images

Library of Congress Cataloging-in-Publication Data is on file with the publisher.

ISBN-13: 978–1–62336–483–0 direct

2   4   6   8   10   9   7   5   3   1   hardcover

We inspire and enable people to improve their lives and the world around them.
For more of our products, visit **rodalestore.com** or call 800-848-4735

To those who've always helped me keep my perspective:
Christine and David
James and Vicky
Julie
Kay and Paul
Kelvin
Michael and Gloria
Steve and Amanda

CONTENTS

Part 3:
THE SIX-WEEK PROGRAM BEGINS

INTRODUCTION

How Did I Get This Way?

I t's a reasonable question to ask when you see a vacation photo that gives you a pang of shock at your appearance.

You may have a photo like that. You'd been happily going along, ignoring the deep indentation that the waistband of your jeans was leaving in your skin (so much for "relaxed fit") or the appearance of new numbers or letters in your bra size.

But there's no getting around this photo, which looks nothing like the image you see in your mind. Somehow, at some point, you became too large for your comfort. Now you know the truth, but you aren't sure what to do about it.

How Did I Let My Home Get This Way?

Another common question. As with your body, the state of your household can sneak up on you. Sure, you know that things are a little messy. But when your aunt arrives at your door unexpectedly—or your pastor, or the new neighbors, or the air conditioner guy—you suddenly see the place through that person's eyes. You didn't really let yourself think about it before, but now you can't avoid it: Your home embarrasses you.

So how did you get here? Given the environment we live in, I'd say a more useful question is this: How can your body and home *not* get to this point?

If you're an American—or have the good fortune to live in a similarly modernized country—you're surrounded by abundance. Advertising messages whisper, plead, and shout at you all day long to buy, buy, buy. Buy something to eat! Buy something to put in your hair! Buy something to put in your kitchen cabinet! Clever marketing tells you that your life is *good*, but if you'll buy this one thing, it'll be *great*! Or, more pointedly, that you can have the life you want if you just buy the right things.

You're also surrounded by easy choices. Why dirty your pots and pans when you can go out to eat and someone will make your meal for you? Hold that thought. Why take an entire hour to eat at a sit-down restaurant when you can roll your car through the drive-thru? Wait . . . even better: Order a sub sandwich from your smartphone and have it delivered to your home. You don't even have to get up.

On that note, why spread your own mulch when the landscaper who left a flyer in your mailbox will do it for you? Why stand up and go for a jog when you're comfortable sitting on the couch? Why go to the hassle of throwing out a bunch of stuff when you can just stash it in the garage and park your car outside?

These have all become perfectly normal decisions for many people.

That's not to say that Americans don't like to work. In 2013, the average American worker put in 1,788 hours on the job. We spent more time working than our counterparts in France (1,489 hours), England (1,669 hours), and even Germany (1,388 hours). And Americans receive less paid time off, in the form of vacation days and paid holidays, than people in many other nations. Surveys have found that many workers can't even tear themselves away from the job to take all their vacation days over the course of the year.

If you're putting in long hours at the office—then juggling work issues over your phone and computer in the evening while you're trying to raise a family— it's not surprising that you would look for shortcuts whenever you can. If society offers a way for you to eat faster, handle a chore more quickly, or feel better about yourself for just a few bucks, how can you resist? Everyone else seems to be doing it.

So you wind up living like the average, everyday people around you. You buy a lot of stuff, and you take things easy when you can. Most days, it won't occur to you to examine the effect these "normal" choices are having on your life.

Perhaps you don't notice that your pants size has grown because you see other people your size every day. If you pluck three American adults out of the crowd at random, only one will have a normal, healthy weight. The second will be overweight. The third will be obese, or in other words, extremely overweight. When two-thirds of those around us are heavy, then heavy becomes the new normal. The one who's at a healthy weight is *unusual*.

Manufacturers are adjusting their products to keep up with the nation's growing girth. The world around you now offers extra-large ambulances and stadium seats and movie theater seats and operating tables and caskets—all built to be extra spacious and strong to accommodate the typical modern user. Like the ever-growing portion sizes at restaurants, these subtle enlargements in your surroundings seem normal now. They can reinforce the idea that there's no reason to change your eating habits, your exercise habits, or your size.

And just as you might not notice your growing weight because your surroundings mask it, you may not notice how overstuffed your home has become. Your friends and neighbors, and your counterparts in other affluent countries around the world, tend to have a *lot* of stuff crowding their homes and their lives, too. The portion of American adults who meet the criteria of hoarding disorder is now estimated to be a little over 5 percent. This means that every year, about **23 times** more people in the United States have a hoarding problem than have a heart attack!

I'm convinced that the number of Americans who *don't* meet the definition of hoarding, but who have so much household clutter that it's hampering their lives, is much, much higher. If you doubt me on this, I challenge you to drive down any suburban American street on a sunny spring day when garage doors are often up. How many garages do you see in your neighborhood that are so overstuffed with clutter that it's impossible to park a car in them?

These aren't the people who are clinging to floor-to-ceiling stacks of moldy newspapers, but they're not comfortable inviting company over. They may never need a team of workers in hazmat suits to empty the contents of their home into a Dumpster, but they could easily fill a bunch of trash cans, then throw a terrific yard sale with the items they no longer need, use, or want.

As I'm writing this, my Facebook page shows me standing in someone's backyard in my native Australia. I'm over there fairly often as the decluttering and organising (that's how they spell it Down Under!) expert on an Australian TV program. In the photo, which is taken from a distance, you can see a tiny Peter Walsh standing in a sea of furniture, boxes, and general *stuff*. This giant trove of material possessions was taken from just three rooms of the house I was working in. More than 300 boxes of books, memorabilia, craft supplies, clothing, shoes, toys, and paperwork . . . from just three rooms in one home.

The house was quite cluttered—but I wouldn't say it's that far outside the norm. It's an example of what many people would call a normal life, just as being overweight or even obese is now quite average.

Everywhere we look we see people living in cluttered homes. Most of the bodies maneuvering around inside those homes are also overcluttered with extra flesh around the waist and under the chin.

These homes typically aren't small. The average size of a new house in the United States has swelled by more than 60 percent since 1973. That's a lot of extra room to contain more stuff. More clutter. More stress. (But many people tell me that they feel an ever-present sense that they *still* don't have enough room.)

People struggling with too-heavy bodies and overstuffed homes often have heavy mental and emotional burdens, too. This is also a type of clutter, even though it's not as visible as the clutter in our homes and on our hips. In 2010, more than 20 percent of American adults were taking a medication to treat mental health issues—often depression and anxiety.

You can see this unhappiness in the faces in checkout lines. You hear it from your co-workers in the morning. You can feel a low buzz of people's tired impatience as they wish they were somewhere other than where they are right now.

If you're unhappy, frazzled, and dissatisfied, then you're like many of the people around you. If the thought of feeling energetic, excited to be alive, and truly interested in the well-being of others seems foreign, perhaps it's because you don't see enough examples of people living that way.

Household clutter, obesity, and mental health concerns often travel together. In many cases, people are wobbling under the weight of more than one of these kinds of clutter. Often, they have all three.

I've seen this connection with my own eyes. Many of the clients I've worked with—and the people I've met in my many years as a professional organizer—weigh more than they'd like. They've talked to me about the stress and sadness they feel, both in relation to their household clutter and their general state of mind.

How about you? How would you describe the state of your home, your body, and your mind? What has become your "normal"? As I run through some contrasting scenarios, where do you fall on the scale from terrific to terrible?

Your Home

When you walk into your home, do you . . .

 . . . have that "I'm on vacation" feeling you get when you walk into a freshly cleaned hotel room?

Or do you . . .

. . . feel the full weight of all your possessions crush your spirit when you walk in the door?

Your Body

Does your body . . .

 . . . feel light and free? Could you go for a brisk walk for an hour? Can you lean over and touch your toes? Can you get into and out of your car easily?

Or do you . . .

. . . drive around for a few minutes to find the closest parking space to your shopping destination? Do you see those electric carts at the supermarket and feel a pang of concern that your weight will cause you to need one someday?

Your Mind

Would you say that you . . .

 . . . generally take note of the beauty and potential in the world around you? Do you feel grateful for the good things in your life? Do you make most of your choices deliberately and with your full attention? Are you alert and awake during the day? Do you feel no more than the occasional sadness or stress?

Or are you . . .

. . . tired . . . distracted . . . bored . . . anxious . . . or depressed? Do you often buy something to eat or drink, to read or wear, or to hang on a wall or put in a cabinet because it will ease your discomfort or make your life seem better? Do you feel a closer bond to the people in your life than to your *stuff*?

Perhaps these questions make you realize that you've been following the crowd for years, doing the same things they do, and you've ended up somewhere you don't want to be. How do you create a new "normal"—one that reflects the life you want and yearn for? How do you abandon all these habits? How do you start making the choices that aren't typical but that lead you to a better place?

Let Go of Your Overstuffed Life

As a professional organizer, I've been into hundreds of homes and offered advice to thousands—if not tens of thousands—of people on how to tame their messy, cluttered, disorganized spaces.

Whether from the clients I work with personally or from the large audiences I interact with online, through media, or at public events, I've fielded many questions that have the same answer. "My closet is stuffed full of quilts that Grandma left me. I never use them but can't bear to get rid of them. What should I do?" Or, "As I approach retirement, I'm thinking about downsizing to a smaller home. I have all the artwork and toys and books that belonged to my kids. I've kept this stuff for them all these years, but they don't want it. What do I do with it?"

Often, we exchange a long look, and tears spring to their eyes. This is not a casual moment in their lives. The answer has great importance to them right now. Yet they're letting a near-total stranger make the decision.

My answer is frequently the same: "If the stuff you own is not helping you create the life you want, then let it go."

And with those words, I typically see the weight that's been crushing and smothering them disappear. They nod their heads and let themselves laugh as their sense of paralysis or guilt vanishes and their anxiety evaporates. They admit that yes, they knew that was the answer. They just needed permission to realize it.

This doesn't mean that the problem has magically disappeared. It's never that simple! Similarly, just reading this book won't solve your difficulties. With *Cut the Clutter, Drop the Pounds*, my goal is to offer you a clear direction for the changes you're seeking in your life. The words are mine, but the hard work has to be yours. This program is ambitious and at times tough. I don't apologize for that. It demands your commitment, focus, and effort. You deserve happiness and a full life, and I share that goal with you.

The lives that each of us live are built on our actions and choices, such as:

▸ The items we've purchased

▸ The foods and drinks we've consumed

▸ The way we've chosen to spend our time

▸ The way we've interacted with others

If your home is littered with items that don't bring you happiness or peace of mind, it's probably because you focused on the immediate pleasure that your purchases might bring you; you couldn't pass up an unbeatable bargain; or for whatever reason, you thought incorrectly that you just *had* to have them.

If you weigh more than your body can comfortably carry, it's not because you made a series of deliberate choices to take in more calories than you burned off. Instead, you made a pattern of decisions that felt good in the moment. You ate to comfort yourself when you were uncomfortable or just bored. You distracted yourself with television or the Internet because it was easier than getting up and moving around. In that moment, you chose the easier option rather than the one that would have been healthier for you.

I'm here to share two very important truths that I share with every client I work with:

1. You're not overweight and cluttered because you're a bad person or a weak person.

2. It's not too late to change.

In fact, here's the good news. You can let go of the stacks and bins of material things that have overstuffed your home. You can let go of that layer of excess padding under your skin that bulges tightly against your clothes. You can make mindful choices that more accurately reflect the life you want. But first, you'll need to examine the way you interact with the world around you. You have to identify the habits and small daily choices that led your home and body to become overstuffed, and you have to let go of those, too.

As you cultivate a new way of living with less household, physical, and mental clutter, I predict that you'll enjoy improvements across *all* these areas, seeing a new home, a new body, and a fresh outlook emerge.

Every January on Facebook, I host a program I call the 31 Days to Get Organized challenge (#31Days2GetOrganized). I set daily 10-minute tasks and provide short videos every day that show people how to root the clutter out of 31 areas around their home. After the 2014 challenge, a reader named Carol told me that she noticed a surprising side effect. (Or at least it was surprising to *her*. I've gotten used to readers and listeners discovering this benefit.)

"I lost 8.4 pounds! What's remarkable is that the success I had in one month is almost what I had during the entire previous year at Weight Watchers. I still did my usual exercise and my usual eating. What else changed in January? That's the only thing I changed!" the 56-year-old Michigan resident said.

She was moving around more as she dug through drawers and hauled out needless stuff, which provided more physical activity. But she also kept telling me about the sense of freedom, lightness, and energy she felt from decluttering. These improvements in her spirit carried over to her body.

"The older I get, the less I want to be bogged down with *stuff*," she said. "Now I don't have to step over piles of clothes in the closet to get to the workout drawer. I feel more energetic, and I don't feel trapped. Before, I would just feel overwhelmed knowing I should be doing something about my home. I think that caused me to be still, watching TV and overeating. I got rid of my inertia and got stimulated!"

That's the type of feeling that inspired *Cut the Clutter, Drop the Pounds*. This is the first-ever step-by-step manual that helps you deal with the physical clutter that's invaded your home, the food choices that have led to extra pounds, the lack of exercise that has left you less fit than you'd wish, and the lack of focus that keeps you from living the fullest, richest life possible. The 6-week program in this book will give you the tools you need to look deeply into your household and into yourself, and then make the changes that will create a healthier, happier new normal.

Look afresh at your unwanted heirlooms and abandoned hobby materials, and learn exactly why you're still holding on to them. Cast your gaze onto your body in that photo you despise and consider the emotions that immediately flare up—then look deeper. Understand the behaviors and acknowledge the choices that led to your current physical state. By following the plan in *Cut the Clutter, Drop the Pounds,* you'll develop a new appreciation for the items you own, the choices you consciously make, the person you are, and the life you fully choose to live. You'll identify the elements of the unsustainable, overstuffed life you've been living and learn to turn away from those choices.

If you're familiar with my earlier work, you may be aware that I touched on the connection between your household clutter and your weight in a book I wrote a number of years ago. Several factors prompted me to return to this topic.

First, in the years since the publication of that book, the science linking an overcluttered lifestyle to poor health and fitness has become especially compelling. Researchers have been digging ever more deeply into the emotional causes of clutter and obesity, and they're finding many mutual factors. This new research is simply too good not to share.

Secondly, I had an opportunity to assemble a multidisciplinary team to develop a very detailed program to un-stuff your household and your body. We built a dietitian-approved eating program that will help you make simple food choices directed at weight loss. An exercise physiologist created a fitness plan that burns calories and strengthens your body using simple movements you can do at home without having to buy *any* workout equipment.

Keeping with my desire to promote a simplified, streamlined life, I designed this program using factors that are important to me. The program adds no clutter to your life. That means no calorie-counting, no artificial rules to memorize, and no gadgets that will shortly disappear into the back of a closet or a dresser drawer.

To verify that this program actually works, I assembled a test panel of regular folks to go through the 6-week weight loss and decluttering program you'll find in these pages. When my editors and I put out a notice in the media, we received an immediate flood of responses, and we quickly recruited 22 enthusiastic (and a little nervous) volunteers. These people tended to be overweight and *way* too attached to the idea of filling their homes with material possessions. In other words, they were good representatives of the modern American lifestyle.

Several were also struggling with anxiety and low self-esteem. This didn't surprise me, as I've seen many clients carrying these burdens.

As they went through this program, the test panel members learned how to make fundamental changes to their homes and their lives. Six weeks after I first met them, I was thrilled—and to tell you the truth, even a bit amazed—for how much weight they'd lost and how much control they'd gained over their clutter.

You'll meet many of these participants in the following pages, where you'll see just how much better their lives became. Along the way, they'll talk about the parts of the program that worked especially well for them, and they'll share tips on how they got past their challenges.

While my work has acquainted me with the wide variety and amount of clutter that can fit into a home, I've also witnessed something far more memorable: people's remarkable ability to make significant and permanent changes in their lives. *Cut the Clutter, Drop the Pounds* is the product of many years of working closely with people to declutter every aspect of their lives. It comes from a belief that people, including you, can change—if only they're shown how.

Somewhere deep inside, you have a sense of what you need to do in order to live a life that's free, rewarding, and unencumbered by stuff that doesn't make you happy. It's time to identify those changes—and allow yourself to finally make them.

Part 1

How Clutter Invades Your Home, Your Body, and Your Mind

Chapter 1

THE HIDDEN FORCES THAT MAKE YOUR HOME A MESS

Imagine a team of future archaeologists carefully examining the remains of one of today's typical homes. Hundreds of years from now, what would they think of the objects piled up in our rooms? Would they understand why we let our belongings take over so much of the space in our homes?

We don't have to wonder how archaeologists would interpret our early 21st-century homes. They're already trying to make sense of them *now*.

Earlier in her career, UCLA professor Jeanne Arnold, PhD, did the kind of work that the word *archaeology* more often brings to mind: examining bits of material left behind by ancient Native Americans. More recently, though, she shifted her focus to a very different society: modern-day Southern Californians. As part of an extended study, she and a team of researchers made in-depth explorations into 32 homes. They carefully photographed the rooms, noted exactly what types of household possessions the families treasured, and observed in real time how the residents used their homes. She wanted to find out what leads so many people to pack so much stuff inside and, once they bring it in, what they *do* with all of it.

All the families in these homes had kids. In all the homes, both parents worked. These were typical families with busy schedules and not a lot of time for cleaning and sorting. But Dr. Arnold and her colleagues didn't go out of their way to include homes that were especially cluttered. (They accepted families into the study without first seeing their homes.) Nor did they see evidence that the homeowners cleaned up before the team visited.

They found that many of these homes were so crowded that some of the rooms couldn't be used for their intended purposes. In three-quarters of the houses, the garage was so packed with items like sports equipment, boxes of files, lumber, and plastic bins filled with clothing that the cars were parked outside. The garage was too full to hold them.

Dr. Arnold and her team took nearly 20,000 photos in the homes, some of which ended up in a book that she co-authored about the project, *Life at Home in the Twenty-First Century*. One shows a shower stall where no one can bathe because it's stuffed knee-high with clothes. In another photo, no one

▶ CLUTTER DEFINED

The notion of "clutter" has different meanings. A household scene that looks like squalor to one might be "just a bit of a mess" to another. In this book, I'll use the word *clutter* a lot, and I'd like you to understand what I mean by this word.

Dr. Jeanne Arnold, the archaeologist who explores the modern world, and I see eye to eye on the three factors that turn household objects into clutter:

1. **It's a lot of stuff.** As you cast your eye around the room, it's hard to make sense of all the visual noise of colors and shapes. Merely owning an abundance of possessions doesn't necessarily mean that your home is cluttered, but it's a good start.

2. **It's out of place.** Here's where clutter begins. If you see a fork in the middle of your floor, you know it doesn't belong there. That's because forks have a very specific home, and it's not on the floor. A pile of clothes in the shower (where a person belongs) looks like clutter. Cases of sodas on the washing machine (where clothes should temporarily go) become clutter.

3. **It's untidy.** "A beautifully arranged bookshelf with hundreds and hundreds of books doesn't look like clutter—it looks like a nice collection, right? Whereas if the books are all falling out of the bookcase and some of them are stacked and things are sticking out of the books, it starts to look like clutter, since it's not tidy," Dr. Arnold says.

The totally uncluttered definition: Clutter is too much stuff scattered in the wrong place.

can sit comfortably in front of the computer because the home office is so jammed with clutter. No one can relax on a couch because it's littered with stuffed animals. No one can sort laundry on top of the washer or dryer because they're covered with stacks of groceries.

"Something like two-thirds of households had, based on a simple visual observation, an uncomfortable amount of stuff," she says. And by "uncomfortable," she means how an average visitor might feel upon entering the home. Most of the families living in these spaces, on the other hand, didn't seem to be too upset about the clutter around them or even to notice it.

"Many of the men in the households expressed no concern whatsoever about the untidy spaces or having lots of stuff. Moms more often commented on it, but only some of them commented on it using language that suggested that it caused them considerable stress," she said.

But it's hard to be truly blissful, calm, and relaxed in an untidy environment. Psychologists on the team found signs that a cluttered house could pose a threat to a peaceful state of mind. Women whose homes were more stressful—based partly on their home's clutter levels—had a pattern of changes in their cortisol levels that showed more chronic stress. Their levels of depressed mood also increased over the day.

When you truly need cortisol coursing through your system, it's great to have around. It shifts your body into a different mode—like shifting your car into a higher gear—so it's ready to fight or flee from an attacker. But long term, you don't want too much cortisol and other stress hormones flooding your system. Revving up your car for too long isn't good for the engine, and excess stress hormones in your system can, over time:

▸ Keep you from sleeping

▸ Make you feel sick to your stomach

▸ Throw off your mental focus

▸ Hurt your heart

▸ Make you feel more anxious or depressed

▸ Contribute to weight gain

A cluttered house isn't a good enough reason to do this to your body and your mind.

After many visits to messy homes, I've come to realize that clutter is a customary part of most families' lives and that many families have given up on trying to keep it under control. I've also learned that the accumulation of too much stuff in people's homes has more serious and negative effects on their lives than they realize. Clutter has:

A financial impact: Take, for example, the father who traveled constantly for work. He was wracked with guilt because he rarely spent time with his children, so he bought them toys to make up for his absence. When I started working with the family, all their credit cards were maxed out and the huge plastic containers of untouched toys that filled their garage had long ago begun to spill out into their yard.

An emotional impact: I met a mother who became obsessed with collecting plastic action figures and other memorabilia from a national restaurant franchise. Her 8- and 12-year-old daughters had never shared a family meal at the kitchen table because it was so cluttered with this stuff that they couldn't even see it.

A social impact: A young mother couldn't say no to the offers of hand-me-down clothes from her family and friends. Once she had the clothes, she felt too guilty to part with them. With three children under the age of 6, her home was so packed with kids' clothing that she felt too embarrassed to have anyone in for a visit. She became increasingly isolated and depressed.

A relationship impact: A couple collected "gifts" for family and friends, but never actually gave them away. Their surroundings were so cluttered that their grandchildren had never even visited their home.

While many of the homes I visit are much, much worse than the homes in Jeanne Arnold's book, in all of them I find families that are stressed, less happy than they could be, and unable to live the kind of lives they'd like. They're drowning in too much stuff. When we talk about their surroundings, without exception these conversations dredge up powerful emotions like guilt, loss, regret, betrayal, worry, and anger.

If your house is an overstuffed mess, I've learned that more often than not, it's a warning sign that you have some type of trouble—large or small—in your mental and emotional well-being. In turn, a chaotic home that leaves little room for you and the other people inside can threaten your mental and physical health.

Stuff that overfills a home is usually a symptom of some deeper, more significant issue that has not been addressed by an individual or the family. It's easy to be distracted by the stuff—but the real issue is never the stuff itself. As I often tell people, it's not about the clutter.

My work is based largely around one simple yet powerful premise that I know to be true: You can't make your best choices, your healthiest choices, your most life-affirming choices in a cluttered, messy, disorganized house. You can argue with me as much as you want, but I can tell you with absolute certainty that it just doesn't happen.

If you were to invite me into your home, and I were to see that it's packed full of objects that you don't truly need, use, or want—but can't get rid of—I would be concerned that:

▸ Your mind isn't as happy, relaxed, and focused as it could be.

▸ You are feeling overwhelmed by your possessions and unable to get them under control.

▸ Your weight is likely higher than you would like it to be.

▸ Your relationships with your spouse, kids, and other loved ones in your home aren't as strong as they could be.

▸ The stuff you own has become more important than your and your family's well-being.

▸ You simply don't know where to start making a change.

Does this sound like a typical morning at your home?

When you wake up, the very first thing your eyes see is a cluttered, messy bedroom, which immediately sets an unpleasant tone for your day. You get up and can't find the outfit you know is somewhere in your closet (thus starting your day with a failure). Your kids' homework has disappeared, you're out of milk for breakfast, and your car keys are nowhere to be found. You've had more frustration by 8 a.m. than some people feel all day. If this sounds like you, is it any surprise that you feel tense and on edge before you step out of the house?

I can show you how each room in your home can drag down your happiness in its own special way.

If your kitchen counters are cluttered and your drawers are overflowing with gizmos that you bought in a moment of culinary enthusiasm—but haven't used once—then you're not likely to cook a healthy meal that brings your family together. It's just too stressful an exercise.

If your home office is such a mess that it keeps you from getting your finances in order, it's no surprise when stress, uncertainty, and fights about money disrupt your marital happiness and keep everyone in the home worried.

The clutter in your house may be a cause of deeper personal and emotional issues in your life, and it will almost certainly contribute to stress within your family. This clutter can also directly affect your weight and serve as a warning light that you're making decisions that threaten your health.

Since a cluttered home can so completely drag down a family's quality of life, why do so many people bring so much stuff into their homes, use it so little, and find it so difficult to let go? A more useful question might be: In today's society, how could people *not* do this?

A Culture of Clutter

In the United States, consumer spending makes up about 70 percent of the nation's overall economic activity. The same is true in other developed countries: Of all the spending that goes on, everyday consumers account for most of it. As a result, the forces that run the place where you live—the government, big businesses, the media—keep a very, very close eye on whether *you,* the consumer, are spending enough.

Did you catch that? The powers that be don't necessarily view you as a citizen, a voter, or a person. You're a *consumer.* You're someone who buys products, then consumes them. After you eat it, use it up, or wear it out, you buy more.

As I sit at my desk writing this today, the headlines on my computer are very excited about how much Americans have been spending recently. "If You're Average, You'll Spend $98 Today," *Time* magazine tells me. The typical consumer spent $98 a day last month, pushing the average to its highest in 6 years. That doesn't count things like your mortgage, car payment, or utility bills. It's a measure of your purchases at places like coffee shops, convenience stores, department stores, and online retailers.

If you're contributing to this daily flow of commerce, the newscasts will speak of you in glowing terms. Your neighbors may look at you with envy. But this spending, I fear, will continue to keep you overweight, overcluttered, and *under*happy.

This pressure for consumers—I mean *people*—to keep spending has been building since before you were born. Thousands of years ago, humans evolved in an environment of scarcity, says Peter Whybrow, MD. He's a psychiatrist at UCLA whose main interest these days is trying to figure out why people need to buy so much in the pursuit of happiness.

Our ancient ancestors spent their time seeking the three things their brains told them to chase: food, shelter, and sex. At least two of these were typically hard to find. These primitive people spent a lot of time and energy chasing down a tasty animal to eat or looking for a safe place to spend the night.

When they succeeded, their brains' reward centers released chemicals that made them feel happy and content. Another day as successful as that might not happen for a long time, Dr. Whybrow says.

Even in the 1700s, when philosophers and economists were setting up the foundation of our free-market economy, even basic necessities were still scarce for most. "You can only harness your horse and go to the market once a week," Dr. Whybrow explains. "The constraints of work, the climate, the mountains, all of those things that constrained people were so dominant that they could never imagine the situation where we live now."

Our economy was set up with the expectation that these constraints would always limit our ability to get our hands on food, clothing, and tools. So would our desire to not look greedy in front of our neighbors, says Dr. Whybrow, who covers these issues in his book *American Mania: When More Is Not Enough*.

But that all changed, even though our brains haven't. Now we live in an environment of plenty. Most people can afford more than they need, and even if they can't really afford it, credit cards aren't usually hard to get. On the one hand, we can divide expensive items into monthly payments, and on the other hand, the stores we visit are flooded with cheaply priced items we can buy without a second thought.

"The only thing that constrains you now is your dorsolateral prefrontal cortex, the part in the brain that enables us to say, 'That isn't a good idea,'" says Dr. Whybrow. "'Even though that chocolate cake is attractive, I don't really want to weigh 200 pounds at the age of 14.' But the trouble is, that is a very weak inhibitor."

This little part of your brain, just behind your forehead, is now up against some powerful adversaries, from big business and the federal government to genius-level marketers to Hollywood actresses and reality TV stars. If you've ever felt like a war is going on inside your own mind, you're sort of right!

"There are a lot of things that contributed to this growth of consumerism and our self-identity being overly associated with being consumers," says Annie Leonard, the founder of the Story of Stuff Project. She's especially concerned with the damage that manufacturing all our stuff causes the environment and the damage that *buying* all that stuff causes our well-being.

"After World War II, our economic and business planners, including folks in government, were trying to figure out how to keep a humming economy going when you're not having to make all these *war* things," she says. "The way is to make toasters, blenders, cars, couches, and all this stuff. Prior to

1950, people didn't have such a desire to buy endless consumer stuff, so that desire had to be stimulated."

And who better to stimulate our desires than marketers? After WWII, "the real science of advertising came to fruition," says James Roberts, PhD. He's a Baylor University professor and marketing expert who focuses on the psychology of consumer behavior. He's also the author of *Shiny Objects: Why We Spend Money We Don't Have in Search of Happiness We Can't Buy.*

Nowadays, two-thirds of advertising dollars pay for messages that are broadcast on TV, computers, and handheld devices. These messages had much less impact on people's lives—or were nonexistent—in 1950. That year, only 9 percent of Americans had a television, which carried a couple of black-and-white channels and didn't broadcast at night. And zero percent, of course, had Internet access or handheld devices.

Today, marketers will direct somewhere between 2,000 and 5,000 messages at you, Dr. Roberts says. They'll do the same tomorrow and the next day. Just as any flat surface in your home is a magnet for clutter—from your refrigerator door to your bedside table—any open space in your environment that could catch your eye now attracts advertisers.

"I was recently in Boston on the subway platform, and you can't wait for the subway without looking at these giant new TV screens bombarding ads at you from across the tracks," Leonard says. "There's increasingly fewer places where we can rest our eyeballs without getting commercial messages. It's relentless!"

Marketers often exploit your insecurities, Dr. Roberts says. They make you wonder, "Do I smell bad? Am I unattractive? Is everyone else having fun somewhere because they bought a certain object, and I'm left out? What can I buy so I'll be more accepted?"

But above all, marketers sell the promise of happiness. "Buying new jewelry or pants or a car makes us feel better about ourselves. If we have low self-esteem or we're depressed, we get a lift from the purchase," Dr. Roberts says. "I think it simply has to do with distraction. When we're spending, we're not thinking about things at the core of our unhappiness. We don't have to think about problems with our spouse or kids or problems at work."

It's often difficult to know exactly what we're buying when we hand over our cash or swipe our credit card. You might *think* you're buying a specific item, but I'd challenge you to think about this a little differently.

When we buy a "product," we frequently—and unwittingly—hand over our money for the *promise* we hope that product will deliver on. We buy:

- A treadmill (the product), but what we're really investing in is the dream of losing weight and being fit (the promise)

- A beautiful set of pots and pans (the product), but what we're really hoping to get are the wonderful dinner parties and the appetizing food that will amaze our family and friends (the promise)

Remember: Every product you buy comes with a corresponding promise that you invest in. Your heart is set on attaining both. But while you'll definitely come home with the object in your hands, you may or may not get the promise you see in your daydreams. Always look beyond the product to understand what's really motivating your purchases.

Here's another force that's accelerating the pressure on us to keep consuming: the people we want to look like. Both Dr. Roberts and Leonard pointed out that we're no longer trying to keep up with the Joneses. After all, the Joneses live across the street from you and are more or less in the same boat. They have pretty much the same size house and the same class of car as yours and generally the same educational background, and they're in a similar tax bracket.

"The gold standard now is keeping up with the Gateses," Dr. Roberts says. He's talking about billionaire Bill Gates and his family. You may not want to dress like him or adopt his haircut, but his mansion, toys, and checking account would certainly be fun to have.

If you don't have a roof over your head or enough to eat, you *do* need more, Leonard says. But once their basic needs are covered, people tend to decide

▶ DARE TO COMPARE

My mother used to tell me that no matter what I had, someone out there would always be better off than me. I didn't fully realize how true that was until I started meeting people around the world in my current job, and I saw them exhausting themselves trying to attain what others had. The moment you start judging what you have against the possessions of others is the moment you set yourself on a road of dissatisfaction and unhappiness.

The things you own should help you create the life *you* want—and that shouldn't have anything to do with other people's lives. "Comparison is the death of joy," a wise person once said. (This is sometimes attributed to Mark Twain, while Teddy Roosevelt is quoted saying a similar sentiment. Whoever said it, it's true!)

whether they have enough stuff by comparing themselves with not just their neighbors but also the celebrities on TV. "Now instead of comparing my shoes to my neighbor's, I'm comparing them to Angelina Jolie's or Kim Kardashian's, because our media is so focused on these celebrities and we have such access to their inner lives," Leonard says. "Television disproportionately shows wealthy people. The more media we watch, the more substandard we feel by comparison."

Can you learn to resist all this pressure to buy, buy, buy?

Sure.

Is it easy?

No. But you can do it, and I'll help you like I've helped many other people. It starts with developing an *awareness* of how you feel about material possessions and an *awareness* of the factors that influence your urge to shop.

"I live in Berkeley, California, where people wear clogs and flip-flops year-round," says Leonard. "In Berkeley, my clogs feel totally fine. But when I'm in New York City, where the women have the *best* shoes, I get overwhelmed with this desire to buy shoes." She used to think she actually needed new shoes in those moments, so she'd buy them. But now she realizes she's comparing herself to wealthier, glitzier people, so when she gets a case of shoe lust, she tells herself, "There's that thing happening again" rather than "Oh, I need new shoes."

I love that line: "There's that thing happening again!" That is exactly the kind of awareness and insight I'm hoping you'll gain during the 6 weeks of this program. As you read this book, you'll have the chance to make these sorts of discoveries and gain a deeper understanding of your own motivations.

You've been manipulated for too long by clever marketing and the allure of owning more. However, with more stuff comes more stress, more demands to clean and care for objects, and more credit card statements with scary numbers—realities you might not have pictured while you were dreaming of all those "promises" this stuff would deliver!

Though marketing plays a substantial role in making you want more stuff, it's not the only factor driving you to add to your clutter.

Needless Acquisitions

That "promise" you see in your mind when you think about buying a new possession is just one of many thoughts you attach to objects. We also apply powerful emotions to the things we buy or receive as gifts. And once one of these hard-hitting emotions gets attached to an item—even a cheap, ridiculous item you should *never* treasure—it surrounds the object like a magnetic field that sticks to you. Some examples:

You can't say no. People express their love, their respect, and their admiration by giving *stuff*. You get married, you have a baby, or you move into a new home, and people will buy you things. When you simply invite people over for a meal, they'll bring you something. Even if it's just a bottle of wine, you have to make room for this gift somewhere.

You might tell your close friends and family members that you don't want all this stuff. But they're likely to blink nervously and think, *How can we express our love, respect, and admiration if we don't buy something for her? Anyway, she's just being polite. We'll keep buying her gifts.* Or you might feel like it's rude to tell people not to buy you gifts. You might think, *Why go to this hassle? Why not just accept the gift? I can always find room somewhere.*

You buy stuff for your family to show your affection. On the other window open on my computer screen right now, I'm looking at two lists of customary anniversary gifts—traditional and modern. The traditional list starts with a paper gift on the first anniversary, then builds to gold on the 50th and diamond on the 60th. The modern list is front-loaded with more expensive stuff for the first 10 years of marriage, like china, appliances, silverware, and diamond jewelry (perhaps because so few stay married for 60 years?).

These lists suggest that society takes gift-giving seriously. Perhaps you've bought into it. Maybe you buy an anniversary gift for your spouse, as well as birthday gifts, holiday gifts, a Mother's or Father's Day gift, cheering-up gifts, and gifts "just because." You buy stuff for your kids on important holidays, gifts for good behavior, gifts for good grades, gifts when they're sick, gifts because you feel guilty that you were impatient that time, and gifts because you want them to hug you.

This adds up to a lot of stuff over the year. It all takes up space in your house. *I can always find room somewhere,* you sigh.

You buy stuff to feel better. How often are you fully and completely free of unpleasant sensations? You're well-rested and well-fed. You're not sleepy, hungry, or thirsty. Your mind is occupied, and you're not bored. You're happy. You're not annoyed with someone. You're not feeling bummed-out or worried about a work deadline. Nothing itches. You're thoroughly pleased and satisfied.

Such moments are rare. Usually *something* is bothering you, even just a little. If you're like most people, the thing you can do to fix this problem—or at least distract yourself from it—is to buy something. Maybe you go to the vending machine for a pack of gum. Maybe you type in the first few letters of your favorite online retailer and the computer takes you the rest of the way there. Or you hop in the car and drive to the store, daydreaming the whole way.

These purchases that fix a momentary unpleasantness create a river of stuff that flows into our homes. *I can always find room somewhere*, you think, but you know you can't.

You're out of room.

But your house isn't overcluttered and out of room only because you bought and received too much stuff. It's also because you held on to stuff when it was no longer doing you any good or serving any real purpose. A whole other set of factors may lead you to do that. Let's take a look at them.

Cluttered Mindset

I'm not sure why we still make such a big deal about spring cleaning. Every February and March or so, reporters want to interview me for feature stories about new and improved ways you can clear out your house so it feels spring-fresh.

At one point, people actually *did* spring cleaning. The ritual originated in Europe hundreds of years ago, when winter snows finally receded and people could open up their stale, cramped, smoky hovels. The reason the concept of spring cleaning doesn't sit well with me is that:

▶ Few people actually do it. They might open their windows (until it gets too hot and they turn on the air conditioner) and do some dusting. But few people make large-scale efforts to haul out clutter.

▶ It reinforces the idea that cleaning/decluttering is a once-a-year event, when it should be an ongoing process.

Think about it. Over the course of an average week, do you bring more objects into your home than you take out? Society's attitudes about "clearing out" tend to be fairly indifferent and fleeting. For all the rituals we have in which buying things is expected—holidays, anniversaries, graduations—we don't really have customary times throughout the year when we take stuff out of our house. On the other hand, people's feelings about *keeping* their stuff are often numerous and powerful.

As a decluttering expert, the work I do sometimes overlaps with the efforts of researchers who study hoarding. As I'll explain in the next chapter, there are differences between people who are merely *heavily cluttered* and those who are *hoarders*. But they're not always far apart when it comes to specific attitudes. If you have too much stuff around your house, the factors that follow may help explain why.

You feel like it's your job to take care of these objects. "Many individuals, whether they meet the criteria for hoarding disorder or not, keep objects from their childhood. Why do we hang on to mementos that may not be useful or monetarily valuable?" asks Kiara Timpano, PhD, a hoarding researcher at the University of Miami. "People have all sorts of reasons for saving things. Sometimes it's because of the potential for future usefulness, or perhaps you don't want to be wasteful. Sometimes people are emotionally attached to an object and will feel *responsible* for it."

All these reasons for saving—including that sense of "I wouldn't want anything bad to happen to the object" or "If I'm going to get rid of it, I want to know that it's going to a good home"—are actually normal ways to feel about objects, she says. But *how strongly* you feel this way can make the difference between hoarding disorder and customary reasons for saving. It can also make the difference between a neat, streamlined home and a place that's chaotic and full of clutter.

Some people I've worked with talk about many of their possessions as if they were their pets or even their children. When they adopt this mindset, it becomes easy for them to claim that no one else could possibly care for these objects as well as they can. They get sad, upset, and even angry at the thought of these objects being neglected or unappreciated. Unless they're convinced (and they seldom are) that these objects are going to "a good home," it's close to impossible for them to part with them.

The ex-journalist I worked with who saw her books as an extension of herself—"my babies," as she called them—found it impossible to look at the books as anything other than living, breathing beings she was charged with nurturing and protecting.

At first glance, this may seem ridiculous. But haven't all of us at some point held on to an object that meant far more to us than the physical thing itself—often for reasons we couldn't fully articulate? The stuff people own has power, and they feel many reasons for not letting it go, even when they know they should.

You don't want to be wasteful. David Tolin, PhD, is a longtime colleague of mine and one of the preeminent hoarding researchers in the world. He says he has spoken to many clients who feel that "if they let go of something without finding a good use for it, they're being wasteful. By extension, they worry that if they're being wasteful, that makes them a bad person. The irony is that they don't then follow up with actually *using* the object. Creating a landfill in your home does not mean that you're saving the environment. You just moved the garbage. It's no less wasteful to do that in your own home."

I vividly remember working with a teacher who specialized in environmental education for elementary school children. She taught a wonderful curriculum that focused on respect for the environment, recycling, and responsible use of resources. She felt wasteful letting go of anything and thought she should be personally responsible for the recycling efforts of her whole neighborhood. Her garage was overrun with cans, bottles, and all manner of recyclables because she didn't trust the city recycling program. Her intentions were wonderful, but her overzealous sense of responsibility for avoiding waste left her buried in clutter.

I see this all the time. People bring stuff into their home and then keep it forever because:

▸ It cost money. Who wants to throw out or give away a perfectly good appliance? I paid good money for this!

▸ It was free or a bargain. How could I pass up such a great deal? I'm an incredible shopper for snagging this before someone else got it!

▸ It would just become more trash on an overpolluted planet if they threw it away.

▸ It has significance for someone else, so it should have meaning for them (even though it doesn't).

You feel guilty. Someone thought enough of you to buy you a clever T-shirt from a catalog or a concrete statue of a squirrel for your garden. Your mother drove hours to bring you her suits so you could wear them to interviews when you were between jobs. Your grandmother left you her teacup collection in her will.

Our homes are filled with things that loved ones, friends, and co-workers gave us. You probably don't go more than a few months without receiving a gift you never asked for. And when you think about giving it away, you picture the gift-giver's face falling in sadness. Even worse, what if they come to your house someday and don't see the gift displayed? What if they ask when you're going to wear that tie? What if they go to Goodwill and see the grandfather clock? How disappointed and hurt would they be?

This misplaced sense of obligation is very common with my clients. A close friend of mine recently asked my advice for dealing with his mother-in-law. Despite repeated requests to stop, every time she visits my friend's home she brings gifts for his son. Birthdays and Christmas see a virtual flood of presents. He loves his mother-in-law and feels guilty letting anything go. The result: His home is overrun with toys his child doesn't enjoy.

My response to questions like this is simple and direct, but tough. If a gift has come to you wrapped in obligations and tied tightly with a ribbon of guilt, then it's not really a gift at all. It's a manipulation. A gift should be something freely given that enhances your life and reminds you lovingly of the giver. If it's not, you simply should not give it a place in your home.

I understand that you're a nice person who doesn't want to hurt others' feelings, and so you hang on to these items for longer than you should, even if you don't like them. But such behavior doesn't help create the life or home you want.

Your sense of guilt can pressure you to hang on to the most worthless of items. Dr. Tolin recalls his wife feeling torn over what to do with a flyer asking their kids to collect pledges or names or *something* for a fund-raiser. "We've done like 8 million of these for every organization the kids belong to, and here's one more and my wife said very clearly, 'I don't want to do this.' So she puts it on a stack of papers, and I asked her, 'Why aren't you throwing it out?' She said, 'I feel too guilty to throw it away right now, but I will later.' When you hang on to something, it allows you to feel like things are different from how they really are. It's almost a way of tricking yourself," he says.

You think a thing has more value simply because it belongs to you. Experts called behavioral economists have noted an issue they call the endowment effect, Dr. Tolin says. Merely owning an item causes you to exaggerate its value, or "endow" it with more worth. One common example is when people want to sell their homes for more than they're worth. But the endowment effect can make even insignificant items feel more important to you.

"There was a great study where the researchers got a bunch of people in a room, and they showed them all a coffee mug," Dr. Tolin says. "They asked, 'Would you please tell us how much you would pay for this coffee mug if you were to buy it from us?' Everyone wrote down a figure. Later on, the researchers actually gave them the coffee mug as a present, but they added, 'We're interested in buying it back from you. How much would you sell it for?' And everyone's numbers went straight up."

I see this all the time. Even when people don't talk about feeling responsible for an item and they don't feel guilty or wasteful at the thought of parting with it, they simply feel like the item is too important to get rid of because it's *theirs*—and that's all there is to it.

I recall one woman I worked with a few years ago. Soon after her daughter was born, she began carefully collecting a certain brand of dolls with the intention of one day selling them to finance her daughter's college education. By the time I met this woman, her daughter was well out of college, yet more than 2,000 virtually worthless dolls were stashed in a spare bedroom, gathering dust.

Though a quick check of an online auction site clearly showed the value of the dolls, she refused to believe the facts or get rid of the dolls. The collection had taken on a value that had nothing to do with market rates or sale prices. These dolls were valuable—more valuable than anyone could possibly appreciate, as she pointedly told me—because they were *hers*. End of story!

Extreme? Maybe. But stop a moment and look at your own behavior. Aren't we all a little like this on occasion?

You have an emotional connection to the stuff. We tend to connect our memories of the important moments in our lives, the places where we lived, and the people we loved to *objects*. Seeing these things allows us to replay and refresh those memories.

There are a few downsides to attaching memories to possessions. Often people feel that if they part with an object, they'll lose the memory attached to it, along with a special moment in their life. Or that a person now only living on in their memory would be forgotten completely and disappear forever.

A few years ago at a speaking engagement, a gentleman in the audience told me that he had 22-year-old twin boys in college. He was obviously very proud of them. He had kept—and stored in every available nook and cranny in his home—every single piece of schoolwork his sons had ever done.

▸ Every test

▸ Every quiz

▸ Every project

▸ Every book report

▸ Every piece of artwork, writing assignment, and math problem

▸ Every workbook, notebook, and homework task

▸ Every. Single. Item.

This wasn't about the stuff. Each of these items represented a milestone for the dad. Each was a tangible example of his sons' progress, their growing intellectual ability, and his pride in their success.

So dads keep homework and moms keep baby gifts. A man will hang on to the jacket he was wearing the last time he went out with his brother before the accident. Millions of middle-aged people cling to heirlooms they don't even want, because these items bring back images of long-gone parents and grandparents whose faces grow ever more distant and hard to recall.

Our homes become like photo albums of the past. But these "photos" aren't images that take up little space in a photo album or zero physical space on a computer. They're items of furniture and wood carvings and cars and blankets and clothes. These memory objects can take up lots of room in your home. This is space you can't fill with useful, functional items or *new* memory-associated items.

Often, when people are overly attached to too many memory-related items, I detect a real sadness in the way they talk. Like my client whose grandmother died 26 years ago. She put every single item from her grandmother's home into storage. I mean *every* item. She then preserved it like a museum for 26 years! She never dealt with the loss, and her grandmother's possessions were an attempt to not let go. I have little doubt that unresolved grief and depression play a particular role in this type of clutter.

My major concern with these possessions is that they can become what I call *malignant* clutter. This is a term I'm going to be using often later in the book as a way of identifying items that can have a negative, even harmful, effect on your mood, spirit, and outlook. Rooting out such items will be an important task as you go through the 6-week program of rebooting your home, your weight, and your attitudes.

Malignant clutter is the stuff around your home that you hold on to even though its very presence is harmful to you. It's possible that you can feel the hurt when you look at it. It eats away at your spirit. It spreads bad feelings through your mind, and these bad feelings can harm your body.

We generally associate the word *malignant* with cancer, and I don't use this term lightly. A malignancy, either in our home or in our body, is something that needs to be identified and removed for the sake of our mental health and physical well-being. I have found that *malignant clutter* is the best way to describe objects such as:

▸ The medical equipment that filled the room of a child who passed away from a long illness. Although I didn't start to work with the grieving family until 2 years later, these memories of a devastating time still lingered in their home and were made real every time they looked at the equipment.

▶ The divorce papers piled on an office shelf more than 3 years after the contentious breakup had been finalized. Just glimpsing the papers brought back heartbreaking memories of the failed relationship.

▶ The household goods that were boxed up and stored in the garage after a family had to downsize into a smaller home following a job loss. Their circumstances didn't promise to turn around anytime soon, and those boxes served as a constant reminder of what they'd lost.

Malignant items don't have to be reminders of bad times, like a breakup or a health crisis. They can bring back memories of loved ones or high points in your life. But if these memories leave you feeling sad or feeling that your life isn't as good now, then the objects are causing you mental and emotional harm and have no place in your home.

The things you own should help you create the home and the life you want. The key to enjoying happiness and good health in a warm, welcoming home is to live *in the present moment* surrounded by items that you cherish and that have meaning for you and your family. If too much of your time is spent replaying your greatest hits or struggling with old pain, you're not making new memories of your present life.

You think, *I might need this thing someday.* This is a common response from my clients as I tackle the clutter and disorganization in their homes. They don't want to throw out paperwork, clothing, books, magazines, paper clips, dish towels, or old sheets because "I might need this someday." They're absolutely correct. They might indeed need some of these things, and I'll never convince them otherwise.

If the "memory clutter" I just mentioned ties you to a past that's gone, the "I might need this one day" clutter wraps you up in a future that might never happen. When people demonstrate this undue preoccupation with the future, I see anxiety bubbling to the surface. While remembering the past and preparing responsibly for the future are perfectly normal things to do, when your stuff takes over and limits your ability to function in your home *now*, you have a problem.

Thanks to all the bulk purchase discounts offered by huge warehouse stores, people are taking their "I might need this one day" up to the jumbo level. They bring home towers of toilet paper and giant tubs of mayonnaise that they wouldn't have bought if they weren't so inexpensive. Then they have to figure out where to wedge these stockpiles of items they may not finish for years.

Every single item you touch could conceivably be useful to you someday. It's true. You can save a considerable amount of money when you buy your toothpaste in six-packs. Also true. But keep in mind that you have limited space in your home.

All your "someday" objects have an extra cost you may not be considering: They're taking away space from items that you could be enjoying *right now*. They're occupying room you could be sharing with family members *right now* or using to build a happy, connected life with others *right now*.

When it comes to your home's cleanliness and livability, it's best to devote your resources to the current moment—which is a very real time that is actually occurring—rather than to some future event that may never happen.

Time to Make a Choice

During this 6-week program, you'll learn to recognize when *any* of these factors are spurring you to buy or accept stuff you don't need and then hang on to it longer than you should. You'll learn how to resist these pressures. You'll learn to control them instead of them controlling you.

You'll learn how to fill the empty spaces in your life with better things than *stuff*. As you haul the clutter out of your home, you'll create more space. You'll have more physical room in your home for family activities. You'll have more time in your schedule (since you won't have to shift around clutter just to clean house) for activities that feed your spirit.

That's exactly what several people in the test group who went through the *Cut the Clutter, Drop the Pounds* program told me. The changes they made over 6 weeks opened up time for exercise. They cleared stress out of their mind, leaving room for happier feelings. They rooted out sources of conflict in their marriage, creating a better place to meet in the middle with their spouses.

"I can tell you unreservedly that yes, materialism is related to happiness. People who are *more* materialistic are *less* happy," Dr. Roberts says. It could be that people who are in love with stuff are unhappy because they're trying to find meaning in their possessions, which is the wrong place to look. Or perhaps unhappy people tend to buy stuff because society tells them that objects will cure their sadness.

I don't want you to get rid of all your stuff and go live in a hippie commune or a monastery. I don't want you to wear worn-out clothes. I don't want you to be deprived of the joys of modern living.

Here's what I *do* want you to have after you go through the 6-week program in this book. I want you to:

▸ Be surrounded by objects in your home that you value and cherish

▸ Have a home that meets your needs, not a home that serves as your boss

▸ Feel a deep sense of gratefulness for all the good parts of your life

▸ Feel good about how you look and feel

▸ Have strong relationships with your loved ones that bring you peace and security

▸ Think and act in ways that move you closer to the vision of the good life you've set for yourself—and no longer make choices out of sadness, stress, boredom, or inattention, or under pressure from the media or the people around you

But all these things only scratch the surface of what you can gain from this program. That's because the clutter in your home and the emotions you attach to it have a tremendous impact on your life that we have barely even discussed. When you develop a mindset that allows you to gain control over the clutter and your associated emotions, your new power can also spark improvements in your waistline and your overall health.

This program is called *Cut the Clutter, Drop the Pounds*. Those two concerns in your life are closely linked together. When you fix one, you're in a great position to fix the other. In the next chapter, I'll explain why.

Chapter 2

THE SCIENCE LINKING CLUTTER AND WEIGHT

I received an interesting e-mail recently from David Tolin, PhD, the hoarding researcher I introduced in the last chapter. He's an adjunct professor at Yale University and the coauthor of the classic book *Buried in Treasures* (an image that applies to the lives of not only people with hoarding disorder, but often even standard-issue people with too much stuff).

Dr. Tolin sometimes invites people with hoarding disorder to lie in an MRI machine to see whether their brains are somehow different than the brains of people without this disorder. In his e-mail, he mentioned that for his most recent study, he and his team had to switch to a larger MRI scanner because participants often couldn't fit into the standard machines.

Clutter and excessive weight make a perfect match for each other, and they often trample through people's lives hand in hand. In a sense, they're really the same problem: Household clutter gathers in piles on your tables and bulges out of closets because your home was only built to carry so much stuff, and your possessions go over the limit. And if you weigh too much, you're carrying more fat than your body is designed to hold.

In addition, they both represent an imbalance. You brought too much stuff *into* your home but not enough *out*. So it's cluttered. If you're overweight, you took too many calories *in* but didn't burn enough *off*.

Over the years, I have noticed that very often when I knock on homeowners' doors, the people living in these cluttered homes are struggling not only with the volume of stuff in their homes but also with the physical weight on their bodies. Please understand: I'm not suggesting that cluttered people are automatically overweight, or that all overweight people are struggling with clutter. It's not that simple. But my experience tells me that this clutter-weight connection is no coincidence. In some cases, one problem may encourage the other to develop.

▸ The chaos in your house nudges you toward making poorer eating and exercise choices.

▸ If you're out of shape, you may become too easily fatigued and winded to tackle a big decluttering project. If your home is heavily cluttered, it may literally hold *tons* of extra stuff that you'd need to haul out. Decluttering is definitely a physical challenge.

But often, I think, other factors fuel the growth of clutter and body fat at the same time.

▸ As you're standing in the checkout line to pay for items—groceries to eat or clothes to hang in your closet—you're buying them for reasons you don't realize.

▸ If you're habitually unfocused and daydreaming, the decisions you make while you're mentally checked out can gradually push your home toward chaos and your body into obesity.

▸ If you feel like you never have the time or energy to make substantial improvements to your weight or your home, and your busy schedule leaves you no time for exercise, the best you can seem to do is shift around piles of clutter. You lie awake at night stressed, and you start the next day already tired.

I'm not the only one making these connections. A growing body of scientific research offers support for my suspicions.

The Hoarding-Obesity Connection

Other researchers are noticing the same thing as David Tolin: Excessive clutter and excess pounds may be related.

In a small 2011 study that included 12 people with a diagnosis of hoarding, researchers noted that 11 were overweight or obese. How come? Here's one possibility: A cluttered environment can lead you to make poor food choices. In 2013, researchers asked 34 students, one at a time, to answer questionnaires while sitting for 10 minutes in an orderly or a messy room. The messy room had the components found in many cluttered homes: extra furniture, papers strewn about, and objects piled where they didn't belong. The clean room was streamlined and tidy, with everything in the right place and no needless clutter. When they left, the participants were given their choice of two snacks. Those leaving the clean room were more likely to take an apple than a candy bar as opposed to those leaving the cluttered room.

People who merely have too much clutter, but *don't* have hoarding disorder, may be more likely to have weight problems. A 2008 study included a group of people who said they struggled with clutter, but didn't meet all the criteria of hoarding disorder. These people were 77 percent more likely to be overweight or obese compared to participants taking part in the study who had a family member with hoarding-type behaviors.

Another study found that people who met the criteria for hoarding were significantly more likely to have a higher body mass index (BMI), and to be obese. Your BMI is a measurement of your weight in relation to your height. This number gives a sense of whether your weight is at a healthy level or not. In this study, the researchers found some evidence that a genetic link might help explain both hoarding and obesity. People with a specific type of variation in a gene called *BDNF* were more likely to have more severe hoarding behaviors. They also tended to have higher BMI scores.

▶ YOU'RE WORTH IT!

I often hear people say "I don't have time to exercise" or "I don't have time to plan my meals in advance." This makes me cringe, because I hear something very different than what they're saying.

A healthy, well-maintained body requires personal commitment and effort. When someone tells me that she doesn't have time, I wonder why she feels that she's not valuable enough to make the effort.

You give time to what you believe is important—it's that simple! If you find yourself using this excuse for your inaction, I challenge you to think differently. You *are* important enough to invest the time and energy needed for the change you want. Commit to becoming the person you wish to be and carve out the time for what needs to be done!

The particular gene the researchers examined helps produce a protein that's active in your brain, including the parts of your brain that control your eating and your weight. But it's important not to jump to conclusions. None of this *proves* that if your house is cluttered, you're also going to be overweight—or vice versa.

Kiara Timpano, PhD, a hoarding researcher and assistant professor at the University of Miami, tells me that "our average patients are in their fifties and sixties, and statistics have shown that we tend to put on weight as we age, regardless of whether we have hoarding or not. Does that mean we're going to quit studying this connection? No, but we'll have to be careful about jumping to conclusions, since I don't think the data's clear yet."

Also, the *BDNF* study, which Dr. Timpano led, only included people with obsessive-compulsive disorder (OCD). In some way, this condition could have influenced the hoarding-obesity connection the researchers found. In addition, it's important to note that researchers have spent very little time looking at the health effects of garden-variety clutter. They instead focus on people with hoarding disorder. These individuals' way of looking at possessions (as well as the activity going on in their brain) doesn't always apply to the person with a run-of-the-mill messy home. But, as you saw in the sidebar above, some research supports my notion that "cluttered" and "hoarding" are two points on the same line.

With all that said, a psychologist can make a good case for why clutter and obesity might show up together. Shared factors may help fuel both concerns, like the same stream of electricity running two appliances. "While the relationship is probably really complicated, one theory is that they share a common mechanism of deficient self-regulation. That's a sciencey way of saying 'discipline,'" Dr. Tolin says.

"If you think about it, some of us are naturally slender, but for a lot of us, not being obese actually requires some effort. You have to regulate your diet, and you have to get exercise. Similarly, for some of us, cleaning just comes easy, but for a lot of us, *not* building up clutter is a matter of effort. If you don't have the psychological wherewithal to identify that a problem exists, *then* make a conscious decision to do something about it, and *then* actually stick to a plan even when it doesn't feel good, it's likely that lots of different things could pop up, obesity and clutter being only a couple of them."

Plenty of research has also found that some of society's most common emotional and mood problems may raise your risk of both obesity and clutter.

The Power of Thoughts and Emotions

Not so long ago, many experts thought that hoarding was a specific type of obsessive-compulsive disorder, a problem typically marked by intrusive mental images and a powerful urge to do certain behaviors. Today, hoarding and OCD are generally regarded as separate issues. But experts are finding that when people have difficulty with extreme levels of clutter, often other psychological issues, such as the ones that follow, are also present.

ANXIETY

Researchers looking back at a number of studies on people who hoard found that more than half of these people also had an anxiety disorder. One of the most common types of anxiety they show is social anxiety disorder. With this condition, you often worry that you'll do something to embarrass yourself, and you fear that other people are judging you. Many people who hoard are embarrassed by the chaos in their homes.

Another common type of anxiety in people who hoard is called generalized anxiety disorder. If you have this type, you often worry uncontrollably about a variety of issues.

DEPRESSION

In a study that included 217 people with hoarding disorder, more than half also had major depression. Another 5 percent had a milder form of depression.

ATTENTION-DEFICIT/HYPERACTIVITY DISORDER

Researchers have found evidence of ADHD in about one-fifth to one-third of people with hoarding disorder. Adult ADHD is marked by difficulties with:

▸ Focusing on details

▸ Staying organized

▸ Controlling a chaotic lifestyle

▸ Starting tasks and seeing them through to completion

In addition, poor impulse control—another symptom of ADHD—is evident in many people with hoarding disorder. In one study, nearly three-fourths of people who hoard reported that they compulsively bought stuff. In another, more than half would compulsively purchase things for sale or pick up free things.

ADHD isn't just for kids. More than half of children diagnosed with ADHD may still be dealing with the condition as adults. But adults with ADHD don't have a monopoly on lack of focus, lack of organization, and a "chaotic lifestyle." I think *much* of the population has developed these qualities.

The Terrible Two: Anxiety and Depression

Full-fledged anxiety and depression are very common in adults. Major depression affects about 16 million American adults during any given year, and about 40 million have an anxiety disorder. Millions more have milder versions of these problems that affect their lives but don't warrant formal diagnosis and treatment.

This increasing awareness of the links between the stuff we own and our mental landscape is something that has long fascinated me. I'm not a mental health professional, but I have noticed something compelling during my many years of working with people whose clutter has overwhelmed them: You can see people's sadness and fears in the clutter around them.

Remember that anxiety and depression are two of the most common mental health challenges in our communities today. Think about this: Anxiety is often characterized as an undue preoccupation with the future, with excessive worry about situations that might happen and the impact they could have. Depression is often characterized as a preoccupation with things past, with a concern about what might have been and the "if only's" of one's life.

Remember those two types of clutter we looked at in Chapter 1? There's memory clutter, which reminds you of an important person, achievement, or event from the past. I think memory clutter often gathers in the homes of people with some degree of depression. And then there's "I might need it one day" clutter, in which people hang on to stuff in anticipation of an imagined future. Among these folks, I've noticed a recurring theme of anxiety.

I find it interesting that these two kinds of clutter so closely parallel two common types of mental health problems in our society. Maybe it's possible that the stuff we own and obsess over is the physical manifestation of the mental health issues that challenge our minds.

When I have tough conversations with people about the clutter in their homes, they often tell me that their worries, their sadness, and their inattention played a major role. Again, it's never about the stuff. The focus, instead, should be on the factors that led the stuff to accumulate. Clutter develops because of your mood, your emotions, your attitudes, and your behaviors—and each is intimately connected to the others.

And on a related note, it's not about the *fat* either. Just as you didn't say, "I'm going to deliberately bring more stuff into my home than I really need, then hang on to it longer than I should," I'm certain you didn't say this:

I'm going to overfeed my body with more calories than it needs. I'm also going to be sure to sit around so I don't burn off too many of those calories. Eventually I'll have such a thick layer of food, alcohol, and sodas around my body that I won't be able to fit into my current clothes.

▶ WHERE ARE YOU ON THE CLUTTER SCALE?

The degree to which we accumulate clutter can be thought of in terms of a sliding scale on which most of us can locate ourselves. I've found it useful to think of the different stages of the scale like this:

| MESSY | DISORGANIZED | CLUTTERED | PACK RAT | HOARDER |

Each of these stages on what I call "The Clutter Scale" is marked by increasing levels of clutter, more difficulty discarding things or letting them go, more severe trouble in relationships with family and friends due to clutter, increased social isolation, and increasing mental health issues.

No single factor can predict whether a person will struggle with clutter, though many factors may come into play: genetics, family history, environment, social conditioning, and one's upbringing. Sometimes a childhood trauma associated with personal belongings can play a role.

I vividly remember a woman I worked with who found it impossible to let go of

anything that came into her home. She told me that as a child, her family had moved across the country. Her parents guaranteed that she would find all of her belongings in their new home, but when they proved too expensive to move, her parents threw them away. In many ways, that grown woman was still the traumatized 8-year-old who'd been betrayed. As an adult, she made sure that no one—including herself—would ever separate her from her things.

Some people just never learned the simple routines of maintaining a home when they were kids. Once, working with a young family, I asked why they threw their laundered clothes into the corner of their

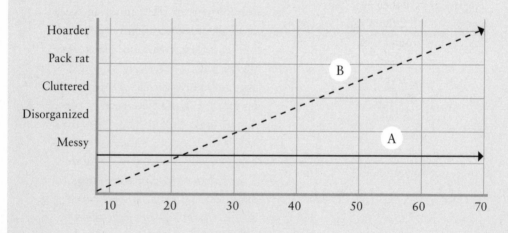

master bedroom. The wife said this was how she was raised. She was surprised—and a little amazed—when I showed her how to fold clothes and iron a shirt. She'd never before seen or done either!

Organization is a skill like any other that must be modeled and taught from an early age, or else kids are more likely to struggle with clutter later on. Many of my clients have confided that their clutter has gotten worse with age, and that an intervention when they were younger might have caught the problem before it became extreme.

Consider a small lesson contained in my Clutter Scale, which you can see once we plot the scale on a graph along with age.

It's not unusual for people to deal with some level of clutter (or messiness) their entire life. Sometimes they struggle with the same level of clutter over long stretches of their lives (represented by the A line). Others see the piles of possessions around them grow deeper over the years (as seen on the B line).

Whether you've been following the A line at any of these clutter levels for years, or you've been riding the B line into more severe problems, the program in the following pages is going to help you steer your arrow downward.

If you're overweight, that's *not* how it happened. Instead, you lifted snacks, entrées, and drinks to your mouth thousands of times. Only some of those times was your action driven by true hunger or thirst. It's quite likely that the same types of emotional upset or inattention that led to your cluttered home also played a role in the current state of your waist and hips. That's because excess weight can be associated with depression.

One study of more than 2,400 obese and overweight adults found that those with abdominal obesity—in other words, a big belly—were more than twice as likely to have symptoms of major depression. In another study that followed nearly 66,000 middle- aged and older women for 10 years, those who were depressed at the beginning of the project were more likely to become obese later. On the other hand, those who were obese at the beginning were more likely to become depressed later.

Anxiety also may influence people to become overweight. In a U.S. study of whites, African Americans, and Latinos, people in any of these groups who'd had an anxiety disorder in the past year were more likely to be obese. And among more than 2,100 Dutch people, those who had symptoms of depression or anxiety at the beginning of the study were more likely to be bigger around the waist 2 years later. (Their HDL, or "good" cholesterol, also fell, which could pose a threat to heart health.)

And let's not forget the issue of inattentiveness. Whether you have ADHD or you simply don't pay attention to your food, inattentiveness may boost your odds of being overweight.

A number of studies on people seeking treatment for their obesity found that a higher percentage of them had ADHD compared to the general population. (These studies, however, weren't set up to prove that one caused the other.) In another study, researchers compared men who'd had childhood ADHD with men who *didn't* have childhood ADHD. The men who'd had ADHD were significantly more likely to be obese (about 41 percent compared to 21.6 percent in the non-ADHD group).

And women who remembered having more ADHD-like symptoms in childhood—such as inattention, poor impulse control, and hyperactivity—have been found to have a higher risk of obesity in adulthood.

I'd like to recap two main points here, since they're crucial for confronting—and conquering—your clutter and your weight in this program:

1. Anxiety, depression, and ADHD may raise people's risk of hoarding and becoming overweight. Since hoarding and regular excessive clutter aren't necessarily far apart, this research very well may apply to you, dear reader, even if you don't have hoarding disorder.

2. You don't need to have a full-fledged, diagnosable case of depression, anxiety, or ADHD for this to apply to you, either. Milder relatives of these problems—respectively, feeling blue, stressed, unfocused, or impulsive—can affect your purchasing and eating habits.

Knowing whether any of these issues are lurking in your mind will put you in a better position to confront them and separate them from your eating habits and your attitudes toward acquiring and hanging on to possessions.

In the next chapter, you'll put your mind to the test to see what kinds of factors may be driving your clutter and weight. Make that *several* tests!

Chapter 3

WHERE AM I NOW (AND HOW DID MY MIND BRING ME HERE)?

The 6-week program at the heart of *Cut the Clutter, Drop the Pounds* will keep you pretty busy. You'll be emptying dressers. Hauling bags of trash to the curb. Carrying trunkloads of goodies to the donation center (a *lot* of them, if you're anything like the test panelists who went through the program). Going on calorie-burning walks. Hoisting household objects until your muscles grow stronger.

If you *only* did these tasks, I think the physical activity alone could change your body and home enough that a bystander would notice the progress. But the improvements likely wouldn't last very long. After all, you've probably lost weight before. You've probably tamed the mess in areas of your home many times. But the changes didn't stick. Your body size went up, and the clutter piled up on your counters again.

I don't want that to happen to you this time. I want the changes you observe in your body and your home 6 weeks from now to stick around for a long time. I want you to have even *greater* success over your weight and your clutter in the months and years after the program is over.

But for that to happen, you can't just *do*. You also have to *think*.

So many of the people I work with—people who struggle with varying degrees of clutter in their homes and lives every day—have one thing in common:

They are frequently not engaged in their own lives. By this I mean that much of their daily activity is conducted almost by rote. They buy things without really thinking about it, eat food without really tasting it, watch TV without noticing what they're seeing, and interact with people around them in a distracted way. Put simply, they're preoccupied by so many distractions they're just not *thinking*.

If your mind continues to force you to overeat, overshop, and hang on to household items long after they've stopped being useful, your body won't be able to exercise and declutter fast enough to keep up. If your mind continues to be unhappy, overstressed, and unfocused, your drive to maintain your improvements will fade.

To make deep, lasting changes to the appearance of your body and home, you're going to have to use your mind differently than before. I want you to do the following:

▸ Work *with* your mind, not *for* it. Avoid blindly following your impulses.

▸ Observe the things your mind is telling you, without immediately obeying its commands or spending time arguing with it.

▸ Recognize when your mind is viewing the world as a darker, scarier place than it really is.

▸ Stop confusing the memories attached to your household items with the items themselves.

▸ Stop envisioning catastrophe in your future.

▸ Celebrate your successes rather than focusing on your shortcomings.

Your attitude plays a crucial role here. I am constantly surprised by the negative perspective so many people have about themselves and their homes. Often when I am in the middle of a decluttering project, a word or look or comment will give this attitude away. When I get a sense of it, I always ask, "Do you think you deserve to be happy?" The response I frequently get first is shock that I would even *ask* such a question, followed by tears, and then a negative shake of the head.

So many people who struggle with clutter have filled their homes with "stuff" in hopes of finding some peace or happiness—always without success. Understand this: You do deserve to live in a tranquil, happy, peaceful home. You do deserve to be happy.

Both your body's weight and your home's appearance evolved to their current state largely because of the thoughts, perceptions, and attitudes in your mind. So you'll need to use your mind differently—in the next 6 weeks and the years to follow—to keep your body and your home in shape.

Taking Stock

But before you can develop a new relationship with your mind, you need a better sense of what's going on in there right now. In this chapter, I'm asking you to fill out a few simple questionnaires that measure your mood, your focus, and your attitudes toward your possessions. The information you gain from these tools will help you declutter more effectively—and permanently— and examine your relationship with food and exercise in a new way.

Ready? Grab a pencil. You might want to scan or photocopy the quizzes first in case you want to repeat them later to measure improvements in your mental outlook. I strongly recommend that you do these quizzes now, and again after you go through the program. The improvements you're likely to see will give you more successes from the program that you can celebrate.

MEASURING YOUR CLUTTER

The first survey you'll take provides a sense of how much your clutter affects your life. It also draws attention to the attitudes that seem to be fueling your clutter. Hoarding expert David Tolin, PhD, says this is a well-regarded tool for measuring the way you feel about clutter. I asked all our test panelists to take this survey. Once you're finished, you can compare your score to theirs.

SAVING INVENTORY—REVISED (MODIFIED FORMAT)

Your score will give you a better sense of how badly you want to bring items home and how much you have to struggle to get rid of them later. For each of these questions, circle the number that corresponds most closely to your experience during the past week.

0	1	2	3	4
None	A little	A moderate amount	Most/ much	Almost all/ complete

1. How much of the living area in your home is cluttered with possessions? (Consider the amount of clutter in your kitchen, living room, dining room, hallways, bedrooms, bathrooms, or other rooms.)   0   1   2   3   4

2. How much control do you have over your urges to acquire possessions?   0   1   2   3   4

3. How much of your home does clutter prevent you from using? 0 1 2 3 4

4. How much control do you have over your urges to save possessions? 0 1 2 3 4

5. How much of your home is difficult to walk through because of clutter? 0 1 2 3 4

For each of these questions, circle the number that corresponds most closely to your experience during the past week.

0	1	2	3	4
Not at all	Mild	Moderate	Considerable/ severe	Extreme

6. To what extent do you have difficulty throwing things away? 0 1 2 3 4

7. How distressing do you find the task of throwing things away? 0 1 2 3 4

8. To what extent do you have so many things that your room(s) are cluttered? 0 1 2 3 4

9. How distressed or uncomfortable would you feel if you could not acquire something you wanted? 0 1 2 3 4

10. How much does clutter in your home interfere with your social, work, or everyday functioning? Think about things that you don't do because of clutter. 0 1 2 3 4

11. How strong is your urge to buy or acquire free things for which you have no immediate use? 0 1 2 3 4

During the past week:

0	1	2	3	4
Not at all	Mild	Moderate	Considerable/ severe	Extreme

12. To what extent does clutter in your home cause you distress? 0 1 2 3 4

13. How strong is your urge to save something you know you may never use? 0 1 2 3 4

14. How upset or distressed do you feel about your acquiring habits?   0   1   2   3   4

15. To what extent do you feel unable to control the clutter in your home?   0   1   2   3   4

16. To what extent has your saving or compulsive buying resulted in financial difficulties for you?   0   1   2   3   4

For each of these questions, circle the number that corresponds most closely to your experience during the past week.

0	1	2	3	4
Not at all	Mild	Moderate	Considerable/ severe	Extreme

17. How often do you avoid trying to discard possessions because it is too stressful or time-consuming?   0   1   2   3   4

18. How often do you feel compelled to acquire something you see (e.g., when shopping or offered free things)?   0   1   2   3   4

19. How often do you decide to keep things you do not need and have little space for?   0   1   2   3   4

20. How frequently does clutter in your home prevent you from inviting people to visit?   0   1   2   3   4

21. How often do you actually buy (or acquire for free) things for which you have no immediate use or need?   0   1   2   3   4

22. To what extent does the clutter in your home prevent you from using parts of your home for their intended purpose? For example, cooking, using furniture, washing dishes, cleaning, etc.   0   1   2   3   4

23. How often are you unable to discard a possession you would like to get rid of?   0   1   2   3   4

Scoring: To find your score, first add up your answers to questions 1, 3, 5, 8, 10, 12, 15, 20, and 22. These questions make up the clutter component of this questionnaire. This score will give you a sense of how much trouble the physical clutter around your home is now causing you.

My clutter score = _____

Next, add up your answers to questions 4 (reversed), 6, 7, 13, 17, 19, and 23.

Be sure to reverse your score for question 4 because of the way it's written. For example, if you circled 0, switch it to 4, and vice versa. If you circled 1, switch it to 3, and vice versa. If you circled 2, it remains the same.

This score measures how intensely you feel the need to save objects, or the intensity of the difficulty you have discarding them.

My difficulty discarding/saving score = _____

Finally, add up your answers to questions 2 (reversed), 9, 11, 14, 16, 18, and 21.

Again, make sure to reverse your score for question 2.

This score measures your need to buy new items or get them for free, as well as how your desire to acquire has affected your life.

My acquisition score = _____

Now add all these scores together to get your total score.

My total score = _____

If you gave this questionnaire to a general crowd of people, on average their scores would be:

▶ Clutter—8.1

▶ Difficulty discarding/saving—7.8

▶ Acquisition—8.1

▶ Total score—24

On the other hand, if you gave these questions to people with hoarding problems, their scores would likely be:

▶ Clutter—more than 17

▶ Difficulty discarding/saving—more than 14

▶ Acquisition—more than 9

▶ Total score—more than 40

When we gathered our test panel, we asked them to take this survey, and I suspected their scores would be high. Much to my surprise, however, their average clutter, difficulty discarding, and aquisition scores were in the hoarding range, or just below it.

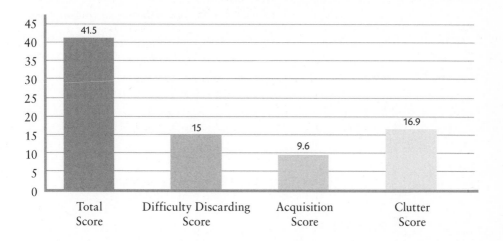

Their total score, on average, was 41.5—just into the range you might see in someone with a hoarding problem. Some had a total score well under 40, and some had a score that was substantially higher.

Keep in mind that a high score on this quiz *doesn't* in itself mean that you have hoarding disorder. You'd need to go to a qualified mental health professional for a diagnosis of that.

The Diagnostic and Statistical Manual of Mental Disorders (DSM) underwent a big revision before its current version, the DSM-5, was released in 2013. This is the manual that guides mental health experts on recognizing and diagnosing hundreds of mental health problems. To be diagnosed with hoarding disorder, the DSM-5 says you need to:

▶ Have persistent trouble getting rid of or giving away possessions, whether or not these are things other people find valuable

▶ Have this trouble because you feel a strong urge to save items and/or you feel distress when parting with them

▶ Have so much stuff in your home or workplace, as a result of these issues, that you can't use at least some of the spaces for their intended purpose

▶ Experience significant distress or problems functioning as a result of these symptoms

I included this survey as a tool to help pinpoint where you have particular problems related to your stuff. Clutter comes from bringing too much stuff *into* your home (your acquisition score), not getting rid of enough of it (your difficulty discarding/saving score), and allowing it to spread throughout your home where it doesn't belong (your clutter score).

An especially high score in one or more of these areas suggests you should pay particular attention to what's causing you to acquire stuff, hold on to stuff, or be messy. If they're all equally high, then you'll know to seek answers across the board.

Remember that your score may well go down after you go through the program. The participants who finished the program saw their scores fall steeply! I'll talk more about how much they improved a little later in the book.

MEASURING YOUR ANXIETY

Next, it's time to test your anxiety levels with a commonly used tool called the GAD-7. This is a fairly recently developed survey, and research has found it to be a "valid and efficient" way for doctors and mental health professionals to check for generalized anxiety disorder.

I'm including it here as a way for you to quickly and easily get a general sense of how much anxiety you're carrying around. I also asked the test panel to answer these questions.

GENERALIZED ANXIETY DISORDER 7-ITEM (GAD-7) SCALE

Over the last 2 weeks, how often have you been bothered by the following problems? Circle a number for each answer.

0 Not at all	1 Several days	2 More than half the days	3 Nearly every day			
1. Feeling nervous, anxious, or on edge			0	1	2	3
2. Not being able to stop or control worrying			0	1	2	3
3. Worrying too much about different things			0	1	2	3
4. Trouble relaxing			0	1	2	3
5. Being so restless that it's hard to sit still			0	1	2	3
6. Becoming easily annoyed or irritable			0	1	2	3
7. Feeling afraid as if something awful might happen			0	1	2	3

Scoring: Add up all your zeroes, ones, twos, and threes at the bottom of each column. Now add all your columns together. This gives you your total score.

Your score can range from zero to 21. Here's what your score means:

0 to 4—you appear to have minimal anxiety

5 to 9—you appear to have mild anxiety

10 to 14—you appear to have moderate anxiety

15 to 21—you appear to have severe anxiety

Remember, this quiz doesn't *diagnose* you with an anxiety problem. It merely draws your attention to a possibility. In my experience, people who are struggling with clutter tend to show higher degrees of stress and anxiety. A frequent part of my work with clients is to help them deal with a sense of anxiousness or foreboding. Addressing clutter inevitably raises surprising issues and emotions. Expect that to be a normal part of this process. Accept and work through your feelings. If anxiety is interfering with your life, seeking professional help may be your best course of action. Anxiety, left untreated, can be seriously debilitating.

Our test panel also saw improvement on their anxiety scores, as you'll see in the graph below.

If you scored high on the GAD-7, keep in mind that addressing your anxiety will likely help you better manage your home and your weight.

▶ TEST PANELIST GAD-7 SCORES
BEFORE AND AFTER PROGRAM

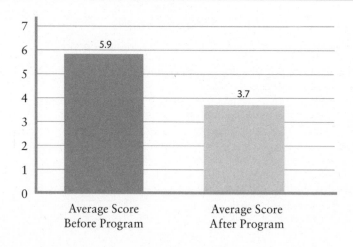

MEASURING YOUR MOOD

Now let's take a look at whether you're dealing with depression, using a similarly structured scale called the PHQ-9. Depression means more than just sitting around feeling sad: It can also lead to physical symptoms and changes in your behavior that you might not realize are due to depression.

Researchers conducting depression-related studies often give participants the PHQ-9 to track their outlook. Since symptoms of depression can play such a big role in your relationship with your home and weight, I'd like you to explore whether any of the elements of this questionnaire relate to you. Having this knowledge can give you more power over your clutter and waistline while you're doing the 6-week program.

PATIENT HEALTH QUESTIONNAIRE-9 (PHQ-9)

Over the last 2 weeks, how often have you been bothered by any of the following problems? Circle a number for each answer.

0 Not at all	1 Several days	2 More than half the days	3 Nearly every day

1. Little interest or pleasure in doing things	0	1 2 3	
2. Feeling down, depressed, or hopeless	0	1 2 3	
3. Trouble falling or staying asleep, or sleeping too much	0	1 2 3	
4. Feeling tired or having little energy	0	1 2 3	
5. Poor appetite or overeating	0	1 2 3	
6. Feeling bad about yourself—or that you are a failure or you have let yourself or your family down	0	1 2 3	
7. Trouble concentrating on things, such as reading the newspaper or watching television	0	1 2 3	
8. Moving or speaking so slowly that other people could have noticed? Or the opposite—being so fidgety or restless that you have been moving around a lot more than usual	0	1 2 3	
9. Thoughts that you would be better off dead or of hurting yourself in some way	0	1 2 3	

Scoring: Add up all your zeroes, ones, twos, and threes at the bottom of each column. Now add all your columns together. This gives you your total score.

Here's what your score means:

0 to 4—you appear to have minimal depression

5 to 9—you appear to have mild depression

10 to 14—you appear to have moderate depression

15 to 19—you appear to have moderately severe depression

20 to 27—you appear to have severe depression

If you got a high score on this quiz or you've been struggling with symptoms of depression, consider talking to your doctor or a mental health professional.

Also, as you go through the program, remember that feelings of depression can influence how you collect new possessions, hang on to old ones, and maintain your home. Improving your home environment will likely require you to address these feelings.

MEASURING YOUR FOCUS

Moving on, let's focus on your *focus*. If you have ADHD-like symptoms, such as trouble paying attention or controlling your impulses, these can play a role in your weight and the orderliness of your home. That's because if you're living your life on autopilot rather than controlling your choices, you're going to drift toward eating and shopping habits that feel good but aren't necessarily good for your health or your home.

The following tool, called the ASRS, can quickly shed light on whether ADHD or its symptoms are likely to be a problem for you. This questionnaire was developed by the World Health Organization, with the help of experts on adult ADHD.

The symptoms in this survey—especially the first four—are likely to impact how well you can create and stick with a plan to address your weight and your household clutter. These issues are all fairly common in today's society, and you certainly don't have to have ADHD for them to affect you.

ADULT ADHD SELF-REPORT SCALE—V1.1 (ASRS-V1.1) SYMPTOM CHECKLIST

Check the circle that best describes how you have felt and conducted yourself over the past 6 months.

	Never	Rarely	Sometimes	Often	Very often
1. How often do you have trouble wrapping up the final details of a project, once the challenging parts have been done?	○	○	○	○	○
2. How often do you have difficulty getting things in order when you have to do a task that requires organization?	○	○	○	○	○
3. How often do you have problems remembering appointments or obligations?	○	○	○	○	○
4. When you have a task that requires a lot of thought, how often do you avoid or delay getting started?	○	○	○	○	○
5. How often do you fidget or squirm with your hands or feet when you have to sit down for a long time?	○	○	○	○	○
6. How often do you feel overly active and compelled to do things, like you were driven by a motor?	○	○	○	○	○

Scoring: Place a check mark in the appropriate circle for each answer. Add the number of check marks that appear in the shaded area. Having 4 or more check marks in the shaded area suggests that your symptoms might point to adult ADHD. You may want to ask your health care provider if you should be evaluated for the condition.

© World Health Organization, 2003

MEASURING YOUR EMOTIONAL EATING

Finally, I'd like you to test one more area in which your emotions influence your health.

Whenever you're making decisions, the emotions you feel during those moments affect the choice you wind up making. This is true for decisions about buying or picking up free items (Do I take this home or not?) and how you're going to eat (salmon steak or regular steak?).

In the last chapter, we learned that anxiety, depression, and lack of attention can make you more likely to grow overweight. In part, that's because it's common for people to reach for food when they're feeling an unpleasant emotion, says Edie Goldbacher, PhD, an assistant professor at La Salle University in Philadelphia. She's a psychologist with an interest in emotional eating, and she often works with people who have both weight and mood issues. Emotions that can trigger a desire for food include:

▸ Stress

▸ Sadness

▸ Guilt

▸ Shame

▸ Boredom

You may also reach for food when you're sleepy or fatigued, which are more physical sensations than emotions. *Positive* emotions can certainly trigger emotional eating, too, such as when you're celebrating at a party or you're ushering in the weekend with a Friday dinner with friends.

According to author Jenny Taitz, PsyD, author of *End Emotional Eating,* when you're eating for emotional reasons, you don't necessarily realize it. But the following situations generally have an emotion lurking in them:

▸ Snacking when you aren't even hungry

▸ Feeling a sense of emotional relief while you're eating

▸ Feeling a powerful urge for a particular food

▸ Eating during or just after a stressful event

▸ Using food to make your emotions feel less powerful

If you have a tendency to eat in response to emotional triggers, you may have been developing this behavior since childhood, Dr. Goldbacher says. Perhaps you learned it from your family, your culture, or your own choices (you felt bad one day, ate a brownie and felt better, and stuck with this routine).

Now when an event occurs that makes you feel worried, or sad, or bored—or you even *think* about these emotions—you reach for the food that you know will help you feel better. Some people are so scared of feeling strong emotions that they're especially likely to use food to quell these feelings or provide a distraction, according to Dr. Taitz.

If you feel ashamed or guilty after you splurge on treats to tame your emotions, you may eat even more to cope with *these* negative emotions that arise. This can turn into a very troublesome cycle.

There's a large overlap between *emotional* eating and *mindless* eating. Mindless eating means you're eating food without enjoying it or even noticing what you're doing. Do you have any experience with eating a box of candy—without even tasting it—when you're under a work deadline? Have you ever emptied a pint of ice cream on autopilot while you were caught up in a nerve-racking TV show? That's emotional, mindless eating.

Not everyone who eats because of emotional triggers is overweight. All sorts of people do this, no matter their body weight, Dr. Goldbacher says. And it's not necessarily harmful to enjoy a cookie here and there when you're feeling down. Emotional eating only becomes a problem when it has a negative effect on your life, Dr. Taitz says.

As you progress through the 6 weeks of the *Cut the Clutter, Drop the Pounds* program, I want you to start living your life more deliberately. I want you to bring new objects into your home only when you have a good reason to do so. I want you to only keep possessions in your home that truly belong there. And when you eat, I want you to eat for a specific purpose.

If you're suffering from a moment of sadness, or you're so excited that you must celebrate, I'm not going to tell you that you must get through this moment without food. But I do want you to be deliberate about what you're doing. I want you to be in control of how much you eat. And I want you to fully enjoy the taste and the texture of your food without feeling guilt and shame afterward.

In the next chapter, you'll find strategies for eating mindfully, including when you're in the grip of strong emotions. Right now, I'd like for you to fill in the following chart, which will give you a better sense of how often you rely on food during emotional moments.

Specific situations—like feeling stress during holidays—can act as triggers for emotional eating. So can certain feelings, like anger, boredom, or frustration. Identify three situations and three feelings that commonly lead you to eat as a coping mechanism.

EMOTIONAL EATING TRACKER

Situations

1. _____

2. _____

3. _____

Feelings

1. _____

2. _____

3. _____

Simply being aware of these triggers can help you take a *huge* step toward positive action. Some people deal with these moments not by eating or buying, but by going for a walk or organizing a drawer or other small area of their home! Try different ways to distract yourself, and when you feel a strong emotion coming on, use a new approach.

Looking Ahead

Very soon, I'm going to introduce you to the 6-week program that will start reversing the impact that all these emotions and attitudes have had on your weight and your home.

But first, I'd like to take the next chapter to discuss a powerful mental tool that can supercharge the program and boost your success over the coming 6 weeks . . . and for the rest of your life.

Chapter 4

CLUTTER AND FAT ARE NO MATCH FOR YOUR MIND

Your mind is a powerful tool. You can summon the names of hundreds—perhaps thousands—of people when you see their faces. You can learn to use bewildering new gadgets, from VHS recorders to self-scan supermarket checkouts, as they change over the decades. Perhaps you can detect hidden jokes in Shakespeare's verses or follow Stephen Hawking as he explains the mysteries of the universe.

As smart as it is, though, your mind isn't always easy to use. It can want different things at the same time. It propels you into situations that you know aren't good for you. It swings between logic and emotion. The choices it makes aren't always predictable.

If you're overweight and cluttered, *your mind led you to be that way!* Some people never learn how to create a healthy partnership with their mind. That's too bad. When they let their mind meander through life, they don't necessarily wind up where they want to be. They also miss big stretches of scenery along the way.

In this chapter, I want to talk about a tool that's as simple to describe as a hammer. It's called mindfulness. You can use mindfulness in different ways in your life, just as you can do different things with a hammer. If a squeaky board in your floor is annoying you, you can fix it in a few minutes with that hammer. Or you can use your hammer to build a beautiful home.

Mindfulness isn't about controlling your mind, but simply watching what it does so you learn how it works. By tracking its movements, you can:

- Break the cycle of consuming foods and buying possessions because of emotional triggers

- Find more joy by becoming more accepting of your life and discovering more inner contentment

- Learn to avoid the poison of depression and anxiety that your mind tries to sneak into your life

Mindfulness can help you limit all three components of clutter:

- You can better examine whether you truly want to bring new clothing, new furniture, or a new knickknack into your home.

- You can become more aware of how tidy your home is (rather than letting clutter blend into the background).

- You can better assess, without emotion, whether it's time to get rid of any of your possessions.

In some ways, your mind is like a toddler. It demands to get what it wants. It won't tolerate you ignoring its tantrums. But it's likely that your mind's demands have led you to become overweight in a cluttered home. And if you don't change your relationship with your mind, you'll stay that way. Let's not let that happen.

The Science of Mindfulness

Historically, spirituality and science haven't always coexisted peacefully. But they do—in a way—in PubMed, the online database of medical studies. There you'll find that a central practice borrowed from an ancient religion has become a well-researched treatment for physical and emotional problems.

It's called mindfulness (or mindfulness meditation), and researchers have investigated its use in the full spectrum of ailments that can strike our bodies and minds. They've studied it for joint-replacement pain. For addiction. For sexual desire in women. Researchers have looked at the benefits of mindfulness for cancer patients, African American men with high blood pressure, and Marines about to be deployed. That's just a tiny taste of a few months' worth of mindfulness research.

Mindfulness has great potential. I believe it can help you reduce the burden of most—if not all—the problems that brought you to this book: a cluttered home, out-of-control weight, and mental distress.

Mindfulness has come a long way, both geographically and in social attitudes, to get to this place of acceptance by mainstream scientists. Over the last half of the 1900s, Buddhism—which previously occupied a toehold in American culture—gained more of a foothold. Turmoil in Asia brought refugees and their practices to the United States, along with returning GIs who had become interested in the beliefs they encountered overseas. By the early 1980s, American psychologists and physicians were inquiring whether mindfulness meditation, a practice that lies at the core of Buddhism, had any health benefits.

But this Westernized practice doesn't involve statues of the Buddha. You don't chant. You don't spend years seeking enlightenment in a monastery. You can practice mindfulness wearing your regular clothes in your bedroom, in your backyard, in your car, or while you're walking.

Mindfulness meditation is for people with any religious belief, and for people with *no* religious belief. Despite its origins, it is in itself a nonreligious activity. In that regard, it's akin to yoga, which gives you a good stretch no matter your beliefs.

Jon Kabat-Zinn, PhD, founder of the Mindfulness-Based Stress Reduction Program at the University of Massachusetts Medical School in 1979, has defined mindfulness as "the awareness that emerges through paying attention on purpose, in the present moment, and nonjudgmentally to the unfolding of experience moment to moment."

This seems like a simple idea, but improving your mindfulness is not necessarily easy. Most of us haven't been raised to be mindful, and modern life certainly doesn't encourage it.

Let's examine Dr. Kabat-Zinn's definition a little more closely. Mindfulness simply involves:

Observing what's going on right now. When you're mindful, you're aware of the thoughts going through your mind, the sensations in your body, and the happenings in the world around you at this moment. You're aware of where you are and what you're doing.

Making these observations with more tolerance. You notice these things without wanting to change them or complain about them. The day may be hot . . . but you're okay with it. The teenagers next to you at the stoplight are blasting their music . . . but you realize that you won't be hearing it for long. An unpleasant memory pops into your head . . . but it doesn't bring you down. These things merely are what they are.

Living in the real world, not the world your mind creates. When you're replaying an argument with a relative, you're living in your mind. You're not living in the real world. The same is true when you spend a day in dread while you wait for a call from your doctor. You're also engaged in your mind—not living in the real world—when you're displeased with how an event is unfolding because it doesn't match your preferences.

Most of us confuse our preferences, biases, and fears with the real world. They're not. And it's this confusion that causes major problems. For example, two people might face the same stressful situation. One person grows physically sick from worrying about it. The other remains calm and untouched until it's over. Or, more to the point of this book, one person might look at a tattered old shirt and see it for what it is: an unusable object that has no reason to be in the closet. Another might cling to it just because he wore it to a party on the last night of high school 20 years ago.

Mindfulness keeps you centered and aware. It helps you be present and focused. It keeps you firmly rooted in your life and living in the real world. I believe it also helps you to have an uncluttered home and a happier, more organized life.

Understanding the Present Moment

Can you think of any particular moments in your life when you were especially aware of what was going on around you? Maybe:

▶ You were floating on a raft on a slowly moving river when you were 12, and as you smelled the trees and felt the warm sun on your face, you were completely happy.

▶ The phone rang with the job offer that would send your career in a wonderful new direction, and you remember every word of the conversation.

▶ You saw your child's face for the first time, and you knew you would never forget that instant in time.

Can you think of any moments from your own life when you were fully aware of what was happening? Jot down your thoughts here.

_____

_____

_____

_____

_____

Our lives may take place over decades. But they're made of one long string of present moments like these. Of course, not all of these moments are this memorable, nor do they have to be. But they're all equally *real*. You're having a present moment right now. Now you're having another one.

This can be a challenging concept if you've not heard it before. We're taught to think about what will happen tomorrow or what plans we need to make for next week. The idea that our time is made up of individual moments, that we live our life from one moment to the next, can take some thinking about. The present moment, the *now* as it's often called, is all that we have. The rest is either past or yet to come—neither of which we have any control over.

The present moment is when *everything* in your life happens. It's the only real time you ever have. But we miss too many of these moments. Instead, we're rolling over some old hurt in our mind. We're missing someone who's gone from our lives. We're reliving a past event. And the past is gone. It's not real.

Or we're worried that we're going to lose our job. We're fretting about our health and imagining the worst. We're analyzing evidence and building a case for a catastrophe that will surely happen. At these times, our minds are in the future. The future hasn't happened. It's not real.

Or we're daydreaming that we're a superhero. Or we're caught up in the sheer unending noise of our mind as it chatters and bounces around like a monkey, zipping from one topic to another. Our mental noise isn't real, either.

In these moments, you might be making yet another decision that affects your weight or your home, and you choose poorly because you aren't really paying attention to the real world around you.

Do you wonder *why* you became overweight or *when* your home became unlivable? I'd guess it happened because you weren't paying attention when you ate those snacks or when you made those purchases. It happened while your mind was elsewhere.

I'm not a religious guy. I'm not New Agey. I'm as practical and no-nonsense of a person as you'll find, whether in my own life or when I'm offering advice to others. I promote swift, efficient changes that actually work. But I'm here to tell you that if you're fat, unhappy, and cluttered, mindfulness can help you move toward a lower weight, a happier outlook, and a more pleasant home. I've seen life-altering changes brought about by a more mindful approach to life. Mindfulness helps create the permanent positive changes that so many people desire.

Now, mindfulness isn't a cure-all. It's not magic. It's not a contest that you can "win." There is no specific end to it. The more you learn about it, the more you find there is to it.

I'm not asking you to devote your life to mindfulness. But for the next 6 weeks, all I ask is that you give it a try. Because when it comes to your home, your body, your emotions, and your self-image, a little bit of mindfulness can lead to big improvements.

▶ MINDFULNESS: WHY AND WHEN?

The practice of mindfulness will enhance your life—for lots of reasons and in loads of circumstances. Here's a quick rundown.

Why practice mindfulness?

- We're constantly distracted.

- We often can't go 5 minutes without checking e-mail, texts, or social media.

- Multitasking divides our attention.

- Thinking is hard, so we often zone out and go through life on autopilot, missing good things.

- We're so busy we're often not fully engaged in *anything*.

When to practice mindfulness?

- When we're making decisions

- When we're feeling depression or anxiety growing

- At the end of the day when we're exhausted and turn to the TV to "veg out." (It's no accident that infomercials are on late at night and in the early-morning hours.)

Getting Started

In *Fully Present,* authors Susan L. Smalley, PhD, and Diana Winston—mindfulness educators at UCLA—offer these suggestions to newcomers on how to begin a mindfulness practice.

Focus on your breathing. During mindfulness meditation, simply focus your mind on an "anchor" rather than letting it float adrift on the roiling stream of noisy thoughts that flow through your consciousness.

It's actually more difficult to do than you might imagine. (It's like playing the game where you try *not* to think of a pink elephant. As soon as you try not to do it, your mind will post a picture of a pink elephant and refuse to let it go.)

Mindfulness experts often suggest that you anchor your focus on your breathing. Our ancient ancestors around the world associated our breath with life itself. Breathing is also closely linked to the present moment, since both pass at a constant stream. Both your present moment and your current breath replaced the previous one. New ones then replace them. And both occur largely without your awareness. By focusing on your breath, you can become more aware of the present moment.

Start small. Trying to sit for a long session at the beginning can be tiring and discouraging (also, you're going to have plenty of other stuff to do during your 6-week program). So keep your first sessions short, like 5 to 10 minutes.

Find a comfortable, nondistracting spot. Sit somewhere that allows you to relax. Your surroundings should be relatively quiet, and no one should be trying to get your attention. Find a place that's comfortable, but not so comfortable that you'll get sleepy. Sit on the floor, on a cushion, or in a firm chair. Meditate with your eyes closed, or open and fixed on an object that won't distract you (*not* the TV).

That's pretty much what you need to start. Simply sit and feel your breath move in and out of your body, noticing the rise and fall of your abdomen or chest, or the sensations of the air moving through your nostrils. Just let your breath come as it will, without trying to hold it or speed it up.

If a thought pops into your head, distracting you from your breathing—and trust me, it will—turn your mind away from the thought and back to your breath. The distracting thought is like a buzzing fly. It will go away. Another will take its place,

> ## Quick Tip!
> You can practice mindfulness meditation in noisy environments or while you're moving. You don't always have to sit in a quiet space. But for now, I'd recommend keeping it simple.

begging for your attention. Turn your focus back to your breathing and that thought will pass, too.

If you find you've spent some time caught up in a string of thoughts, with one turning into another and another, your next step remains the same: Direct your focus back to your breathing. Try not to get frustrated or mad that you're doing it "wrong." Your mind simply likes having your attention—sort of like a 2-year-old—and it'll make noise if it doesn't have it. With practice, you'll be better able to maintain your focus on your breathing. Then, as you're going about your daily routine, you may find that you're able to hold your focus

▶ TEAM WALSH: BUILDING MOMENTUM FOR MINDFULNESS

Mindfulness isn't always easy, but the benefits can be great. I heard from a number of the test panelists that they struggled with the mindfulness portion of this program (especially the 5-minute sessions of mindfulness meditation).

On the other hand, I also got good feedback from people who embraced the practice. Brenda (you'll see her story on page 88) found that mindfulness took the emotions out of her decision making. She saw her clutter as it really was, rather than allowing her sentiments related to these objects to distract her from the choices she needed to make.

She also noted:

The mindfulness of the program has helped me during these weeks. I have found myself "thinking" about the popcorn or the brownies I made for someone else. I find myself imagining I'm eating the food. I think, Do I want to do this . . . or not? I think about what will the popcorn do for me (or not do for me), the progress I've *made so far, that the food doesn't really taste that great sometimes anyway. I then drink water, go to my favorite healthy treat (fresh oranges or frozen strawberry smoothie), or run in place for 100 steps— and the temptation seems to pass. It's hard, but it has helped me.*

Other comments from test panelists included:

Marcia T.: "I realized some time ago that mindless spending is how I got into this clutter mess. I don't bring anything other than what I absolutely need into the house."

Elizabeth: "I have noticed that my legs and ankles are no longer swollen at the end of the day. I can't stress how huge this is for me, and I am so incredibly grateful for the skills and mindfulness I'm learning on this program!"

Jan: "I am making myself stop and actually notice when I take a bite, and for those few seconds don't do anything else but eat."

better on the present moment. The idea is to keep doing your special sessions of mindfulness meditation but also stay more mindful in real time.

As you progress, you'll spend fewer of your waking hours on autopilot or daydreaming. You'll make fewer eating and shopping choices while you're distracted (the choices you make on autopilot are more likely to take you away from your goal of fitness and tidiness). And when you stay more mindful, you'll be more aware of the factors that are trying to influence your decision. You'll have the mindfulness and presence to ask yourself:

▸ Am I truly hungry? Or do I recognize that an emotion is setting off an automatic desire to eat?

▸ Do I really want to keep that stack of magazines I haven't read? Or am I just reacting to the guilt I feel over the money I spent on the subscription?

▸ Is my heart pounding and my face flushed? I could be anxious. Do I need to find a course of action to lower my anxiety?

Mindfulness helps you be more aware of *how your mind works* and *what's going on in your body and the world around you.* That awareness can help you tame your household, your weight, and your emotions.

Mindfulness in the Marketplace

If you want a fun companion to go shopping with—someone who will encourage you to fill up your cart and pull out your credit card—you probably shouldn't call Diana Winston. But if you want to get a better sense of how to separate your emotions from your purchasing behaviors, she's definitely your expert.

Winston, whom you met earlier, is also the director of mindfulness education at the Mindfulness Awareness Research Center at UCLA. In the late '90s, you could have found her in a forest in Burma, where she lived for a year as a Buddhist nun. More recently, you might have seen her wandering the aisles of a major home goods store in Los Angeles, where she was teaching students about "greed management."

The students could walk around, pick up items, read the boxes, and take in all the joyful colors of the store. What they *couldn't* do was buy anything. Instead, she wanted them to simply take note of the desire they felt for items and how the mind reacts when it doesn't get what it wants.

The urge to possess an appealing object starts off strong. "It's coming into you—it's grabbing you by the throat. We think that in order to get rid of that 'I have to have it' feeling, we have to buy that object," she says. Too often, people don't ever get the chance to see what happens if they notice the feeling without acting on it. They usually buy the item to make the uncomfortable feeling go away.

But as her students learned, an interesting thing happens if they pay attention to the urge. It may grow worse for a while. Then it fades. Winston calls this *urge surfing*. "The concept is used in mindfulness-based treatment with people with addictions—Mindfulness-Based Relapse Prevention—but it's also relevant for people without addictions," she says. "When the urge comes, you feel it, you bring your self-awareness to the experience of having this urge, and you notice it like a wave. It has a crest and it passes through us."

When she says to "bring your self-awareness," she's merely advising you to be mindful. You need to be aware of what's happening in your mind and the effect it's having. You're not kicking yourself for wanting another pair of dress shoes. You're not building a logical argument against the purchase ("I can't afford a new lawn mower!"). You're not guilting yourself. You're simply observing the desire without judgment and watching what it does, like a bird you notice on a tree limb. Eventually, that bird will fly away on its own; you don't have to exhaust yourself chasing it away.

"Because it's hard to tolerate the uncomfortable feeling, whatever it is, we go straight to the behavior that numbs it out or the behavior that we think is going to satisfy the need. In a way, we're so often on automatic pilot," she explains. "When we're at the bakery, we see a cookie, we reach in our pocket, we pay, and that cookie's gone and suddenly we wake up from that trance, right?"

But that "autopilot" action doesn't really make our wants go away. "We find out it never really works," she says. "We're always hungry for the next thing, the next object. Bringing mindfulness into your daily life can intercept this automatic pilot and can really be helpful when you're dealing with cravings, whether it's for food or 'stuff.'" The following are important observations that apply to your weight, your mood, and your home.

▸ You are seldom going to be completely at ease. Frequently, you'll be tired, frustrated, worried, sad, bored, or unfocused to some degree. You will almost always have some type of itch that a snack or a purchase could relieve for a moment.

"There's a bumper sticker that I love," Diana Winston says, "and I talk to my students about it: 'Don't believe everything you think.' Our thoughts are very powerful, and we have many thoughts that are extremely positive and helpful thoughts. But we have a lot of thoughts that can lead to quite a bit of suffering. They have a grip on us. We're taught to believe everything we think, so if you have this thought that, 'Oh, I failed at such and such,' you believe it."

▸ The things you buy will never provide you lasting contentment. That's because a new sensation of discomfort will come along soon enough.

▸ You will never have *everything* you want. There will always be something new that you would like to have. Even if you look around and feel satisfied with what you own, a catalog can arrive showing you something you never knew existed but feel like you've *always wanted*.

Mindfulness teaches us that our thoughts are not necessarily reality:

▸ Just because our mind tells us to do something doesn't mean we have to obey!

▸ Just because our mind tells us that something is good or bad doesn't mean it actually is!

▸ Just because our mind is uncomfortable with an emotion doesn't mean we have to take action to turn off the emotion or create a distraction!

This concept may be new and even strange to you, but your mind is not your boss. You don't have to obey the thoughts in your mind or get upset about them. That can lead you to become overweight, cluttered, in debt, and unhappy.

On the other hand, you don't have to *argue* with your thoughts, either. That can be exhausting, and while you're arguing, you're not observing the real moment around you. Instead, mindfulness teaches you to merely observe your thoughts and let them pass by as if you're watching, say, fluffy white clouds in the sky. A cloud won't hurt you (we're assuming, of course, it's not a thundercloud) and won't affect your life. Conversely, you won't change *it*, either. You'll glance at it, and it will disappear over the horizon on its own schedule. Another will come by, and you'll do the same.

And that leads us back to the marketplace. Think about what happens when we shop. The process is usually straightforward.

I see ⟶ I want ⟶ I buy

An item draws your attention, your mind tells you to buy it, and you do so. You may have some thoughts about its price or fit or design or suitability, but the choice often happens without much reflection in the moment.

When you get an urge to toss an item into your shopping cart, I'd like you to observe the thought mindfully rather than acting on it without reflection. *Why* do you want this item? Do you truly need it? How are you feeling right now? Are you buying it just to buy something? Will that urge pass on its own, as in Winston's "urge surfing" description? By introducing this step of mindfulness, the process now looks like this:

I see ⟶ I want ⟶ Will this item help me create the life I want? → No → Walk away / Yes → I buy

If you truly need this thing—if it will actually do something useful for you that your other possessions don't do, if it will move you closer to the life you want, and if you have the money and space for it—then buy it. If you don't need it, use the moment of mindfulness to sort through your emotions and desires, and let the urge pass. Your mindfulness saved you from a bit more additional clutter!

This is especially important if you scored high on the "acquisition" questions in the Saving Inventory questionnaire in Chapter 3. By being more mindful, you can tame this element that's contributing to your clutter.

Now try this: Look around your house and find an item you've tried to discard before but just couldn't. Examine it and think about letting it go. What other thoughts arise? Does your mind struggle to stop you from getting rid of this item? Remember: You really don't have to obey your mind's command to hang on to it. If your "difficulty discarding" score from the Saving Inventory questionnaire is high, this kind of self-examination may be especially helpful for reducing your clutter.

During the 6-week program, I'll share a few mindfulness exercises that I'd like you to do regularly. Later, you can continue these activities and mix in some more, such as the ones in this chapter. I just ask that during this program you:

STOP AND TAKE STOCK

Try this mind-focusing strategy whenever you want to make a purchase. It's called the **STOP** exercise. "This is a great acronym to help you remember to be mindful when you're in the grip of a desire," Diana Winston says. It stands for:

- **Stop.** Take a moment to process what's happening.

- **Take a breath.** Literally, take a breath and focus on it entering and exiting your body.

- **Observe.** Winston suggests you take note of what's happening in your body and mind in this moment. Is your heart racing, your stomach clenched, your face flushed? "You can even observe the sounds around you," she advises, "or just notice your feet on the floor." This gets you to recognize what's happening in your mind, body, and the world around you in this moment.

- **Proceed.** Now you can take action—best of all, an action that carries you closer to a fitter body, a happier mind, or a less-cluttered home.

▸ Spend a few minutes a day doing mindfulness meditation. During the rest of your day, try to be more aware of your thoughts and how they influence your behaviors, especially inside stores.

▸ Avoid seeing mindfulness as a time-consuming burden to add to the more important activities in the *Cut the Clutter, Drop the Pounds* program. You will be doing quite a bit of decluttering, as well as eating differently and getting more exercise. But I'm hoping you'll see your mindfulness activities as a supplement to these other changes that fits nicely into the spaces when you're not busy.

▸ See mindfulness as the important activity it is. We value action so much that simply sitting still and centering ourselves can easily be viewed as wasted time. Mindfulness is worth the effort, and it will pay huge dividends in enabling you to be more focused on the life you want to live.

▸ Don't be hard on yourself if you're not taking time to be "mindful enough" or if you're not doing it "right." Remember, mindfulness involves judging yourself less.

Mindfulness at the Table

How many of the calories you consume every week are because you're actually hungry? Or because you've determined that a food item helps you meet your fitness goals?

On the other hand, how many of your weekly calories do you take in because you're in the grip of emotional triggers that compel you to eat? How much of the food and drink that you take in over the course of a week vanishes into your belly without your awareness because you're distracted?

When you eat mindfully, you improve your ability to eat out of *need*, rather than because of a fleeting *want*. If unhealthy eating habits have led you to become overweight, mindfulness may help break this relationship.

In 2014, researchers collected 21 earlier studies to review how mindfulness activities affect people's obesity-related eating behaviors, such as:

▶ Emotional eating

▶ Binge eating

▶ External eating (eating because food looks or smells so good, even if your body doesn't need it). This can be a major factor in obesity, because we're surrounded by food that's been carefully manufactured to appeal to us.

The majority of the studies that focused on each of these types of eating found that mindfulness led to improvements. The authors concluded:

> *The outcomes from the reviewed studies provide evidence to support the use of (mindfulness exercises) for obesity-related eating behaviours.... Given the extent of the obesity epidemic, novel approaches to support weight loss are needed. (Mindfulness exercises) are poised to complement obesity prevention and treatment efforts.*

Jenny Taitz, PsyD, the psychologist who focuses on managing emotions and mindful eating—whom you met in Chapter 3—guides patients through eating very slowly so they taste each bite. If you ever eat, for example, a single Twinkie over 10 minutes, nibbling one morsel at a time and focusing the full power of your mind on absorbing every flavor and aroma, you probably won't crave a second one.

During the 6-week *Cut the Clutter, Drop the Pounds* program, whenever you're eating, that's all I want you to do. If the TV is blaring, you're playing a game on your phone, or you're eating while driving, you're not paying attention to your food. Refueling your body is an important moment. I'd like you to be mindful so you can be aware of what you're eating.

Take note of what the food tastes like. If you've eaten a thousand hamburgers in your life, you probably won't pay much attention to the 1001st. So take an extra moment to be mindful of *this* one. Prepare it with care, and perhaps add some herbs and spices or a marinade to the meat. What subtle flavors do you pick up? What smells are you noticing? What enjoyable details of this burger-eating experience would you have completely missed if you weren't paying attention?

When you eat, do it in a place that supports this kind of mindfulness. During the first week of the program, you'll declutter and reorganize your kitchen and dining room to reduce distractions and give new purpose to these spaces. The first step, before you do anything else, will be to decide on a vision of how you want to use these rooms and how you want them to support your health. I encourage you to make your kitchen and dining room the places where you prepare and consume most of the food you eat, rather than eating in a recliner or hunched over a living room end table.

On the flip side, these rooms should primarily be used for cooking and eating, rather than for storing stacks of mail or serving as your home office. When you walk into these uncluttered spaces that are organized with intention, you'll know you're there to refuel your body and nourish your family.

I'll introduce a brief daily exercise early in the program that will help you develop eating mindfulness. I encourage you to try the following mindfulness activities, too, either during the program or after you move on to long-term maintenance.

Check your emotions. When you realize you'd like a treat, assess the emotions you're feeling, Dr. Taitz advises. (Consult the questionnaire on page 45 for a list of emotions often linked to eating.) Rate the emotion on a scale of 1 to 10. Also rate your sense of hunger, again from 1 to 10. If your emotion is at an 8 and your hunger is at a 2, reconsider whether you truly need that snack or if you're simply eating as a way to cope with the emotion.

Savor a treat. In her greed-reduction classes, Diana Winston often has her students unwrap one Hershey's Kiss, then do an "eating meditation." "What they're encouraged to do is first think about all the conditions that led to this chocolate being here. They think about the farmers who grew the cocoa beans and the sugar. They reflect on the plants, animals, and elements of nature such as soil and rain. Then I have them eat it very, very slowly, paying close attention to the impulses that are happening. Usually when we eat things we like, we shove it into our mouth without paying attention. In this exercise, you only have one Hershey's Kiss. You can't eat more. So you have to take it slowly and savor it."

Not only does this exercise teach you to get more satisfaction from less, it reminds you that a *lot* of work and resources go into the food you eat and the material goods you buy. So purchase (or eat) something only if you really need it. And if you buy it, put it to good use.

Mindfulness and Your Happiness

Becoming more mindful may also reduce some of your burden of depression and anxiety. A recent review of meditation programs published in *JAMA Internal Medicine* found some evidence supporting this practice. The authors included 47 earlier studies that involved more than 3,500 participants. They found "moderate" evidence that mindfulness meditation programs can improve anxiety and depression for up to 6 months.

In their book *Fully Present*, Dr. Smalley and Diana Winston discuss an approach, abbreviated RAIN, for using mindfulness to work through your emotions. It stands for:

Recognition. When you're upset, take a moment to observe your emotions and label them. Simply putting a label on how you feel can help you start to feel calmer and more in control.

Acceptance. Instead of judging yourself for having these emotions, simply accept that you have them: "Yep, I'm mad. But I'm not going to be ashamed of myself or feel guilty that I've once again lost my patience." That doesn't mean you should *act* on your anger or other negative emotion. Just let it pass along on its own, like the thoughts that crowd into your mind while you're practicing mindfulness meditation.

Investigation. Often emotions cause sensations in the body: Your face gets flushed, your pulse races, you feel dizzy or dazed. By learning to recognize their physical signs, you can get a better understanding of how your emotions affect you.

Non-identification. With this final step, you distance yourself from your emotions. Your feelings of sadness, frustration, or fear aren't something you deliberately ordered. You didn't *ask* for them to happen. They're simply things that are passing through your mind. One way to think about it is to say "I have anger," rather than "I feel angry," the authors write. These thoughts are just something that you have temporarily. They don't affect who you are. They certainly aren't *you*.

By the time I work with people to bring order to their homes, they're generally unhappy with themselves. They feel like they've done something wrong by letting their homes get so messy. Also, though it's not the main topic of our conversation, if they're overweight, they're often disappointed in themselves for letting their bodies get out of control. As a result, they often have a negative outlook on their physical attractiveness, their self-control, and even their value. They talk to themselves as if they deserve the harshest of criticism.

I heard hints of this self-talk in some of the feedback I got from the test panel. Before they started the program, they rated their self-esteem and self-confidence on a scale of 1 to 10. Their responses ranged from 2 to 9, but on average, they came in at 6.7. That suggests they didn't feel too good about themselves in general.

Although on the whole they stayed enthusiastic and had great success, at times during the program some of the participants were pretty hard on themselves. They didn't feel they were decluttering "fast enough." They were upset that they weren't doing their mindfulness exercises. They felt that they'd tackled too many changes at once. If they didn't finish their tasks for the week, they took it out on themselves.

People often try to motivate themselves through unforgiving self-criticism, says Kristin Neff, PhD, associate professor at the University of Texas at Austin and author of *Self-Compassion*. But being hard on yourself doesn't move you toward the changes you want. It discourages you and slows down your progress. It can also be bad for your physical and mental health, she says. "All the research shows that self-criticism, while it comes from a caring place, raises your cortisol levels," she explains. (Cortisol is a "stress hormone" that harms your body if it stays elevated over the long term.)

Even if it's only you being hard on yourself, part of your brain will react as if someone else is physically attacking you. Your fight-or-flight mechanism will kick in, your heart rate may rise, and you may feel jittery and queasy. But since you can't flee yourself, there's nowhere safe to retreat. "You become anxious and depressed," Dr. Neff says, "and both of those are highly linked to self-criticism. It kind of undermines your faith in yourself. It's like pulling the rug out from underneath you, and it ends up making it harder to be motivated to make a change."

Dr. Neff told me that it's possible to be aware that you need to make changes to your weight or your home, yet do it in a way that doesn't involve criticizing yourself. "You want to be happy, you want to feel better in your body, you want to have a more peaceful environment," she says. "You're much more likely to change for those reasons than change because you call yourself a fat, lazy slob! You absolutely can change, and the research shows that self-compassion is a more effective motivator than self-criticism. It makes you less afraid of failure, because it's safe to fail, which allows you to learn from your failures and mistakes."

Because it's so important that you motivate yourself through kindness rather than harsh words, I'd like to make two requests as you jump into the program:

Focus on the positive. Be happy with the results you obtain over the next 6 weeks, rather than focusing on the ways you think you fall short. The test panelists enjoyed incredible results. But they didn't all reach their goal weight. They didn't all completely declutter their homes. I feel confident, however, that they picked up the tools and the motivation to keep moving in the right direction in the weeks, months, and years to come. If they're kind to themselves, they'll be more likely to stay engaged in those changes. I believe that's true for you, too.

Say good-bye to the negative. I'll be encouraging you many, many times over the next 6 weeks to get rid of things in your home that tell you "You failed." I want you to clear out clothes that are too small, so that every time you open your closet they're not reminding you that you didn't succeed at losing weight those previous times. I want you to empty your garage of stuff that didn't sell at the last yard sale. I want you to get rid of purchases hiding unopened in the back of a cabinet because you felt guilty about buying them.

In Week 3 of the program, I'll offer a quick exercise that Dr. Neff recommends for improving your self-compassion. In the meantime, keep in mind the three components she suggests for how to speak to yourself in a kinder, more encouraging way.

1. **Apply your mindfulness.** "A lot of people aren't even aware of the constant barrage of self-criticism they give themselves, they're so used to the voice," she says. Pay attention (in other words, be mindful) when you're using a nasty tone of voice with yourself. In this instance, you don't need to just accept it. Instead, change your tone. "You might say that compassion is how you respond when you're mindfully aware of your own pain," she says.

2. **Be kinder.** If you catch yourself being overly critical, shift to a more caring and supportive tone. Talk to yourself as kindly as you would a friend or a small child.

3. **Remember that no one's perfect and that everyone else in this world is falling short, too.** "Often when people see something about themselves they don't like, they think something has gone wrong. If all of these *other* people have normal happy lives, then it's *me* who's failed, it's *me* who's overweight," Dr. Neff says. "Remembering that human experience is supposed to be imperfect helps reduce those feelings of isolation that can come from feeling inadequate."

Looking Ahead

I can't stress enough that when you look at your cluttered home or your weight: *It's not about your stuff . . . and it's not about your fat.* The clutter filling your home got there because of factors related to your emotions, your mood, and your point of view. I feel confident in saying that if you're overweight, those pounds accumulated for many of the same sorts of reasons.

So remember what you've learned about the contribution your mind has made to your weight and your clutter. Coming up, I'll give you the keys to a very practical program that will help you harness your body and your mind to work together to solve these problems.

Now that you know how to *think*, it's time to start *doing*!

The Clutter Chronicles

Margie Cherry, 59

POUNDS LOST: 7.6

AMOUNT OF CLUTTER REMOVED:
At least 10 bags to Goodwill, plus countless bags of trash

Visitors to Margie's home tell her that it feels "homey, warm, and inviting," she says. However, she sensed a general atmosphere of disorder throughout the home. Though she regarded much of it as "creative clutter" that she generated while working as a comedian, cartoonist, and life coach, "It became too much for me," she says.

"When you have clutter in your home for so long, it blends into the background like wallpaper," Margie explains. "You don't recognize it's there, or you have a subconscious sense that it *belongs* there."

During the program, Margie learned to see her surroundings through new eyes, even though she struggled with the mindfulness exercises. ("I have *shpilkes*—the Yiddish word for people who are

Before

restless and can't sit still!") With her new awareness, though, she noticed a bread machine that was taking up valuable kitchen counter space (and collecting clutter on its flat surface). Her husband had bought it 10 years ago, and though he frequently used it at first, it soon fell into disuse. As Margie looked at the machine, she realized it was malignant clutter. "What is this thing doing on my counter?" she asked herself. "I don't use it, and I don't need it." She moved it to the basement and laughingly notes that it was like "excising a tumor."

Her bathroom scales may deserve a trip to the trash bin, as they weren't very accurate in helping her stay aware of the present moment. "My scales showed that I'd lost like *1 pound*. When you think you're working hard and not getting anywhere, it's frustrating," she says.

When she checked in for her follow-up photo at the end of the program, she had a pleasant surprise. She'd actually lost more than a pound *per week*, as well as 4½ inches from her waist. And that success unleashed her inner Christie Brinkley. "As soon as that camera started clicking, I found myself striking sassy poses that I didn't know I had in me!" she exclaims. "Could it have been the 5-inch heels, the skinny jeans, or the discovery that, despite fearing I had failed at my diet plan, I actually lost over 7 pounds and multiple inches?"

Along with her improved sassiness, Margie says she's better able to see her surroundings as they really are—and she's willing to make any fixes that are necessary. And she's applying these skills to other parts of her life. "I'm able to look at things that my eyes glossed over before. The lens through which I was viewing shifted. I can take control over things I didn't think I had control over before. I know I can slowly but surely chip away at things like my weight," she explains. "The main change is that I feel empowered. Just knowing you have power can change the way you do everything for the rest of your life."

Part 2

The Cut the Clutter, Drop the Pounds Blueprint

Chapter 5

HOW THE
PROGRAM WORKS

Six weeks isn't very long, but if you have determination and a good plan, even this brief period can become a momentous turning point in your life.

In just a month and a half, it's possible to turn an unmanageable maze of a home into a well-organized refuge *while* you're melting away stubborn pounds *while at the same time* you're shaking loose upsetting emotions and deeply ingrained ways of looking at yourself.

If you're skeptical that you can accomplish all this at the same time, I understand. Simply trying to keep your home clean at a surface level can be exhausting. If just straightening up the mess you've made over the past few days takes so much effort, how can you possibly sort and haul out years (or decades) of accumulated stuff that has packed the deepest nooks and crannies of your home?

Add to that the challenge of losing weight, which may feel even more difficult than decluttering your home. The work that goes into weight loss can be time-consuming and frustrating. If your approach requires counting calories, carbs, or grams of fat, it adds a substantial chore to your day. If you're steeply cutting back on the amount of food you allow yourself, or forcing yourself to eat unappealing foods, these changes also make each day a new exercise in unpleasantness.

Also, few people make one weight loss attempt, then cruise through the rest of their lives at their ideal weight. If you're currently overweight, odds are good that you remember your history of unsuccessful attempts whenever you're trying to launch a new effort. You likely have a "Greatest Weight Loss Failures" video that's ready to play at any time in your head.

This brings us to the challenge of taming your *mind* at the same time as your body and your home. Your mental processes can be even more stubborn than your weight or your home's organization. Some people who seek therapy to shake their anxiety or depression learn in a dozen or fewer sessions how to use tools to change their behaviors and thoughts. But some stay in therapy for years.

Even given all these challenges, do I *really* believe it's possible for a normal human being to make a lasting improvement in all three of these areas in a short period of time? I truly do. You're holding the directions in your hands, and I've seen people do wonderful things with this plan. That doesn't mean it's easy. Starting the program is a bit like getting a treadmill. Just setting the treadmill in your home (and in many homes, that's *all* the treadmill is doing) won't change your weight. You have to get on it and start walking.

As you start this program, you're going to have to apply a positive attitude, a lot of focus, and some serious commitment. You'll have to power through some challenging moments.

You can do this. I've seen people accomplish these achievements many times, and I know it's possible.

During the next 6 weeks, while you focus on your home, body, and mind, try to keep yourself firmly aimed at the intersection of the three circles in this diagram, so the same effort moves you toward all three goals.

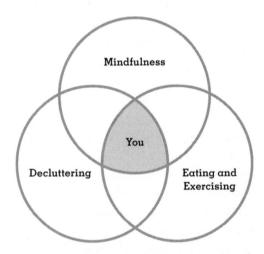

Plenty of people have told me that they've cleaned out their homes, come to feel better about themselves, and watched their clothing size shrink all at one time. Often, they were only focusing on decluttering their home, and the other improvements just sort of happened without any additional work.

But when I was putting together this program, I wanted *proof* that it works, both for myself and for my readers. I wanted to carefully observe which elements were especially helpful and which needed adjustment before I made the program available to the public. I wanted to make sure it provided the right advice and motivation. That's why I assembled the test panel to blaze the trail for you.

Putting the Program to the Test: Meet Our Brave Test Panelists

My editors and I put out a notice in traditional and social media seeking participants who wanted to improve their health and their home environment at the same time. A lot of people must have been feeling trapped under the weight of their homes (and their bellies and thighs), because we received a flood of interest.

Once we assembled the test panel of participants, we saw that many of them had a good reason to want to make these changes. I met with all of them to share the details of the program (as you'll find in Chapters 9 through 14). In return, they opened up and shared a lot of their secrets. They filled out a survey to gauge their anxiety level and another questionnaire to measure their attitudes toward clutter (just like you did in Chapter 3, although you got to keep your results private). They brought me pictures of the interiors of their homes. They allowed a nurse to weigh them and measure their hips and thighs. They rated their self-esteem. Given this level of commitment and openness, you can understand my admiration for them and why I call them brave!

The panelists came in all sorts of body sizes, but most were overweight based on their body mass index, which made them average representatives of today's society. Their average BMI was 32, officially categorized as obese. Overall, their self-esteem and energy levels weren't great. As a group, their relationship with clutter was having a substantially negative impact on their emotions and their quality of life.

So these weren't folks whose homes and bodies just needed a bit of touching up to get to a level that would make them happy. These were real people with real weight and clutter challenges who were going to have to do some heavy lifting, both mentally and physically.

Once the program began, I stayed in touch with nearly all the participants on a weekly or even daily basis online. I celebrated their joys with them and listened to the difficulties they were facing. The following comments captured some of the challenges. But keep in mind that all these participants achieved notable successes with their weight, their decluttering, and their attitudes:

Elizabeth: "I hit an unexpected roadblock with malignant clutter this week in the form of family photos and a filing cabinet of my grandfather's papers. It's malignant now—I'm still grieving—but it won't always be. I'm dealing with photos by putting them in archival photo albums and labeling them. They make me sad now but I know they won't always, so I want to have them accessible but not yet displayed. The paper is way harder because it feels a lot like a last connection to someone who has passed, and the way he thought is reflected in them. My plan is to keep a small representative folder, but I've been dragging my feet. I also came off the spool eating-wise and exercise-wise this week, but I'm starting fresh today."

Linda: "The weight goes down, then up, then down. I find the temptation to eat wrong is too great when together socially with friends."

Melissa H.: "I am running out of motivation to do the decluttering process and am only following parts of the exercise/diet process. I get mad at myself for not following the program and in turn feel bad about myself. It is a daily struggle I dealt with before the program, and here I am again in the same boat. What didn't help was seeing myself in my daughter's prom photos and realizing how much weight I still have to lose."

Robin: "I have made some terrific progress in some areas—but not all four at one time—and I believe that the changes you make in one area directly can influence the others. But trying to think about and focus on all four at one time (diet, exercise, clutter, and mindfulness) may be a bit much with everything else life has to present to me. That said, I have made progress—I'm not throwing in the towel, but I think that you will need to check back with me at 12 weeks and 18 weeks to get the full picture of how these four activities have been integrated into my daily life."

Dayl: "I must admit I am struggling doing all components at once. I work a lot of hours, and when I get home I am exhausted. I have changed my eating habits. No more soda, only diet iced tea or water and of course my one cup of skim milk. Still trying to cut out the sugar (a big, big struggle). I am moving more, taking the time to meditate, and I'm slowly decluttering closet by closet, room by room. Mentally and physically I am feeling much better. I feel the program has definitely helped me, but the realization of doing it all in 6 weeks is not possible for me. Check back in about 15 weeks."

At the end of 6 weeks, the evidence pointing to their improvements astounded me, to put it mildly. I had a spreadsheet tracking their weight and their attitudes toward clutter, along with their stories and the before-and-after photos of their rooms. These folks made remarkable improvements on all their types of clutter: body fat clutter, stuff-on-their countertops clutter, and mental clutter.

On average, their scores on the clutter questionnaire fell by **nearly half.**

SAVING INVENTORY BEFORE PROGRAM

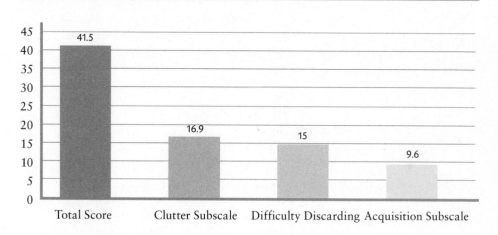

SAVING INVENTORY AFTER PROGRAM

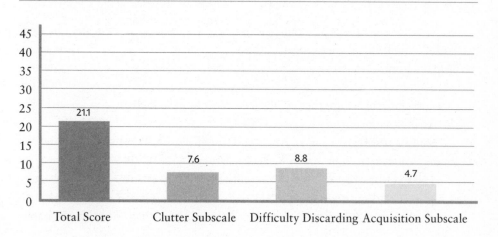

Their average total score at the beginning was a hoarding-esque 41.5. Afterward, their average total score was 21.1—which is what you might see in the general public. (See the graphs on page 77.)

On an individual level, every single person whose original score was at the "hoarding" level was now well below it. Together, they brought out enough unwanted household goods and trash to fill at least one dump truck.

It was just as obvious that the time they spent decluttering didn't stop them from losing weight. On average, they lost nearly 10 pounds apiece. As a group, they lost almost 219 pounds!

Some of the participants pointed out unexpected obstacles that I want to warn you about before you embark on the program. But the general sense I got from them afterward was that the program left them feeling empowered and strong. In just a month and a half, they'd achieved several life-altering victories. They'd lost pounds on the scale, inches from their hips, and piles of trash bags full of clutter from their homes. Here's how you can do it, too.

Your Next 6 Weeks: What to Expect

Every week in the *Cut the Clutter, Drop the Pounds* program, you'll be making changes in the following intertwined areas. I'll provide specific advice and activities that take you through them.

A DECLUTTERING PLAN

Each week during the program, you'll tackle a different room or area in your home. You'll be assigned specific "tasks" for each room or space. Some tasks will take only minutes to complete, and some may take days. To help guide you through these tasks, I've provided tips and techniques for tackling each space and dealing with the types of clutter generally found there. I've specifically plotted out your journey so your efforts:

Make a difference early. You'll start in the rooms that have the biggest impact on your weight and your health.

Start gently. You won't have to address as many emotionally sticky areas early in the program as you sort through your belongings. The last week will require you to dig deep into the spaces of your home where you have probably stashed a high density of objects because throwing them away was too painful. By then, you'll hopefully have the mindset to handle getting rid of these items with more confidence and less distress.

Get your body ready for a challenge. Clearing out your home can be quite a workout. You're lifting, squatting, pulling boxes off high shelves, and perhaps walking up and down stairs. So you'll start the program with rooms that should be less physically demanding. Over the following weeks, you'll have opportunities to grow stronger and more flexible while you improve your endurance. The intent is to get you ready to tackle areas of your home where the items tend to be bigger, heavier, and more unwieldy. You'll likely encounter these items in your final week.

AN EATING PLAN

I wanted the eating plan for the next 6 weeks to be as simple as possible. I don't want to clutter your time or your focus with a lot of dietary rules. I don't want you to count calories or carbohydrates or grams of fat. You have much better things to do with your time. Nor do I want you to have to go to out-of-the-way supermarkets or order foods online. I *certainly* don't want you to have to buy new cooking equipment.

What I *do* want is for you to give your body the right amount of fuel so you stay well-fed and nourished during the coming challenges, but still lose weight. I also want your meals to be pleasurable, so you can sit down and enjoy food that rewards all your senses (it can't be fun to eat mindfully when you have to focus your mind on bland, flavorless food). I also designed this program to be useful and appealing for the long term rather than an ordeal that you can only bear to suffer through for 6 weeks.

In the next chapter, you'll discover dietitian-approved meal and snack plans. All you have to do for the next 6 weeks is pick foods off these charts. So long as you choose a breakfast, lunch, dinner, and any snacks from these lists, you'll stay within a daily calorie range that encourages weight loss.

A FUNCTIONAL FITNESS PLAN

You'll burn off calories every day while decluttering your house. It's quite possible that this amount of physical activity alone would be enough to spark your weight loss. But you'll set yourself up for even better results if you do additional physical activities several times a week. I worked with an exercise

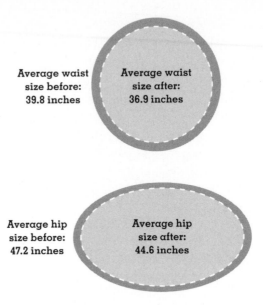

Average waist size before: 39.8 inches

Average waist size after: 36.9 inches

Average hip size before: 47.2 inches

Average hip size after: 44.6 inches

physiologist, Liz Davis, MS, to develop a special workout plan to go with this program.

The test panelists were able to make big changes in their appearance in a hurry. On average, they lost nearly 3 inches from their waists and about 2½ inches from their hips. Their energy level went up, and so did their self-esteem. I'll let them tell you how they felt after 6 weeks.

Elizabeth: "This has been the best thing I have done for myself in a really long time."

Nanette: I've continued to exercise, and I've made some really smart choices in relation to food. I am so thankful that I was able to be a part of this test panel. I have struggled with weight issues for many years, and it wasn't until I made this commitment that I have seen significant results. Although I have more work ahead, I vow to practice your principles."

Melissa H.: "Was I perfect all the time? Um, no. But, if I can survive the Easter holiday and still come away with losing weight, then I think I had success. As for all the ladies (and Joe too!), I heard different variations of success as we gathered together yesterday. We all made improvements in our health and our homes. As for the decluttering, I was not able to declutter my entire house in 6 weeks, but just getting started has motivated me to keep going."

Along with changing your appearance, we wanted the exercises in this program to help your body work more effectively. A current focus in the field of exercise science is on functional fitness. This approach isn't so much concerned with your looks. Instead, the goal is to ensure that you can squat down and pick up a box from the floor, then place it on a shelf. You can spend an active day of grocery shopping, gardening, and playing with your kids or grandkids and not feel exhausted that night and sore the next day. Your muscles and joints stay strong and limber, and your heart and lungs don't become strained during normal use. In short, your body *functions* better.

The idea here isn't to build big muscles or a tiny waist just for appearance's sake, which you then have to maintain with time-consuming workouts. Instead, the *Cut the Clutter, Drop the Pounds* fitness plan aims to make your overall life healthier, happier, and easier.

It's also cheaper than many exercise plans. You'll notice in Chapter 7, which provides the directions for each exercise, that none of these activities requires you to buy any weights or other equipment. You could fill a large gym with all the unused workout equipment I've seen in people's homes. So I was determined that this program would provide all the exercise you need without sending you to the store for a single new piece of workout gear.

You'll start with short walks during the first week and gradually go farther, until you're walking for 30 minutes at a time in the final week. You'll also regularly do strength- and flexibility-building movements using household objects or your own body weight. As you fill bags with castoffs that will go to the donation center, you'll use them to strengthen your legs, back, arms, and shoulders. As you clear countertops and walls, you'll use this reclaimed space for doing pushups!

That's another reason I hope you'll find this program easier and more efficient than previous weight loss plans or housecleaning endeavors you've tried. You're rarely *only* addressing your body, your home, or your attitudes. You're usually working on two or three at any given time.

SIMPLE MENTAL EXERCISES

Changing your outlook is a crucial component of the program. I'll provide a new mental exercise each week that will help you adjust your mindset related to your diet, your home, or your fitness. Doing these mental exercises regularly can help ensure that:

The program will feel less difficult. Often when you're trying to improve your habits, the part of your mind that wants positive change is battling the part that wants things to stay just the way they are.

You may have found weight loss so difficult in the past because you hadn't discovered the core thoughts and behaviors that were leading you to eat too much. Similarly, housekeeping may seem like an endless struggle because you're cleaning on one day but allowing clutter to regather on the next 6 days. The cycle continues over and over.

With these mental exercises, you'll go deep into your mind (like an IT person analyzing a computer), then reprogram your software to make your weight control and home maintenance easier and more consistent. You'll be able to identify the thoughts and behaviors that hold you back, and once you finally bring them out into the open, you can change them.

You'll enjoy lasting improvements. The absolute last thing I want you to do is rid your home of clutter and your body of excess fat over 6 weeks, only to watch all your improvements disappear as soon as the program is over. I didn't write this book in the hopes that you would have another "failure" to kick yourself over. I wrote it so you can start an entirely new phase of your life that's more streamlined, orderly, and rewarding.

To reap those benefits, however, you have to do more than just "do." You can't just sweep all the unnecessary possessions out of your home and expect it to stay uncluttered. You can't just eat differently and move around more for a few weeks and expect permanent improvement.

You also have to *rethink*. You have to develop new ways of thinking about food. You have to identify the meaning that you attach to objects on the shelves at the department store. You have to learn how to not take every action that your mind begs you to do or follow its every command. I want this program to be the start of a much bigger process in your life. To do so, your mind will need to work for you, not vice versa.

AVOIDING PITFALLS

Some of the challenges you'll face during this program are easily predictable. I've seen many people struggle with them, and they've talked to me about these obstacles using the exact same language.

But while I was working with the test panel, some of the participants reported problems that had a bigger effect on them than I was expecting. I'd like to prepare you for some of these particular challenges and equip you with preventive strategies that will minimize their impact.

Pitfall #1:
NOT SEEING ENOUGH IMPROVEMENT

As I mentioned, each week you'll declutter a specific area of your home. If you live in an apartment or a house that's not very cluttered, you can probably do a thorough job on each part of your home within a week.

But I'm guessing you have a high hurdle to get over, or you wouldn't have bought this book. Our test panelists were like you—they had a *lot* of work to do on their homes, which is why they volunteered for the program. As they progressed through the 6 weeks, several of them started telling me that they were falling behind.

They had set their expectations very high and were struggling with rising feelings of discouragement and disappointment. They had anticipated that the program would feel like a great accomplishment, but they were starting to feel like they'd failed themselves.

I don't want this to happen to you. Many people who invited me into their homes over the years told me that their cluttered homes represent just another example of how they failed. As they looked around their homes, they remembered how they quit taking piano lessons as a kid or lost too many jobs. Now, yet again, they were falling short of how a reasonable, capable adult is expected to act.

I suspect that many people who are overweight also feel that their body size is a symbol of how they've failed. Many have a lot of negative, critical self-talk bouncing around in their minds. As you learned in the previous chapter, talking to yourself this way doesn't spur you to make positive changes. It just holds you back. So I'd like for you to follow three bits of advice to prevent these sorts of negative feelings.

Manage your expectations. It is quite possible that your home won't be fully decluttered at the end of 6 weeks. That is very much okay. I simply want you to make a substantial improvement in your home. This is about progress, not perfection. Build on the skills you develop with each room, capitalize on your increased energy, and focus on your achievements—which will be significant—rather than dwelling on what remains to be done.

If you're not at your "dream" weight at the end either, that is perfectly fine, too. I hope you at least lose enough pounds—or that your clothes fit loosely enough—for you to see that you're capable of making progress. *No one* will reach the finish line at the end of 6 weeks and never have to clean their home or watch what they eat again. *Everyone* will have to shift into long-term maintenance mode at some point. If it takes you longer than 6 weeks to get to this stage, that doesn't mean you failed. You're just going on your own timetable. As I often tell people, perfect is the enemy of good.

Keep going. Some of the test panelists started running behind during the program, and they felt overwhelmed when they saw new decluttering tasks arriving before they'd finished all the old ones.

I don't want you to ever panic during this program. You may have to sort through difficult emotions while you're debating whether to part with some of your possessions. Painful memories may arise that you have to address. But I *don't* want the timetable of this program to be a source of stress!

At the end of each week, move on to the next area of your home, even if you're not completely finished with the space you're currently tackling. I want you to keep moving forward without feeling that your tasks are piling up to an unmanageable level. At the end of 6 weeks, or when you've completed a task more quickly than you'd expected, go back and take care of earlier tasks you may not have had time to complete.

Celebrate your successes. If you found you didn't care for certain pieces of my advice, or you had trouble sticking with some of the activities in the program, don't kick yourself over it. It doesn't mean you're letting yourself down, disappointing me, or doing the program "wrong."

I hope you follow the entire program as closely as you can, but I'm not expecting perfection. Some of the test panelists were quite open about telling me how they didn't do certain parts or that they adapted them for their own needs (for example, some did their own workouts instead of following the plan in the book).

Please don't dwell on any "failures." Instead, if you came across particular home-cleaning techniques, exercise movements, or shifts in your mental outlook that you found meaningful and worked into your daily routine, I would rather you focus on those and strive to get the most value from them. At the end of 6 weeks, let the improvements you made stand out in your mind, not the opportunities that didn't quite reach their potential.

Avoid a "miracle" mentality. When it comes to health and fitness, we are often presented with "miracle plans" and "wonder programs." They promise quick, easy, and astounding results. I believe that such programs set you up for failure and disappointment. Your clutter or excess weight didn't accumulate overnight, and it won't disappear overnight. Results will only come from your commitment and consistent effort over time. Small steps yield huge results— it's that simple and that tough.

Pitfall #2:
LACK OF TIME

I tried to design this program around a lot of multitasking and kill-two-birds-with-one-stone efficiency. But even though you're not having to count grams of fat and you're burning calories while you declutter, you are still taking on a lot of changes at once.

These tasks will take some time every day, especially later in the program when you're walking more and tackling more labor-intensive parts of your home, like the garage and basement. I suggest you plan on spending an average of an hour a day on your decluttering, exercises, and attitude-shifting activities. Some weeks may require even more.

Some of the test panelists reported that they simply didn't have time for all of this. Often, the first things they cut were the mindfulness activities (even though these take only a few minutes!).

The idea that you'd need time every day to exercise and unload years' or decades' worth of clutter from your home should not come as a big surprise. I think I was able to keep the program simple, but I couldn't break the laws of physics.

Even if you're busy with the usual demands of work, spouse, kids, parents, or chores, you will need to allocate at least one hour each day for this program. Here are some ways you might be able to find it.

Establish a new mindset. Consider this program an investment in creating a better life. All investments require a little sacrifice today for a brighter tomorrow. This program requires you to invest little to no money. Instead, you merely have to devote some of your time. When your home is finally decluttered, it will be easier to keep clean. I predict that any hours you invest now will be returned to you later, with interest.

Schedule tasks just like you would any other appointment. Set aside the time for this program as if it were an important event you need to attend. Get it on your daily calendar and show up on time for your next task!

Drop an activity. Carve out an hour from the time you spend in front of the television or idling on the Internet. Convert that time that you're wasting passively into active time dedicated to making real, lasting changes in your home and your life.

Start your day sooner. Go to bed earlier and set your alarm an hour earlier in the morning to give yourself more time to complete these tasks. You may have fewer interruptions when you work on this program in the morning—and you can start your day feeling successful. Devoting ample time to this program is critical. If you don't, you're setting yourself up for failure before you even commence.

Pitfall #3:
RESISTANCE FROM FAMILY

If you share your home with a spouse or partner, you're not the only one who filled this space with clutter. You don't have the final say over getting rid of everything, either. And it's quite possible that your other half collects something weird—or unusual quantities of something normal—and won't want to join the program with you.

The husband of one of our test panelists, Tiffany, collects T-shirts (Tiffany's story is on page 240). He has dozens, perhaps hundreds of T-shirts—T-shirts for play and T-shirts for work, she says. (Even though his workplace provides new ones on a regular basis, he still keeps his old ones.) She claims to have no idea why he has so many of them. Perhaps because he feels he looks particularly good in a T-shirt? Perhaps a parent drilled into him the importance of never, ever throwing away a T-shirt? Who knows? But Tiffany's bedroom wasn't going to be clutter-free as long as they were in there. Her solution was to leave one dresser drawer for his T-shirts and put the rest into a large storage bin; she'll dole out new ones as his current ones wear out.

She laughed as she told this story, but in many households, a spouse who hangs on to clutter isn't funny. Sometimes a spouse can give the impression that objects are more important than the relationship. Sometimes a cluttered spouse doesn't seem like a loving spouse. A huge collection of treasured objects can even break up a relationship.

I'm not quite as worried about kids and teens who won't take part in the program. At no point during the 6 weeks do I ask you to declutter your child's bedroom. If you do, that's great. I think it's important for parents to teach their kids to take care of their surroundings. But I want you to focus on areas that you can control—and controlling your child's room may require more time and hassle than you should expend. (If your kids' junk is in *your* bedroom or in shared areas of the home, that's an entirely different matter, and I want you to take steps to address this stuff.)

If your spouse is clinging to clutter and resisting the changes you want to make, keep these ideas in mind.

Remember that it's not about the stuff. If you start arguing about the clutter, you will inevitably find yourself in a battle over who wins the argument. Instead, talk about the vision you both have for your home and the different rooms in it. Agree on a common vision and start from there.

Negotiate. All relationships are about give and take. Reflect on how you decide on your vacation destinations or the movies you'll watch together, and apply those same techniques when discussing what stays and what goes in your home.

Talk in terms of limits. No one likes to think about giving up *everything* they treasure. Instead, focus on the amount of space you're both prepared to allocate to specific items. By decluttering according to the limit that each space will hold—150 books in the bookcase or three bins of holiday decorations in the attic, for example—you're letting your home determine how much you should keep. This takes a lot of the emotion out of the discussion.

Bring in a neutral third party. Ask a trusted mutual friend (avoid other family members!) to referee for you on touchy decisions or to help solve an impasse.

Pitfall #4:
ISOLATION

It's normal to be overweight today. It's fairly customary to live in a chaotic, cluttered home, too. As a result, you're going to be taking steps that get you out of rhythm with the way the people around you are marching.

It's a little weird to be hauling out truckloads of stuff from your home when all your neighbors are bringing in new stuff. (It's very likely that someone will ask if you're moving!) It's odd to be thinking about what you want your home to do for *you* rather than working to meet the demands of your home.

If possible, get people around you who agree with the new way you're living your life. Your choices will seem more like the normal, expected behaviors that everyone should do.

The test panel could lean on several sources of support as they went through the program, to remind them that they weren't going it alone. For starters, I gave them a copy of my DVD *It's All Too Much* that I produced a

(continued on page 90)

The Clutter Chronicles

Brenda Hanna, 58

POUNDS LOST: 12.8

AMOUNT OF CLUTTER REMOVED:
Lost count

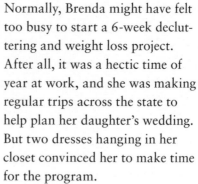

Normally, Brenda might have felt too busy to start a 6-week decluttering and weight loss project. After all, it was a hectic time of year at work, and she was making regular trips across the state to help plan her daughter's wedding. But two dresses hanging in her closet convinced her to make time for the program.

"I'd bought my mother-of-the-bride dress and a rehearsal dinner dress about 5 months earlier. They were really nice, expensive dresses," she says. "However, I'd gained some weight since then, and when I tried on my dresses I couldn't zip them up . . . *at all!*"

Her daughter heard about the *Cut the Clutter, Drop the Pounds* test program and remembered that

Before

Brenda had set a goal to get control over the chaotic areas of her home.

When Brenda met with me, she was feeling emotional. "Being unable to wear those dresses for the wedding, that's the worst thing for a mom," she explains. "I also had tears in my eyes over the clutter in my home. My basement was especially out of control, and it had just been weighing on me. But there were tears of hope, too, to know that maybe I could conquer this clutter and weight."

The clock was ticking, since her daughter's wedding day was just 2 weeks after the program ended. So the 58-year-old owner of a preschool/kindergarten committed herself fully to the plan.

"I felt that all four parts of the program were important to do together. I addressed the decluttering, the exercise, the eating, and the way I was thinking," she says. "One fed into another. Exercising gave me more energy. I was eating better and I felt encouraged, so I decluttered. I felt that you couldn't ignore any component of this program."

Progressing through her house room by room, task by task, kept her from feeling outmatched by the pockets of clutter throughout her home, especially in the basement. "I had been feeling overwhelmed about all the stuff in the house, but the concepts of mindfulness, having a vision, and recognizing benign and malignant clutter helped take the emotion out of the process, which made it easier to face all the stuff."

While she was clearing out the clutter, her pounds were disappearing, too. She lost nearly 4 inches from her waist and 4½ inches from her hips. On Week 6 of the program, she pulled on each dress again. Both times, she grasped the zipper between her fingertips and smoothly pulled it all the way up.

"At the wedding, I got lots of compliments, which was very nice—but it wasn't my primary motivating factor. I just wanted to wear the dress that my daughter and I chose together," she says. "I felt more than happy. I felt joyful."

few years ago with tips on decluttering. Secondly, we set up a Facebook group for them to share their breakthroughs and frustrations. They said they enjoyed the camaraderie and the ability to share photos of their decluttered rooms. I'd suggest that you look for this kind of support, as well.

▸ Do you know of a family member, co-worker, or friend who's living in an overstuffed home? Know anyone who'd like to lose weight? I'll bet you do. If so, share this book and go through the program together. You'll have someone eager to hear your triumphs and interested in sharing ideas that can get you through tough moments.

▸ Look me up on Facebook, whether on my own page (www.facebook.com/ PeterWalsh) or the page for this book. I regularly provide quick videos with how-to advice and links to recent appearances on TV shows, where I get to have fun with audiences and homeowners while we discuss new tips I've discovered and share strategies that work. You'll find a community of people just like yourself who are enthused about living a simpler, fitter, more streamlined life. (You'll also learn a thing or two about Australians, as they make up a big portion of my audience.)

In today's connected world, there's no reason for you to feel like you're alone, especially when you're tackling big concerns like your weight and your home.

Looking Ahead

In this program, there's also no reason to have to do extra work to figure out what to eat. In the next chapter, you'll find the easy-to-use lists that will guide your meal and snack choices for the next 6 weeks.

Chapter 6

HOW TO EAT TO LOSE THE WEIGHT

Many elements you'll find in the typical "diet" don't fit well in the *Cut the Clutter, Drop the Pounds* program. So I stuffed them into a bag and hauled them out to the curb (an activity that will soon become quite familiar to you). The food-related clutter that I refused to include in this program includes:

Counting. Whether it's calories, carbs, or grams of fat, counting takes time and mental focus. That may be okay if your life is otherwise uneventful. But during the next 6 weeks, you'll have other outlets for your energy and attention. That's why the eating portion of this program is very simple. All you have to do is look at the charts on the following pages and pick items for breakfast, lunch, dinner, and snacks. Anything you see in the charts is fair game—the calorie-counting work has been done for you already.

Rules. A central aim of this book is to make your life simpler and more streamlined. I don't want you to have to buy into any special diet-related belief system or memorize a bunch of directions. All you have to do is hold yourself to a few limits when putting together your meals and snacks from these charts, and you can expect to lose weight.

Temporary weirdness. I don't want you to take a detour into a land of unappealing or unfamiliar foods you can only tolerate for 6 weeks. I don't want you to haul a bunch of strange items into your kitchen that you'll throw out half-eaten after the program. Instead, I hope you'll use this book to gain control over your home and your weight for years to come. As a result, you should learn what it's like to feel satisfied eating the typical foods that you see in the supermarket. In the following food charts, I'm confident that you'll find plenty of items that you'll be happy to eat mindfully.

You can mix and match your options into enough combinations that you may want to keep following this plan long after the program is over and you're focused on maintaining your weight loss.

Dieting. The word *dieting* implies all the rules, deprivation, and temporary changes that I tossed out. In this program, you're simply eating in a smart, mindful way. You're beginning new habits that will keep you fit and hopefully will permanently replace the old habits that added those extra pounds to your frame.

The Meal Plan

The plan is pretty simple. With the input of registered dietitians, the program contains an appealing array of foods and drinks arranged in a format that will naturally and easily guide you toward weight loss. You'll find separate lists of:

▸ Breakfast items. Each of these contains 350 to 400 calories.

▸ Smoothies. These 350- to 375-calorie drinks make a nice breakfast.

▸ Lunch and dinner items. These contain 400 to 500 calories.

▸ Snacks and treats. You can have up to two 100-calorie snacks per day.

Just select one breakfast item, one lunch item, one dinner item, and one or two snacks each day for the next 6 weeks, and you will stay in a daily calorie range of 1,250 to 1,600 calories. This calorie range should support weight loss for most women who are active or somewhat active, as well as men who are sedentary.

You can modify how you pick foods from the charts to make this plan fit your individual needs.

▸ In each chart, items are listed from least to most caloric (in other words, items at the bottom of columns have more calories than those at the top). Choose a variety of foods from throughout the columns. If you find that you aren't losing enough weight, start picking foods from higher up on the charts. If you're hungry and losing weight too fast, move down the chart. Choosing from a variety of positions in the charts should yield a proper calorie balance.

▸ Women who are sedentary should limit their snacks/treats to one per day. That's because you aren't burning as many calories as someone who's active. Men who are active should aim to eat higher-calorie foods at mealtime (choose the foods in the bottom rows of the charts). They may also consider eating 50 percent more protein in a meal than what the chart specifies if they're not feeling satiated or they're losing weight too rapidly.

- If you wish, you can "bank" unused snack/treat calories—up to 400 once a week—to accommodate a splurge.

- Please refrain from drinking beverages with calories, like sodas and alcoholic drinks. You can, of course, have a smoothie for breakfast.

- If you eat a meal out, try to find out the calorie count of your options, and choose something that fits into your daily range. I know this calorie-counting requires effort and time, but the trade-off is not having to cook or clean up.

- The items in these charts aren't necessarily all low in sodium or saturated fat. If you need to follow any dietary restrictions for health reasons, be sure to choose items that meet your particular needs. If necessary, talk to a doctor before embarking on this eating plan.

- Plan ahead! Shop ahead of time so you always have plenty of appealing options in your kitchen. If you leave your decisions to the last minute, you're likely to default to less healthy choices.

Now it's time to get started. Here are your simple, easy-to-follow charts. And, exclusive to this edition, you'll find 50 recipes for when you have some time to cook. Use them to put together delicious meals and snacks that will help you create the slender, happy, more mindful life you're seeking!

▶ AND DON'T FORGET . . .

Besides choosing breakfast, lunch, dinner, and snacks off the charts in this chapter, be sure to also follow these principles whenever you eat.

Be mindful. Pay attention to all the good sensations you feel while you're eating. Think about where your food came from and what it's doing for your body. Take a moment to express gratitude for this food.

Avoid multitasking. That means no TV, playing on your phone, or doing work.

Be social. One thing you *can* do while you eat is share the experience with people you care about. People have historically come together over food, but for too many today, mealtimes are a solitary occasion.

Take your time. Give yourself plenty of space to enjoy your meal.

Doing all these things—especially focusing on your food and celebrating it as a special occasion—may help nudge you away from eating processed snacks and fast food. That's because you'll be more aware of what you're eating (and you may feel silly making a special occasion out of eating junk).

BREAKFAST

Start each day off right. Every morning, select *one* of the breakfast items from these charts.

Breakfast Sandwich

EGG	BREAD	MEAT/MEAT ALTERNATIVE	CHEESE
6 Tbsp liquid egg whites (or 2 large egg whites)*	1 sliced bagel "thin"	1 slice (1 oz) bacon, cooked	2 Tbsp feta crumbles
1 large egg	1 English muffin	2 slices (1 oz each) lean deli ham	1 slice (¾ oz) 2% milk provolone cheese
	¾ pita (6½"), white or whole wheat	1 patty or 2 links fully cooked turkey/chicken breakfast sausage	1 slice (¾ oz) 2% milk Cheddar cheese
	2 slices multigrain or whole wheat bread	2 slices (1 oz each) deli turkey breast	1 slice (¾ oz) 2% milk Jack cheese
	8" flour tortilla	2 slices (1 oz each) turkey bacon, cooked	
		2 slices (2 oz each) Canadian bacon	
		⅓ Hass avocado, sliced	
		1 frozen meatless breakfast patty (1.3 oz)	

If using egg whites, double the amount of meat/meat alternative or cheese.

▶DIRECTIONS

Cook the egg as desired in an 8-inch nonstick skillet with ½ teaspoon of olive oil.

Toast the bread, if you like, and heat the meat or meat alternative if necessary.

Sandwich the egg on the bread with the meat, cheese, and toppings (see below) as desired.

▶FLAVOR BOOSTERS

Customize your breakfast sandwich with these "freebie" toppings:

- Hot-pepper sauce
- Salsa
- Baby spinach or kale leaves
- Tomato slices
- Dijon or deli mustard

▶CHANGE IT UP

Try one of these sweeter takes on the breakfast sandwich. In a skillet coated with cooking spray, grill until gooey.

- Two slices of multigrain or whole wheat bread *plus* 2 tablespoons of natural peanut or almond butter *plus* ¼ cup of sliced banana *plus* 1 teaspoon of crumbled cooked bacon
- Two slices of multigrain or whole wheat bread *plus* 2 tablespoons of natural peanut or almond butter *plus* 1 tablespoon of 100 percent fruit raspberry spread *plus* ⅓ cup of fresh raspberries
- Two slices of multigrain or whole wheat bread *plus* 2 tablespoons of natural peanut or almond butter *plus* 1 tablespoon of raisins *plus* 2 pinches of ground cinnamon

Quick Egg Wrap

Makes 1 serving

1 whole wheat flour tortilla (8" round)

1 teaspoon honey-mustard

1 slice smoked turkey breast

¼ cup arugula

2 hard-cooked eggs, sliced

Ground black pepper

1 apple

Place the tortilla on a plate. Spread with the mustard and layer the turkey, arugula, and sliced egg in the center. Sprinkle with the pepper and wrap the tortilla around the filling.

Serve with the apple.

Mediterranean Egg Wrap

Makes 1 serving

1 whole wheat tortilla (8" diameter)

¼ cup spinach

2 eggs, lightly beaten

2 tablespoons crumbled feta cheese

1 cup strawberries

¼ cup fat-free vanilla yogurt

1. Place the tortilla on a plate and top with the spinach.

2. Heat a small skillet coated with cooking spray over medium heat. Cook the eggs for 2 minutes, stirring constantly, until cooked through. Place on the spinach and sprinkle with the feta. Roll to eat.

3. Place the strawberries in a bowl and top with the yogurt. Serve alongside the wrap.

Tex-Mex Burritos

Makes 4 servings

- 4 whole wheat tortillas (8" diameter)
- 1 tablespoon olive oil
- 1 small onion, chopped
- 1 can (15 ounces) reduced-sodium black beans
- ¾ cup salsa, divided
- 1 teaspoon chili powder
- ¼ cup low-fat plain Greek-style yogurt
- 6 tablespoons shredded reduced-fat Monterey Jack or Cheddar cheese
- 2 tablespoons finely chopped fresh cilantro
- 1 avocado, peeled, pitted, and sliced

1. Preheat the oven to 350°F. Coat a small baking dish with cooking spray. Wrap the 4 tortillas in foil and bake for 5 minutes to heat.

2. Meanwhile, heat the oil in a medium skillet over medium heat. Cook the onion for 3 minutes. Stir in the beans (with liquid), ¼ cup of the salsa, and the chili powder. Simmer, stirring occasionally, for 10 minutes. In a small bowl, combine the remaining ½ cup salsa and the yogurt.

3. To assemble the burritos, divide the bean mixture evenly among the tortillas. Sprinkle each with the cheese and cilantro. Roll and place the burritos seam side down in the baking dish. Top with salsa mixture. Bake for 10 minutes, or until heated through. Serve with avocado slices.

Hummus Breakfast Sandwich

Makes 1 serving

- 1 whole pita (6½" inch), 1" cut off one side
- ⅓ cup hummus such as garlic, red pepper, or spicy
- ⅓ avocado, sliced
- ½ cup mixed greens
- ½ cup raspberries

Place the pita on a plate. Fill with the hummus, avocado, and greens. Serve with the raspberries.

Cereal

CEREAL	DAIRY/DAIRY ALTERNATIVE	TOPPING	FRUIT (PICK 2)
1 cup cold cereal (about 150 calories)	5.3 oz 0% plain Greek yogurt	1½ tsp natural peanut or almond butter	½ cup sliced fresh strawberries
⅓ cup granola (about 150 calories)	1 cup 1% milk	1 Tbsp pure maple syrup	½ cup fresh raspberries
1½ packets plain instant oatmeal	1 cup soy milk	2 Tbsp chopped walnuts or pecans	½ cup sliced fresh peaches
1 packet instant whole grain cream of wheat	5.3 oz 0% vanilla Greek yogurt	2 Tbsp raisins	¾ cup fresh blueberries
½ cup plain oats (quick cooking, old-fashioned rolled, steel cut)		2 Tbsp 100% fruit spread	½ cup chopped apple
1 packet instant multigrain hot cereal		2 Tbsp sliced almonds	¼ cup sliced banana

▶DIRECTIONS

Prepare hot cereal per package directions with 1 cup of milk or soy milk. (If preparing with water, serve dairy choices on the side.) Or serve cold cereal in a bowl with your choice of dairy.

Serve with topping and two fruit choices.

▶SMART SHORTCUTS

Breakfast cereals and granolas vary widely in calories and serving sizes. Stick to varieties without a lot of added sugar and aim for a 150-calorie portion.

BRAND	PORTION
KIND Healthy Grains Cinnamon Oat Clusters with Flax Seeds	⅓ cup
Purely Elizabeth Cranberry Pecan Granola Cereal	⅓ cup
Kashi Go Lean Crunch	¾ cup
Kellogg's Special K Multigrain Oats & Honey	1 cup
General Mills Total Raisin Bran	1 cup
Post Shredded Wheat Spoon Size Wheat'n Bran	1 cup
Nature's Path Organic Heritage Flakes	1 cup

Peanut Butter Oatmeal Breakfast

PREP TIME: 5 MINUTES   TOTAL TIME: 5 MINUTES

Makes 1 serving

½ cup quick-cooking oats

¾ cup low-fat milk—dairy, soy, or almond

½ teaspoon vanilla extract

2 tablespoons natural creamy peanut butter

1 teaspoon honey

In a small microwavable bowl, stir together the oats, milk, and vanilla. Microwave at 1 minute intervals, stirring between intervals, until the oatmeal reaches the desired consistency, about 2 minutes. Stir in the peanut butter and honey.

Peach Breakfast Quinoa

PREP TIME: 5 MINUTES   TOTAL TIME: 20 MINUTES

Makes 3 servings

⅔ cup quinoa, well rinsed

1½ cups low-fat milk—dairy, soy, or almond

½ teaspoon minced crystallized ginger or ⅛ teaspoon ground ginger

2 whole peaches, pitted and chopped, or 2 cups frozen peaches, thawed

2 teaspoons butter

In a medium-size saucepan, combine the quinoa, milk, and ginger. Bring to a slow simmer over medium heat. Reduce the heat to low, cover, and cook for 15 minutes, until the quinoa is tender. Immediately stir in the peaches and butter.

Cherry Cream of Rye Cereal

PREP TIME: 5 MINUTES   TOTAL TIME: 5 MINUTES

Makes 4 servings

2 cups water

2 cups apple cider

¼ teaspoon salt

⅛ teaspoon ground cardamom

1 cup cream of rice cereal

2 tablespoons cherry fruit spread

2 tablespoons dried cherries

1⅓ cups 0% Greek-style vanilla yogurt

1. Combine the water, cider, salt, and cardamom in a saucepan and bring to a boil over medium heat. Stir in the cereal, stirring constantly.

2. Cook, uncovered, stirring, for 1 minute until thick. Remove from the heat and stir in the fruit spread and cherries. Top each serving with ⅓ cup yogurt.

Omelets

EGG	CHEESE	MEAT/MEAT ALTERNATIVE	VEGETABLE (UNLIMITED)
¾ cup liquid egg whites (or 4 large egg whites)*	2 Tbsp grated Parmesan	¼ cup meatless crumbles	2 Tbsp sliced scallions
3 large eggs	1 Tbsp goat cheese	1 slice (1 oz) turkey bacon, cooked and crumbled	¼ cup diced bell peppers
	2 Tbsp shredded 2% milk Cheddar cheese	1 oz chopped smoked salmon	2 Tbsp diced onions
	2 Tbsp shredded 2% milk Jack cheese	1 slice (1 oz) bacon, cooked and crumbled	¼ cup diced tomatoes
	2 Tbsp feta crumbles	2 links or 1 patty fully cooked turkey/chicken breakfast sausage	½ cup sliced mushrooms
	2 Tbsp reduced-fat cream cheese	1 link fully cooked pork breakfast sausage	2 cups baby spinach leaves

*If using egg whites, double the amount of cheese or use 1½ times the amount of meat/meat alternative and serve the omelet with 1 slice of multigrain or whole wheat toast.

▶DIRECTIONS

Sauté the vegetables in an 8-inch nonstick skillet coated with cooking spray over medium heat until tender. Transfer to a plate.

In a small bowl, use a fork to beat the eggs with 1 teaspoon of water or milk and a pinch of salt and pepper.

Heat 1 teaspoon of oil in the same skillet over medium heat. When hot, add the egg mixture, stir briefly, then tilt the pan to allow the uncooked egg to run to the side. Loosen the edges with a spatula. Sprinkle the cheese, meat (or meat alternative), and vegetables over half the omelet, fold the other half over the top, and cook for 30 seconds. Slide onto the plate.

▶CHANGE IT UP

Fry, scramble, or poach your eggs if you prefer, and incorporate the additional ingredients or serve them on the side.

SMART SHORTCUTS
FROZEN BREAKFAST ITEMS

PRODUCT	CALORIES	PAIR WITH
Nature's Path Organic Waffles, Ancient Grains	180 (2 waffles)	follow the chart on page 104
Van's Hearty Oats Premium Waffles, Berry Boost	200 (2 waffles)	
Nature's Path Organic Waffles, Chia Plus	210 (2 waffles)	
Kashi Waffles, Blueberry	225 (3 waffles)	
Jimmy Dean Delights Turkey Sausage Bowl	240 (1 bowl)	1 slice multigrain or whole wheat toast + 1 medium orange
Amy's Breakfast Burrito with Black Beans & Tomatoes	270 (1 burrito)	1 medium apple or banana
CedarLane Omelette, Egg White, Spinach, and Mushroom	270 (1 omelette)	

Potato Frittata

PREP TIME: 5 MINUTES   TOTAL TIME: 25 MINUTES

Makes 4 servings

2 tablespoons olive oil
1 bag (14–16 ounces) frozen organic shredded hash browns
8 eggs
½ cup (2 ounces) crumbled goat cheese

¼ cup water
½ teaspoon salt
½ teaspoon ground black pepper
4 bananas, sliced

1. Preheat the oven to 350°F. In a large ovenproof skillet, heat the oil over medium heat. Cook the potatoes for 10 minutes stirring occasionally, or until golden brown.

2. Meanwhile, in large bowl, beat the eggs, cheese, water, salt, and pepper. Pour into the skillet and cook for 5 minutes, or until the edges start to set.

3. Bake in the oven for 10 minutes, or until eggs are set. Serve with the bananas.

Southwest Frittata

PREP TIME: 5 MINUTES   TOTAL TIME: 20 MINUTES

Makes 4 servings

6 eggs
1 can (15 ounces) black beans, rinsed and drained
1 cup corn kernels
1½ cups (6 ounces) shredded low-fat Monterey Jack cheese

¾ teaspoon chili powder
1 bunch scallions, sliced
½ cup reduced-fat sour cream
½ cup salsa

1. In a medium bowl, whisk together the eggs, beans, corn, cheese, and chili powder.

2. Coat a large nonstick skillet with nonstick spray. Add the scallions. Coat lightly with nonstick spray. Cook, stirring, over medium heat for 2 minutes, or until wilted.

3. Add the egg mixture to the skillet. Cook, stirring occasionally, for 8 minutes, or until the eggs are set on the bottom. Reduce the heat to low. Cover and cook for 5 minutes, or until the eggs are set on the top.

4. To serve, cut into wedges and top with the sour cream and salsa.

Vegetable and Bacon Scramble

PREP TIME: 10 MINUTES	TOTAL TIME: 25 MINUTES

Makes 4 servings

3 slices turkey bacon

3 scallions, sliced

½ small red bell pepper, finely chopped

1 cup sliced mushrooms

6 eggs

¼ teaspoon tarragon

¼ teaspoon salt

¼ teaspoon ground black pepper

¼ cup grated Parmesan cheese

1. In a medium nonstick skillet over medium heat, cook the bacon for about 5 minutes, until brown and crisp. Transfer the bacon to a plate lined with paper towels.

2. Add the scallions, bell pepper, and mushrooms to the skillet. Reduce the heat slightly and cook for 5 minutes, or until the vegetables are softened, stirring occasionally.

3. Meanwhile, in a small bowl, whisk together the eggs, tarragon, salt, and pepper. Pour the eggs into the skillet and scramble for 3 to 5 minutes, until set.

4. Crumble the bacon over the eggs and sprinkle with the cheese.

Creamy Eggs with Smoked Salmon

PREP TIME: 5 MINUTES	TOTAL TIME: 5 MINUTES

Makes 2 servings

1 teaspoon olive oil

4 eggs, lightly beaten

1 ounce smoked salmon (lox), cut into thin strips

1 tablespoon finely chopped fresh chives

2 tablespoons sour cream

1 whole wheat bagel, split and toasted

2 tablespoons cream cheese

1. Heat the oil in a nonstick skillet over medium-high heat. Cook the eggs for about 8 minutes, until set on the bottom. Sprinkle with the salmon and chives. Cook and stir gently for about 1 minute, until scrambled. Remove from the heat and gently stir in the sour cream.

2. Spread 1 tablespoon cream cheese onto each bagel half and serve with the eggs.

Waffles

WAFFLE	SYRUP/SPREAD*	TOPPING/SIDE	FRUIT (PICK 2)
2 or 3 frozen waffles (200 to 225 calories total)	2 Tbsp 100% fruit spread	1 Tbsp chopped walnuts or pecans	½ cup sliced fresh strawberries
	2 tsp butter	1 Tbsp sliced almonds	½ cup fresh raspberries
	2 tsp natural peanut or almond butter	1 Tbsp raisins	½ cup sliced fresh peaches
	4 tsp pure maple syrup	1 link fully cooked turkey/chicken breakfast sausage	¾ cup fresh blueberries
	5.3 oz 0% plain Greek yogurt	1 slice (1 oz) turkey bacon, cooked	½ cup chopped apple
			1 Tbsp raisins
			¼ cup sliced banana

*If you prefer, you can skip the syrup/spread choice and serve the waffles with 1 fruit topping, 1 egg, and 1 slice regular bacon.

▶DIRECTIONS

Prepare the waffles per package directions. Serve with a syrup/spread choice, a topping/side, and two fruit choices.

Waffles Florentine

PREP TIME: 15 MINUTES   TOTAL TIME: 15 MINUTES

Makes 2 servings

1 clove garlic, minced (optional)

4 cups baby spinach

4 eggs

4 frozen whole-grain waffles

¼ cup shredded sharp cheddar cheese, divided

1. Preheat the broiler.

2. Heat a nonstick skillet coated with cooking spray over medium heat. Cook the garlic for 1 minute or until golden. Add the spinach and cook, stirring constantly, for 4 minutes, or until wilted. Remove to a plate.

3. Re-coat the same skillet with cooking spray and heat over medium heat. Break the eggs into the skillet and cook, pushing whites toward the yolks to keep eggs separated, until the whites have set but the yolks are still runny, or until of desired doneness.

4. Meanwhile, toast the waffles. Then place the waffles on a baking sheet. Top each with ¼ of the spinach mixture, 1 egg, and 1 tablespoon of the cheese. Broil for 3 minutes, or until the cheese melts.

Smoothies

SMOOTHIE	BASE	PRODUCE
Pumpkin Smoothie	½ cup 1% milk or low-fat soy milk + ¾ cup 0% plain Greek yogurt	½ cup canned pure pumpkin (frozen in ice cube tray) + ¼ Hass avocado (pitted, peeled, and cubed)
Cherry-Berry Smoothie	½ cup 1% milk or low-fat soy milk + ½ cup 0% plain Greek yogurt	1 cup frozen strawberries + ½ cup frozen sweet cherries
Tropical Smoothie	½ cup chilled coconut water + ½ cup 0% plain Greek yogurt	1⅓ cups frozen tropical fruit blend + 1 Tbsp fresh lemon juice
Banana-Avocado Smoothie	⅓ cup 1% milk or low-fat soy milk	½ small Hass avocado (pitted, peeled, and cubed) + ½ medium chopped frozen banana + ⅓ cup frozen pineapple chunks + ⅓ cup baby spinach leaves + 2 Tbsp chopped fresh parsley + 1 Tbsp fresh lime juice
Chocolate Smoothie	½ cup 1% chocolate milk or low-fat chocolate soy milk + ½ cup 0% plain Greek yogurt	½ medium chopped frozen banana

▶DIRECTIONS

Combine the smoothie ingredients (from one row) in a blender and puree until smooth. Adjust the consistency with additional liquid or ice cubes as desired.

BOOST	SWEETENER	ICE CUBES	OPTIONAL FLAVORING/ GARNISH
2 Tbsp ground flaxseeds	1 Tbsp pure maple syrup		½ tsp pumpkin pie spice
4 tsp natural peanut butter	1 to 2 tsp honey	¼ to ½ cup	Pinch of ground cinnamon or dash of vanilla or almond extract
4 tsp natural almond butter	1 to 2 tsp honey		Garnish with toasted unsweetened coconut
1 scoop vanilla whey protein powder			Pinch of minced fresh jalapeño
4 tsp natural peanut butter + 1 Tbsp ground flaxseeds		¼ to ½ cup	1 tsp instant coffee granules

▶CHANGE IT UP

SMOOTHIE	FLAVOR VARIATION
Pumpkin Smoothie	Try molasses instead of maple syrup.
Cherry-Berry Smoothie	Use frozen raspberries, blueberries, or mixed berries in place of strawberries.
Tropical Smoothie	Substitute frozen peaches or mango for the tropical fruit blend.
Banana-Avocado Smoothie	Replace the milk with coconut water.
Chocolate Smoothie	Swap in silken tofu for the yogurt.

Apple Pie Smoothie

PREP TIME: 5 MINUTES   TOTAL TIME: 5 MINUTES

Makes 1 serving

½ cup low-fat milk—dairy, soy or almond

6 ounces low-fat vanilla yogurt

1 teaspoon apple pie spice

1 medium apple, peeled, cored, and chopped

1½ tablespoons cashew butter

Ice

In a blender, combine the milk, yogurt, apple pie spice, apple pieces, and cashew butter along with a handful of ice. Blend 1 minute until smooth. Transfer to a glass.

Melon-Mango Smoothie

PREP TIME: 5 MINUTES   TOTAL TIME: 5 MINUTES

Makes 1 serving

¾ cup frozen mango chunks

½ cup frozen or fresh banana slices

½ cup cantaloupe, diced

⅓ cup low-fat vanilla yogurt

¼ cup vanilla soymilk (or low-fat milk with 1 teaspoon vanilla)

¼ cup low-fat granola, for topping

In a blender or food processor, place the mangos, bananas, cantaloupe, yogurt, and milk and puree until thick and smooth. Spoon into a glass and sprinkle the granola over the top.

Mocha Coconut Smoothie

PREP TIME: 5 MINUTES   TOTAL TIME: 5 MINUTES

Makes 1 serving

1 cup canned light coconut milk

1 tablespoon cocoa powder

1 tablespoon cashew butter

1 tablespoon honey

1 teaspoon instant espresso powder

½ to 1 cup ice cubes

In a blender, combine the milk, cocoa powder, cashew butter, honey, and espresso powder. Blend on low to combine. Add the ice cubes a few at a time, and blend until of desired thickness.

Strawberry Chocolate Smoothie

| PREP TIME: 5 MINUTES | TOTAL TIME: 5 MINUTES |

Makes 2 servings

1½ cups low-fat milk
1 cup low-fat ricotta cheese
1 teaspoon vanilla extract

1 tablespoon honey
1 tablespoon cocoa powder
2 cups frozen strawberries

1. Combine the milk, cheese, vanilla, honey, and cocoa powder in a blender. Process on low for 2 minutes or until smooth.

2. Add the strawberries and process on high for 2 minutes or until well blended.

Gingerbread Smoothie

| PREP TIME: 5 MINUTES | TOTAL TIME: 5 MINUTES |

Makes 1 serving

1 container (7 ounces) 2% Greek-style yogurt
¼ cup frozen sliced banana
1½ tablespoon almond butter

1 tablespoon molasses
¼ teaspoon ground ginger
¼ teaspoon cinnamon
½ to 1 cup ice cubes

In a blender, combine the yogurt, banana, almond butter, molasses, ginger, and cinnamon. Blend on low to combine. Add the ice cubes a few at a time, until of desired thickness.

LUNCH AND DINNER

As the day progresses, you'll find more choices to keep you energetic and productive. Each day, select one item from these charts for lunch and another for dinner.

Burgers

BURGER (UNCOOKED WEIGHT)	BUN	CHEESE	TOPPING	SIDE
2.5 oz veggie burger	Multigrain hamburger bun	2 Tbsp feta crumbles	1 Tbsp ketchup	½ cup grapes
4 oz 93% lean ground turkey patty	Hamburger bun	2 Tbsp blue cheese crumbles	1 Tbsp steak sauce	12 mini pretzels
4 oz ground chicken patty	Potato roll	1 slice (¾ oz) 2% milk provolone cheese	3 sweet pickle chips	2 cups bagged romaine salad blend + 3 cherry tomatoes + 1 tsp olive oil + 1½ tsp balsamic vinegar
4 oz salmon burger	100% whole wheat hamburger bun	1 slice (¾ oz) 2% milk Cheddar cheese	1 Tbsp barbecue sauce	8 baby carrots + 1 Tbsp light ranch dressing
4 oz 90% lean ground beef patty	¾ whole wheat pita (6½")	1 slice (¾ oz) 2% milk Jack cheese	1 Tbsp light mayonnaise	¼ Hass avocado, sliced
		1 slice (⅔ oz) American cheese		

▶DIRECTIONS

Heat a lightly oiled grill or grill pan over medium-high heat.

Grill the burger according to package directions (or see doneness chart), turning once or twice.

Serve on a bun with cheese, topping, and as many flavor boosters as desired (see below).

Pair with a side.

▶FLAVOR BOOSTERS

Customize your burger with these ultra-low-calorie toppings:

- Lettuce
- Alfalfa sprouts
- Baby spinach
- Dill pickles
- Sliced mushrooms
- Raw onions
- Tomato slices
- Hot-pepper sauce
- Fresh jalapeño
- Dijon/deli mustard
- Horseradish

▶DONENESS SIGNS

BURGER TYPE	COOK UNTIL...
Veggie burger	Heated through (see package directions)
Ground turkey patty	Firm and no longer pink inside
Ground chicken patty	Firm and no longer pink inside
Salmon burger	Just opaque (see package directions if frozen)
Ground beef patty	Firm and no longer pink inside (or to desired doneness)

Lamb Burgers with Tomatoes and Feta Cheese

PREP TIME: 20 MINUTES	TOTAL TIME: 30 MINUTES

Makes 4 servings

1 pound ground lamb

2 garlic cloves, minced

1 tablespoon fresh chopped rosemary

½ teaspoon ground black pepper

¼ teaspoon salt

1 cup canned crushed tomatoes

8 ounces mixed greens or baby spinach

⅓ cup crumbled feta cheese, at room temperature

1. In a large bowl, combine the lamb, garlic, rosemary, pepper, and salt. Using a fork, break up the meat and mix in the seasonings. Form into 4 burgers approximately 4" in diameter and 1" thick.

2. Heat a large, heavy skillet over medium-high heat until drops of water skip over the surface. Add the burgers. Cook for 8 minutes, turning once, or until browned on both sides. Pour off the fat, reduce the heat to low, and add the tomatoes to the skillet (the tomatoes will boil briefly). Cook, turning the burgers once, for 10 minutes, or until a meat thermometer registers 160°F for medium.

3. Arrange the greens on 4 plates. Top with the burgers, tomatoes, and cheese.

Pizza Burgers

PREP TIME: 15 MINUTES	TOTAL TIME: 25 MINUTES

Makes 4 servings

1½ pounds extra-lean ground beef chuck

5 tablespoons (1 ounce) grated Romano cheese

½ teaspoon salt

1 teaspoon dried oregano

¾ teaspoon garlic powder

Freshly ground black pepper

4 slices tomato

4 ounces part-skim mozzarella cheese, cut into 4 equal slices

4 whole wheat bagel thins

1. Place the broiler rack 2" to 3" from the heat source and preheat the broiler.

2. Place the beef in a large bowl and break into pieces. Add the cheese, salt, oregano, garlic powder, and pepper. Using a fork, gently combine the beef and seasonings. Form into 4 burgers approximately 4" in diameter and 1" thick.

3. Place on a broiling pan and cook for 10 minutes, turning once, or until a meat thermometer registers 160°F for medium. Top with the tomato and cheese and broil for 1 minute, or until the cheese melts. Serve on the bagel thin.

Reuben Burger

PREP TIME: 10 MINUTES   TOTAL TIME: 20 MINUTES

Makes 4 servings

1 pound ground sirloin or ground turkey

1 teaspoon salt

½ teaspoon black pepper

½ cup sauerkraut, well drained

4 slices Swiss cheese

8 slices rye bread

4 tablespoons reduced-fat Thousand Island salad dressing

1. Shape the meat into 4 large, thin burgers. Heat a cast-iron skillet coated with cooking spray over medium heat. Cook the burgers for 4 minutes or until browned. Flip the burgers and top each with 2 tablespoons of the sauerkraut and a slice of cheese. Cook for 4 to 5 minutes or until a thermometer inserted in the center registers 160°F and the meat is no longer pink.

2. Meanwhile, toast the bread and spread 1 side of each with ½ tablespoon of the dressing. Place a burger on 4 slices of toast and top with the remaining toast.

Dill Salmon Burger

PREP TIME: 10 MINUTES   TOTAL TIME: 30 MINUTES

Makes 4 servings

2 cans (6 ounces each) or 1 can (14.75 ounces) salmon, drained

1 small onion, finely chopped

1 egg

⅓ cup bread crumbs

¼ cup light mayonnaise

1 tablespoon fresh dill, finely chopped (or 1 teaspoon dried dill)

2 tablespoons Greek-style 0% yogurt

1 teaspoon country-style Dijon mustard

4 whole wheat rolls (1½-2 ounces each)

4 lettuce leaves

4 tomato slices

1. Preheat the oven to 350°F. Coat a small baking sheet with cooking spray.

2. In a medium bowl, mix together the salmon, onion, egg, bread crumbs, mayonnaise, and dill. Make 4 burgers approximately 4" in diameter.

3. Place the burgers on the baking sheet and bake for approximately 20 minutes, turning once, until lightly browned.

4. Meanwhile, stir together the yogurt and mustard in a small bowl. Divide the yogurt mixture evenly and spread it on the rolls. Serve the burgers on the rolls and top with the lettuce and tomato.

Grill, Broiler, or Stove Top

PROTEIN (UNCOOKED WEIGHT)	STARCHY SIDE	VEGGIE SIDE
8 oz peeled and deveined shrimp	2 soft white corn tortillas (6"), warmed	1 cup mixed vegetables (cooked from frozen) + 1 tsp butter
4 oz boneless center-cut pork chop	½ cup cooked rice pilaf	⅓ cup cubed fresh Hass avocado
5 oz boneless, skinless chicken thigh	⅔ cup rinsed and drained canned black beans, warmed	12 spears cooked asparagus + 1 tsp olive oil or butter
4 oz flank, top round, or sirloin steak	⅔ cup cooked quinoa	1 cup cooked green beans + 1 tsp butter
6 oz boneless, skinless chicken breast	⅔ cup cooked brown rice	1 cup cooked spinach or chopped kale + 1 tsp olive oil or butter
6 oz pork tenderloin	8" flour tortilla, warmed	1 cup cooked broccoli florets + 1 tsp butter
4 oz wild salmon fillet	6½" whole wheat pita	1 cup cooked sliced carrots + 1 tsp butter
4 oz beef tenderloin	1 cup cooked whole wheat pasta	½ cup pasta (tomato) sauce, warmed
	6 oz baked sweet potato + 1 tsp butter	3 cups bagged romaine salad blend + 5 cherry tomatoes + 2 Tbsp light Italian dressing
	6 oz plain baked potato + 1 tsp butter	¼ cup salsa + ½ cup shredded romaine + 2 Tbsp Cheddar

▶DIRECTIONS

Preheat the grill or broiler or heat a skillet coated with cooking spray over medium to medium-high heat.

Brush/rub the meat or seafood with 1 teaspoon of olive oil and season with salt and pepper. Sprinkle with a flavor booster (see opposite page) if desired.

Cook as desired until the food reaches the proper doneness (see chart). Let stand 5 minutes before eating. Serve with a starchy side and a veggie side.

▶DONENESS SIGNS

FOOD	IT'S DONE WHEN . . .
Shrimp	It turns pink and gets firm
Pork chop or pork tenderloin	Internal temperature reaches a minimum of 145°F, plus a 3-minute rest
Boneless, skinless chicken thigh or breast	Internal temperature reaches a minimum of 165°F
Flank steak or beef tenderloin	Internal temperature reaches 145°F (medium-rare) to 160°F (medium), plus a 3-minute rest
Salmon	It flakes easily with a fork

▶FLAVOR BOOSTERS

Make your meat tastier with these go-to rubs. Mix up a batch and store in an airtight container.

All-purpose (chicken, beef, pork, fish, vegetables)

One tablespoon dried thyme *plus* 2 teaspoons dried oregano *plus* 1 teaspoon smoked paprika *plus* 1 teaspoon cumin *plus* 1 teaspoon onion powder *plus* ½ teaspoon garlic powder *plus* ¼ teaspoon cayenne *plus* ¼ teaspoon salt *plus* ¼ teaspoon black pepper

Sweet and spicy (beef, pork)

Two tablespoons chili powder *plus* 1 tablespoon dark brown sugar *plus* 1 tablespoon ground coffee *plus* 1 teaspoon cumin *plus* 1 teaspoon onion powder *plus* ½ teaspoon garlic powder *plus* ¼ teaspoon cayenne *plus* ¼ teaspoon salt *plus* ¼ teaspoon black pepper

Basic jerk (chicken, pork, beef, shrimp)

Two tablespoons allspice *plus* 1 tablespoon dried thyme *plus* 1 tablespoon ground cinnamon *plus* 1½ teaspoons nutmeg *plus* 1½ teaspoons cayenne *plus* 1 teaspoon black pepper

SMART SHORTCUTS
FROZEN ENTRÉES/MEALS

PRODUCT	CALORIES	PAIR WITH...
Stouffer's Homestyle Classics Beef Pot Roast	230	5.3-oz container 0% vanilla Greek yogurt + ¾ cup fresh blueberries
Healthy Choice Cafe Steamers Top Chef Chicken Fresca with Chardonnay	240	
Blake's Organic Shepherd's Pie	240	
Lean Cuisine Market Collection Salisbury Steak	260	
Healthy Choice Cafe Steamers Top Chef Crustless Chicken Pot Pie	280	½ cup unsweetened applesauce + 2 graham cracker squares
Organic Bistro Alaskan Salmon Cake Entrée	370	1 medium peach

Lemon Chicken

PREP TIME: 10 MINUTES   TOTAL TIME: 25 MINUTES

Makes 2 servings

¼ cup whole wheat flour

1 egg, beaten

2 boneless, skinless chicken breast halves

1 cup white wine

¼ cup lemon juice

4 ounces whole wheat linguine

1 teaspoon butter

2 cups broccoli florets, steamed

1. Place the flour in a shallow dish. Beat the egg in another shallow dish. Dredge the chicken in the flour. Dip into the egg and dredge in the flour again.

2. Heat a large skillet coated with cooking spray over medium heat. Cook the chicken for 10 minutes, turning once, or until browned. Add the wine and lemon juice to the skillet and simmer for 5 minutes, or until the sauce thickens, a thermometer inserted in the thickest portion of one breast registers 160°F, and the juices from the chicken run clear.

3. Meanwhile, prepare the pasta according to package directions. Drain and toss with the butter. Divide the pasta and broccoli onto 2 plates. Place a chicken breast on each plate and drizzle with the sauce.

One-Dish Chicken Dinner

PREP TIME: 10 MINUTES   TOTAL TIME: 1 HOUR

Makes 4 servings

¼ cup reduced-sodium soy sauce

¼ cup honey

¾ cup low-sodium chicken broth, divided

2 tablespoons hot sauce

1 pound boneless, skinless chicken breast halves

1 pound green beans, trimmed

1 pound baby carrots, halved

2 cups cooked brown rice

1. Preheat the oven to 375°F. Coat a 13" x 9" baking dish with cooking spray.

2. Stir together the soy sauce, honey, ¼ cup of the broth, and hot sauce in a small bowl. Place the chicken in the prepared baking dish. Pour about half of the sauce over the chicken. Bake for 30 minutes.

3. Remove from the oven. Arrange the beans and carrots around the chicken. Stir the remaining ½ cup broth into the remaining soy sauce mixture. Pour around the chicken to coat vegetables. Bake for 20 minutes, or until a thermometer inserted in the thickest portion of the chicken registers 160°F and the juices run clear. Serve with the brown rice.

Balsamic Steak Dinner

PREP TIME: 20 MINUTES TOTAL TIME: 30 MINUTES + MARINATING TIME

Makes 4 servings

½ cup frozen apple juice concentrate, thawed

1 tablespoon packed brown sugar

1 teaspoon dry mustard

¾ cup balsamic vinegar, divided

1 pound beef flank steak, trimmed of fat

2 cups sliced onions

1 clove garlic, minced

¼ cup reduced-sodium beef broth

4 baking potatoes (6 ounces each), baked

4 teaspoons butter

1. In a shallow glass dish, stir together the apple juice concentrate, brown sugar, mustard, and ½ cup of the vinegar. Score the surface of the steak several times on both sides with a sharp knife. Place in the dish, turning to coat. Cover and refrigerate for at least 3 hours or overnight, turning occasionally.

2. Just before broiling the steak, heat a large nonstick skillet coated with cooking spray over medium-high heat. Add the onions and garlic. Cook, stirring, for 5 minutes, or until the onions are lightly browned. Add the broth and the remaining ¼ cup vinegar. Cook, stirring, for 8 to 10 minutes, until the liquid has almost evaporated.

3. Preheat the broiler. Coat the rack of a broiler pan with cooking spray. Remove the steak from the marinade and place on the rack. Discard the marinade. Broil the steak 4" from the heat for 8 minutes, turning once, or until a thermometer inserted in the center registers 145°F for medium-rare. Serve with the onions and baked potatoes, each filled with 1 teaspoon butter.

Grilled Cilantro-Tuna Bruschetta

PREP TIME: 10 MINUTES   TOTAL TIME: 15 MINUTES

Makes 3 servings

4 tablespoons olive oil, divided

15 slices crusty baguette (sliced on the diagonal)

2 cans (6 ounces each) light tuna in water, drained and flaked

1 rib celery, finely chopped

¼ cup chopped red onion

¼ cup chopped fresh cilantro

2 tablespoons lime juice

Pinch ground black pepper

1. Coat a barbecue grill or ridged grill pan with olive oil spray and heat to medium-hot. Brush 2 tablespoons oil, evenly divided, on both sides of the bread slices.

2. Grill the bread, in batches if necessary, until one side has dark grill marks, and then turn to toast the other side. Transfer to a platter.

3. In a medium bowl, mix the tuna, celery, onion, cilantro, lime juice, and black pepper. Stir in the remaining 2 tablespoons oil. Spread the tuna mixture evenly over the bread slices.

Glazed Ham with Sweet Potatoes

PREP TIME: 5 MINUTES	TOTAL TIME: 20 MINUTES

Makes 2 servings

2 teaspoons honey

1 teaspoon Dijon mustard

1 boneless fully cooked ham steak (8 ounces)

2 sweet potatoes (6 ounces each), baked

2 teaspoons butter

8 ounces green beans, trimmed and steamed

1 cup unsweetened applesauce

1. Coat the rack of a broiler pan with cooking spray. Preheat the broiler. In a small bowl, combine the honey and mustard.

2. Broil the ham steak for 5 minutes. Turn and brush with the honey-mustard mixture. Broil 5 minutes or until heated through and browned.

3. Serve the ham with the sweet potatoes, each filled with 1 teaspoon butter, the green beans, and the applesauce.

Zesty Steak with Potatoes

PREP TIME: 20 MINUTES	TOTAL TIME: 50 MINUTES + MARINATING TIME

Makes 4 servings

1 tablespoon dry mustard

4 teaspoons soy sauce

2 teaspoons red wine vinegar

1 teaspoon onion powder

¼ teaspoon garlic powder

1 tablespoon olive oil

1 top round or sirloin London broil (1½ pounds), 1" thick

16 ounces organic frozen potato wedges

¼ teaspoon salt

¼ teaspoon ground black pepper

2 cups broccoli florets, steamed

1. In a small bowl, combine the mustard and soy sauce to make a paste. Stir in the vinegar, onion powder, and garlic powder. Whisk in the olive oil. Place the beef in a glass baking dish. Pour the mustard mixture over the beef and rub lightly to coat all over. Cover and refrigerate for 3 hours or overnight. Remove from the refrigerator 15 minutes before cooking.

2. Preheat the oven to 425°F. Place the potatoes on a baking sheet and bake for 15 minutes. Place in a bowl and keep warm. Set the oven to broil.

3. Meanwhile, coat a broiling pan with cooking spray. Place the broiler rack 2" to 3" from the heat source and preheat the broiler.

4. Transfer the beef to the broiling pan, and sprinkle with the salt and pepper. Broil 8 minutes, turning once, or until a meat thermometer registers 145°F for medium-rare.

5. Remove to a platter and let rest for 5 minutes. Thinly slice the steak diagonally and serve with the juices on the platter with the potatoes and broccoli.

Barbecued Chicken and Potatoes

PREP TIME: 40 MINUTES · TOTAL TIME: 1 HOUR 10 MINUTES + MARINATING TIME

Makes 4 servings

1 small onion, minced

1 can (8 ounces) tomato sauce

2 tablespoons brown sugar

2 tablespoons red wine vinegar

2 tablespoons Worcestershire sauce

2 teaspoons chili powder

¾ cup water

4 bone-in chicken breast halves, skinned

4 russet potatoes (6 ounces each)

2 tablespoons olive oil

1 teaspoon dried rosemary, crushed

½ teaspoon salt

1. Combine the onion, tomato sauce, brown sugar, vinegar, Worcestershire sauce, chili powder, and water in a medium saucepan. Bring to a boil over high heat. Reduce the heat to low and simmer, uncovered, for 15 minutes, or until thickened. Remove from the heat and let cool for 20 minutes.

2. Place the chicken in a resealable plastic bag with ⅔ cup of the sauce. Seal and shake to coat. Refrigerate for 1 to 8 hours.

3. Just before grilling or broiling, cut the potatoes lengthwise in half. Cut each half into 3 wedges. Place potatoes wedges in a large bowl. Drizzle with the oil, rosemary, and salt. Toss to coat.

4. Preheat the grill or the broiler. Remove the chicken from the marinade and place on the grill rack or broiler pan. Discard the marinade. Grill or broil for 20 minutes, or until a thermometer inserted in the thickest portion registers 165°F and the juices run clear, brushing with the remaining sauce during the last 15 minutes of cooking. Place the potatoes on the edges of the grill or roasting pan during the last 15 minutes of roasting the chicken. Cook, turning 3 times until tender and browned.

Simple Turkey Cordon Blue Dinner

PREP TIME: 15 MINUTES	TOTAL TIME: 20 MINUTES

Makes 4 servings

1 box (4.9 ounces) quinoa blend
¼ cup whole wheat flour
½ teaspoon salt
¼ teaspoon ground black pepper
4 turkey cutlets (4 ounces each)
1 tablespoon olive oil

4 thin slices (3 ounces) ham, sliced in half
4 thin slices (4 ounces) provolone cheese, sliced in half
8 cups mixed greens
2 tablespoons balsamic vinaigrette

1. Prepare the quinoa according to package directions.

2. Meanwhile, in a shallow dish, stir together the flour, salt, and pepper. Coat the cutlets in the flour and pat off the excess.

3. Heat the oil in a large nonstick skillet over high heat. Add the turkey and cook for 3 minutes, or until brown. Reduce the heat to low, turn the cutlets over, and layer 1 slice of the ham and cheese on top of each cutlet. Cover and cook for 2 to 3 minutes until the turkey juices run clear and the cheese is melted. Serve with the quinoa blend and mixed greens tossed with vinaigrette.

Chicken Teriyaki and Brown Rice

PREP TIME: 5 MINUTES	TOTAL TIME: 25 MINUTES

Makes 4 servings

1 tablespoon olive oil
1 pound boneless, skinless chicken breasts, cut into 1" cubes
2 packages (12 ounces each) frozen oriental vegetables, thawed
1 package (10 ounces) frozen whole grain brown rice

1 teaspoon cornstarch
½ cup low-sodium chicken broth
¼ cup teriyaki sauce
4 oranges

1. Heat the oil a large saucepan over medium-high heat. Cook the chicken for 10 minutes, stirring occasionally, or until browned. Add the vegetables and cook for 5 minutes, or until the heated through.

2. Meanwhile, prepare the rice according to package directions.

3. In a small bowl, whisk the cornstarch into the broth until dissolved. Add the teriyaki sauce. Add to the chicken mixture. Bring to a boil, stirring constantly, for 1 minute, or until thickened.

4. Divide the rice and chicken mixture among 4 plates. Serve each with an orange.

Baked Cod with Roasted Vegetables

PREP TIME: 15 MINUTES	TOTAL TIME: 1 HOUR

Makes 4 servings

4 medium russet potatoes, pierced with a fork

2 cups baby carrots

2 cups broccoli florets

1 package (8 ounces) sliced mushrooms

1 large onion, cut into wedges

2 tablespoons olive oil

½ teaspoon salt

½ teaspoon pepper

4 tablespoons honey

2 teaspoons Dijon mustard

1 pound cod fillets, fresh or frozen, thawed

4 teaspoons butter

1. Preheat the oven to 425°F. Place the potatoes in the oven and bake for 20 minutes.

2. Coat 2 baking sheets with cooking spray. Arrange the carrots, broccoli, mushrooms, and onion on 1 baking sheet, toss with the oil, and sprinkle with the salt and pepper. Bake with the potatoes for 20 minutes.

3. In a small bowl, stir together the honey and mustard. Arrange the cod on the remaining prepared baking sheet. Spread the honey mustard evenly over the fish. Add to the oven with the potatoes and vegetables and bake for 20 minutes, or until the fish flakes easily and vegetables are browned and tender.

4. Evenly divide the fish and vegetables onto 4 plates. Serve with the potatoes with 1 teaspoon butter for each.

Baked Fish and Rice

PREP TIME: 10 MINUTES   TOTAL TIME: 25 MINUTES

Makes 4 servings

1 pound firm white fish such as cod, flounder, tilapia, or halibut

⅓ cup mayonnaise

2 tablespoons grated Parmesan cheese

1 scallion, thinly sliced

½ teaspoon Worcestershire sauce

2 bags (10 ounces each) frozen rice and vegetable mix

1. Preheat the oven to 450°F. Coat a 9" x 13" baking pan with cooking spray and arrange the fillets in the pan.

2. In a small bowl, stir together the mayonnaise, cheese, scallion, and Worcestershire sauce. Spread the mixture over the fish fillets. Bake uncovered for 15 minutes or until the fish flakes easily with a fork.

3. Meanwhile, prepare the rice and vegetable mix according to package directions. Divide rice and fish among 4 plates.

BBQ Pork Chops

PREP TIME: 10 MINUTES   TOTAL TIME: 45 MINUTES

Makes 4 servings

½ cup chili sauce

1 tablespoons orange juice

½ teaspoon garlic salt

4 boneless pork loin chops (4 ounces each)

12 ounces frozen sweet potato fries

1 large bunch cauliflower, cut into bite-size pieces

4 teaspoons butter

1. Preheat the oven to 400°F. Coat a large baking dish with cooking spray.

2. In a small bowl, combine the chili sauce, juice, and garlic salt. Place the pork in the baking dish and brush with the chili sauce mixture. Let stand for 15 minutes.

3. Place the potatoes on a baking sheet. Bake the potatoes and pork chops for 20 minutes or until potatoes are browned and a thermometer inserted in the center of the pork chops registers 155°F.

4. Meanwhile, place a steam basket in a saucepan with 1" of water. Add the cauliflower and steam for 5 minutes or until tender-crisp. Divide chops, fries, and cauliflower among 4 plates. Top the cauliflower with 1 teaspoon butter on each plate.

Pasta

PASTA	SAUCE	PROTEIN	VEGETABLES (PICK 2)	TOPPING (OPTIONAL)
2 oz dry pasta (white, multigrain, whole wheat, gluten-free, etc.)	½ cup jarred pasta sauce	½ cup browned 93% lean ground turkey	½ cup sliced bell peppers	2 tsp chopped walnuts
	1 Tbsp pesto	½ cup chopped or sliced cooked chicken breast	½ cup cut asparagus	2 Tbsp grated Parmesan cheese
	½ Tbsp butter + 2 Tbsp grated Parmesan cheese	2 (1 oz each) frozen turkey meatballs, cooked	½ cup cut green beans	2 Tbsp shredded part-skim mozzarella cheese
	1 tsp olive oil + 2 Tbsp grated Parmesan cheese	½ cup browned 90% lean ground beef	3 cups fresh spinach	2 tsp pine nuts
		3 or 4 frozen vegetarian meatballs (about 120 calories), cooked	½ cup shredded carrots	
		1 link (3 oz) fully cooked chicken sausage, sliced	6 frozen artichoke hearts	
			1 cup small broccoli florets	
			¼ cup frozen peas	
			1 cup chopped kale	

▶DIRECTIONS

Bring a pot of water to a boil. Add the pasta and cook per package directions.

Steam the vegetables until tender in a colander set above the pasta water (or add to the pasta water) during the last 3 to 5 minutes of cooking time.

Drain the pasta and return it to the pot over low heat. Add the vegetables, protein, and sauce. Stir to combine and heat through.

Transfer to a plate and serve sprinkled with topping, if using.

▶FLAVOR BOOSTERS

- Fresh herbs
- Lemon juice/zest
- Red-pepper flakes

▶QUICK PASTA MEASURING GUIDE

2 OUNCES DRY	APPROXIMATE MEASURE	APPROXIMATE COOKED YIELD
Spaghetti (and similar shapes)	⅔-inch diameter (held in fist)	1 cup
Elbows (and similar small shapes)	½ cup	1 cup
Penne (and similar large shapes)	⅔ to ¾ cup	1 to 1¼ cups
Orzo (and similar soup/salad shapes)	¼ cup	⅔ cup

SMART SHORTCUTS
FROZEN PASTA ENTRÉES/MEALS

PRODUCT	CALORIES	PAIR WITH...
Lean Cuisine Culinary Collection Shrimp and Angel Hair Pasta	230	2 Tbsp hummus + carrot and celery sticks 1 medium pear
Lean Cuisine Simple Favorites Four Cheese Cannelloni	230	
Amy's Light & Lean Spaghetti Italiano	240	
Healthy Choice Cafe Steamers 100% Natural Pumpkin Squash Ravioli	260	
Healthy Choice Baked! Lasagna with Meat Sauce	270	3 cups bagged romaine salad blend + 5 cherry tomatoes + 2 Tbsp light dressing/ vinaigrette + 2 Tbsp shredded 2% milk cheese
CedarLane Garden Vegetable Lasagna (10 oz)	280	
Kashi Roasted Garlic Chicken Farfalle Steam Meal	280	
Healthy Choice Top Chef Cafe Steamers Grilled Chicken Pesto with Vegetables	300	1 cup fruit salad

Pasta with Walnut–Basil Pesto

PREP TIME: 10 MINUTES	TOTAL TIME: 20 MINUTES

Makes 4 servings

1¼ cups packed fresh basil

¼ cup walnuts

1 clove garlic, peeled

1 tablespoon extra-virgin olive oil

¼ teaspoon salt

8 ounces multigrain angel hair pasta

¼ cup freshly grated Parmesan cheese

1 pound broiled shrimp, scallops, or chicken breasts

1. In a food processor, place the basil, walnuts, garlic, oil, and salt. Process, stopping the machine once or twice to scrape down the sides, until finely pureed. Scrape into a serving bowl.

2. Meanwhile, prepare the pasta according to package directions. Drain, reserving ½ cup of the cooking water.

3. Stir 2 or 3 tablespoons of the pasta water into the pesto to warm it and make it creamier. Add the pasta and toss, adding more pasta water if necessary. Sprinkle with the cheese and serve with the shrimp, scallops, or chicken.

Warm Pasta Salad

PREP TIME: 10 MINUTES	TOTAL TIME: 20 MINUTES

Makes 4 servings

2 cups grape or cherry tomatoes, halved

4 ounces bocconcini (about 12 small mozzarella balls), halved

½ cup torn fresh basil

¼ cup red wine vinegar

2 tablespoons olive oil

¼ teaspoon salt

8 ounces whole wheat pasta, such as penne, fusille, or bowties

1 cup shredded cooked chicken breast

1. In a large bowl, stir together the tomatoes, bocconcini, basil, vinegar, oil, and salt. Set aside.

2. Prepare the pasta according to package directions. Add the hot pasta and the chicken to tomato mixture, stirring to coat well.

Pizza

CRUST	SAUCE	CHEESE	MEAT TOPPING	SIDE
1 pita (6½" diameter), white or whole wheat	¼ cup pizza sauce	⅓ cup shredded 2% milk Italian/ pizza cheese blend	10 slices turkey pepperoni	1 cup cubed watermelon or cantaloupe
⅕ tube refrigerated thin-crust pizza dough	1 tsp extra virgin olive oil	⅓ cup shredded part-skim mozzarella cheese	½ link (1.5 oz total) chopped fully cooked chicken sausage	1 kiwifruit
1 sandwich-size English muffin (or 3 regular English muffin halves)	2 Tbsp barbecue sauce	1½ oz fresh mozzarella	¼ cup chopped cooked chicken breast	2 cups bagged romaine salad blend + 3 cherry tomatoes + 1 tsp olive oil + 1½ tsp balsamic vinegar
½ naan flatbread	1 Tbsp pesto	⅓ cup shredded 2% milk Jack cheese	¼ cup browned 90% lean ground beef	1 cup sliced bell peppers + 1 Tbsp light ranch dressing
½ mini pizza crust (8" diameter)		¼ cup part-skim ricotta + 1 Tbsp grated Parmesan cheese	2 oz cubed ham	

▶DIRECTIONS

Preheat the oven to 425°F. Prepare the crust per package directions if necessary.

Spread the crust with the sauce. Sprinkle with the cheese and the meat topping.

Bake until heated through and the cheese is melted and golden.

Serve with a side dish.

▶FLAVOR BOOSTERS

Customize your pizza with these fresh toppings, but don't overload the crust or it will get soggy.

- Thinly sliced onion
- Thinly sliced bell pepper
- Thinly sliced scallions
- Thinly sliced mushrooms
- Chopped tomatoes (patted dry)
- Chopped broccoli (or very small florets)

▶CHEAT SHEET

When take-out pizza's on the menu, stick to one slice of a large (14" diameter) plain, veggie, or one-meat-topping traditional New York–style pie; pair it with a salad. Here's what you can expect calorie-wise:

ONE SLICE OF . . .	CALORIES
Cheese pizza	325
Mushroom pizza	325
Broccoli pizza	335
BBQ chicken pizza	380
Pepperoni pizza	390
Sausage pizza	420

Buffalo Chicken Pizza

PREP TIME: 5 MINUTES   TOTAL TIME: 10 MINUTES

Makes 1 serving

- 1 whole grain English muffin, split and toasted
- 1 tablespoons reduced-fat blue cheese dressing
- 1 tablespoons barbecue sauce
- 2 tablespoon reduced-fat crumbled blue cheese
- 3 ounces cooked chicken breast (about ⅔ cup), chopped
- 1 rib celery, chopped
- 1 apple

1. Preheat the broiler. Place the muffin on a small baking sheet.

2. In a medium bowl, stir together the dressing, barbecue sauce, and cheese. Stir in the chicken and celery. Divide the chicken mixture between the muffin halves and place in the oven. Broil for 2 minutes, or until warmed. Serve with the apple.

Hawaiian-Inspired Mini-Pizzas

PREP TIME: 10 MINUTES   TOTAL TIME: 20 MINUTES

Makes 3 servings

- 3 English muffins, split and lightly toasted
- 2 tablespoons mayonnaise
- 1 cup crushed pineapple in juice, drained
- 4 ounces reduced-fat ham, finely chopped
- 1 green bell pepper, finely chopped
- 4 ounces shredded reduced-fat sharp Cheddar cheese

1. Preheat the oven to 375°F. Set the muffins, cut side down, on a baking sheet. Bake for 5 minutes. Remove from oven and turn cut side up.

2. In a small bowl, stir together the mayonnaise and pineapple. Stir in the ham and pepper. Divide among the muffin halves. Sprinkle evenly with the cheese.

3. Bake for 10 minutes, or until the cheese is bubbly.

Greek Salad Pizza

PREP TIME: 10 MINUTES   TOTAL TIME: 15 MINUTES

Makes 2 servings

2 whole wheat pitas

2 tablespoons olive oil

1 clove garlic, minced

1 large tomato, seeded and chopped

1 teaspoon red wine vinegar

1 bag (5 ounces) baby spinach, chopped

6 kalamata olives, pitted and chopped

½ cup crumbled feta cheese

1. Preheat the oven to 425°F. Place the pitas onto a baking sheet.

2. Heat the oil in a skillet over medium-high heat. Add the garlic and cook for 2 minutes. Remove from the heat and stir in the tomato and vinegar, tossing for 2 minutes. Set aside for 5 minutes. Mix in the spinach, olives, and feta.

3. Meanwhile, bake the pitas for 5 minutes, or until toasted. Top with the tomato mixture.

Smoked Ham, Cheese, and Pear Pizza

PREP TIME: 10 MINUTES   TOTAL TIME: 35 MINUTES

Makes 4 servings

1 package (15 to 16 ounces) refrigerated whole wheat pizza dough

2 Bosc pears, thinly sliced

4 ounces thinly sliced Jarlsberg cheese

4-ounce piece Virginia ham (from deli), finely chopped

1 bag (5 ounces) mixed greens

2 tablespoons balsamic vinaigrette

1. Preheat the oven to 450°F. Remove the dough from the refrigerator.

2. Form the dough into a ball and roll or pat out on a large, lightly floured baking sheet until no thicker than ¼". Bake the crust for 15 minutes.

3. Remove the crust from the oven and arrange the pear slices in one layer on the crust. Sprinkle with the cheese and ham. Bake for 10 minutes, or until the crust is lightly browned and the cheese is bubbly.

4. Meanwhile, toss the greens with the vinaigrette. Remove the pizza from the oven and top with the salad. Cut into 8 slices.

Salads

GREENS (2 TO 3 CUPS ANY COMBINATION OF)	VEGETABLES (UNLIMITED)	PROTEINS (PICK 2)
Romaine lettuce	½ cup alfalfa sprouts	⅓ cup shelled edamame
Spring mix	¼ cup sliced celery	1 pouch (2.6 oz) water-packed light tuna
Red or green leaf lettuce	2 Tbsp chopped scallions	¼ cup chickpeas
Boston lettuce	½ cup sliced cucumber	1½ oz smoked tofu, cubed
Baby spinach leaves	¼ cup sliced red onions	⅓ cup chopped (or 1 large) hard-boiled egg
Iceberg lettuce	½ cup sliced mushrooms	⅓ cup chopped cooked chicken
Arugula	½ cup chopped broccoli	⅓ cup flaked pink salmon (from pouch)
Chopped or baby kale leaves	½ cup sliced bell peppers	3 oz cubed or torn deli turkey breast
	½ cup chopped cauliflower	3 oz cubed ham or torn lean deli ham
	2 Tbsp frozen peas, thawed	
	⅓ cup shredded carrots	
	¼ cup sliced cooked beets	
	2 Tbsp corn kernels	
	¼ cup roasted red bell peppers	
	2 Tbsp sliced olives	
	8 cherry tomatoes or ½ cup sliced tomatoes	

▶DIRECTIONS

Toss the greens with your choice of vegetables, two sources of protein, one dressing, and two toppings.

DRESSINGS (UP TO 80-CALORIE SERVING)	TOPPINGS (PICK 2)
2 Tbsp light Italian dressing	1 Tbsp chopped pecans
2 Tbsp light balsamic vinaigrette	1 Tbsp chopped walnuts
2 Tbsp light ranch dressing	1 Tbsp unsalted sunflower seed kernels
2 Tbsp light Caesar dressing	2 Tbsp dried sweetened cranberries
2 Tbsp light raspberry vinaigrette	2 Tbsp feta crumbles
2 Tbsp light blue cheese dressing	8 large croutons
2 Tbsp light Thousand Island dressing	⅓ cup 1% cottage cheese
2 tsp olive oil + 1 tsp vinegar	1½ Tbsp chopped pistachios
	1½ Tbsp goat cheese
	1 Tbsp pine nuts
	¼ Hass avocado, sliced
	2 Tbsp blue cheese crumbles
	2 Tbsp sliced almonds
	3 Tbsp grated Parmesan cheese
	1½ Tbsp unsalted pumpkin seed kernels
	3 Tbsp shredded 2% milk Cheddar or Jack cheese

▶SMART SHORTCUTS
BOTTLED SALAD DRESSINGS

PRODUCT	CALORIES IN 2 TBSP
Bolthouse Farms Classic Balsamic Vinaigrette	30
Bolthouse Farms Chunky Blue Cheese Yogurt Dressing	35
Annie's Naturals Lite Honey Mustard Vinaigrette	40
Annie's Naturals Lite Raspberry Vinaigrette	40
Ken's Steak House Light Northern Italian Dressing	45
Bolthouse Farms Caesar Parmigiano Yogurt Dressing	45
Litehouse OPA Greek Yogurt Ranch Dressing	60
Cindy's Kitchen Creamy Yogurt 1,000 Island Dressing/Spread	70

The salad chart on pages 132–133 budgets in 80 calories, so choose a lower-calorie product if you like your salad generously dressed.

Sandwiches

BREAD	PROTEIN	CHEESE	SPREAD	SIDE
Flatbread sandwich wrap (2 oz)	1 pouch (2.6 oz) water-packed light tuna + 2 Tbsp light mayonnaise	2 Tbsp feta crumbles	1 Tbsp light Caesar dressing	5.3 oz 0% plain Greek yogurt + ½ cup fresh blueberries or raspberries
2 slices multigrain bread	3 oz deli turkey breast	1 slice (¾ oz) 2% milk provolone cheese	1 Tbsp honey mustard	1 medium apple or pear
8" sandwich wrap/tortilla	3 oz deli roast beef	1 slice (¾ oz) 2% milk Cheddar cheese	1 tsp olive oil + 1½ tsp balsamic vinegar	1 cup ready-to-serve vegetable or chicken noodle soup
2 slices 100% whole wheat bread	3 Tbsp hummus	1 slice (¾ oz) 2% milk Jack cheese	2 tsp pesto	12 baked potato or tortilla chips
2 slices rye bread	2 oz cooked chicken breast	1 slice (⅔ oz) American cheese	1 Tbsp light mayonnaise	
Pita (6½" diameter), white or wheat	3 oz lean deli ham		¼ Hass avocado, mashed or sliced	
Kaiser roll				

▶DIRECTIONS

Build a sandwich with bread, protein, cheese, and spread. Pair with one side.

▶FLAVOR BOOSTERS

Customize your sandwich as you please with these ultra-low-calorie toppings:

- Lettuce
- Alfalfa sprouts
- Baby spinach
- Dill pickles
- Sliced mushrooms
- Raw onions
- Tomato slices
- Hot-pepper sauce
- Fresh jalapeño
- Dijon/deli mustard
- Horseradish

Soup (makes 4 servings)

PROTEIN	VEGETABLES (PICK 2)	BROTH/BASE
12 oz cubed ham	1 bag (6 oz) baby spinach	8 cups low- or reduced-sodium chicken broth
1 can (15.5 oz) black, white, or red beans, rinsed and drained	2 cups fresh or frozen cut green beans	8 cups low- or reduced-sodium beef broth
2 cups chopped cooked chicken or 12 oz cubed raw boneless skinless chicken breast	4 cups chopped kale	8 cups low- or reduced-sodium vegetable broth
4 links (3 oz each) fully cooked chicken sausage, chopped	2 cups frozen mixed vegetables (such as soup, stir-fry, and broccoli/cauliflower blends)	4 cups ready-to-serve butternut squash soup*
10 oz raw 90% lean ground beef	1 can (14.5 oz) no-salt-added diced tomatoes (with juice)	4 cups ready-to-serve tomato soup*
	2 cups fresh or frozen sliced carrots	

Cut protein or pasta/grain amount in half with these options.

▶DIRECTIONS

Heat 1 tablespoon of oil in a small saucepan over medium-high heat. Add protein and 1 small chopped onion, 1 rib chopped celery, and/or 1 clove of minced garlic. Cook while stirring until the vegetables soften and the protein is no longer pink (if applicable).

Add your vegetable choices (except spinach or kale, if using) and cook, stirring, until softened.

Add the broth/base and pasta/grain. Reduce the heat to a simmer and heat through, adding additional broth or water if necessary. Stir in the spinach or kale, if using, and cook until wilted.

Season to taste with salt and pepper. Ladle one-quarter of the soup in a bowl (chill the remainder for future meals), top with a garnish, and serve with a side dish.

PASTA/GRAIN	GARNISH (PER SERVING)	SIDE (PER SERVING)
2 cups cooked orzo or elbow macaroni	1 Tbsp 0% plain Greek yogurt	3 reduced-sodium stone-ground wheat crackers
2 cups cooked barley	1 Tbsp light sour cream	1 cup fresh fruit salad
2 cups cooked brown rice	1 Tbsp grated Parmesan cheese	1 small (1 oz) white or whole wheat dinner roll + 1 tsp butter
2 cups cooked quinoa	1 tsp olive oil	3 cups bagged romaine salad blend + 5 cherry tomatoes + 2 Tbsp light balsamic vinaigrette + 1 Tbsp shredded 2% milk cheese
2 cups cooked egg noodles	1 tsp pesto	

▶FLAVOR BOOSTERS

A dash or two of one of these ingredients will amp up the taste of your soup for few or no calories:

- Hot-pepper sauce
- Vinegar
- Lemon juice
- Fresh or dried herbs

SMART SHORTCUTS
PACKAGED SOUPS

PRODUCT	PORTION	CALORIES	PAIR WITH...
Campbell's Home Style Harvest Soup, Ready to Serve, Light, Southwestern-Style Vegetable	2 cups (1 can)	100	Sandwich made from sandwich chart (no side)
Dr. McDougall's Gluten-Free All Natural Black Bean Soup	1 cup (½ package)	150	Half sandwich made from sandwich chart + side option from sandwich chart
Progresso Light Beef Pot Roast	2 cups (1 can)	160	
Pacific Organic Split Pea & Uncured Ham Soup	1 cup (½ package)	160	
Amy's Organic Lentil Soup	1 cup (½ can)	180	
Panera Bread Low-Fat Chicken Noodle Soup (refrigerated)	2 cups (1 container)	280	3 cups bagged romaine salad blend + 5 cherry tomatoes + 2 Tbsp light dressing/ vinaigrette + 2 Tbsp shredded 2% milk cheese

Store-bought soups are often high in sodium, so compare labels and avoid eating salty foods at other meals. Bean/legume soups are filling, so we kept the serving size smaller.

Chicken Vegetable Soup

PREP TIME: 20 MINUTES | TOTAL TIME: 40 MINUTES

Makes 6 servings

2 tablespoons olive oil

1 large onion, chopped

2 green and/or red bell peppers, chopped

1½ pounds chicken breast, cut into thin strips

4 garlic cloves, minced

1 teaspoon Italian seasoning, crushed

2 large carrots, sliced

1 zucchini, chopped

1 can (14½ ounces) stewed tomatoes

6 cups reduced-sodium chicken broth

1½ cups basmati or long-grain rice

1. In a large saucepan over medium heat, warm the oil. Cook the onion and bell peppers for 5 minutes, or until tender.

2. Add the chicken, garlic, and Italian seasoning. Cook for 5 minutes or until the chicken is browned. Add the carrots, zucchini, tomatoes (with juice), and broth.

3. Stir in the rice. Over high heat, bring to a boil. Reduce heat to low, cover, and simmer for 20 minutes.

Turkey Soup

PREP TIME: 20 MINUTES | TOTAL TIME: 35 MINUTES

Makes 4 servings

2 tablespoons olive oil

2 carrots, chopped

2 ribs celery, chopped

1 onion, chopped

2 parsnips, chopped

1 tablespoon freshly grated ginger

2 cloves garlic, minced

8 cups reduced-sodium turkey or chicken broth

⅔ cup orzo pasta

3 tomatoes, seeded and chopped

1 pound cooked turkey breast, chopped

1. Heat the oil in a large saucepan over medium-high heat. Cook the carrots, celery, onion, parsnips, ginger, and garlic for 5 minutes, stirring until lightly browned. Add the broth and bring to a boil. Reduce the heat to medium-low, cover and simmer for 10 minutes. Add the orzo and cook for 10 minutes or until the pasta is tender.

2. Add the tomatoes and turkey. Cook for 5 minutes until heated through.

Chili Soup

PREP TIME: 25 MINUTES   TOTAL TIME: 45 MINUTES

Makes 4 servings

- 1 tablespoon olive oil
- 1 pound 95% lean ground beef
- ½ pound reduced-fat pork sausage, crumbled
- 1 can (28 ounces) diced tomatoes
- 1 can (15 ounces) tomato sauce
- 1 can (15 ounces) no-salt-added kidney beans
- 2 tablespoons chili powder
- 1 teaspoon cumin
- 8 cups shredded romaine lettuce
- 3 tablespoons light ranch salad dressing

1. Heat the oil in a Dutch oven over medium-high heat. Add the beef and sausage. Cook for about 10 minutes, until cooked through. Drain off the fat.

2. Add the tomatoes, tomato sauce, beans, chili powder, and cumin, and cook for 30 minutes. If the mixture begins to look too thick, add a small amount of water.

3. Meanwhile, toss the romaine with the dressing. Serve with the soup.

Hamburger Stew

PREP TIME: 10 MINUTES   TOTAL TIME: 40 MINUTES

Makes 4 servings

- 1 tablespoon olive oil
- 1 medium onion, chopped
- 2 cups sliced mushrooms
- 1 pound lean ground beef
- 1½ cups baby carrots
- 1½ tablespoons flour
- 1 teaspoon dried thyme
- ½ teaspoon salt
- ½ teaspoon ground black pepper
- 1½ cups fat-free reduced-sodium beef broth
- 1 cup whole grain couscous

1. In a large saucepan over medium-high heat, warm the oil. Cook the onion and mushrooms, stirring occasionally, for 10 minutes, or until browned.

2. Scrape the mushroom mixture to one side of the skillet. Crumble in the beef. Cook, stirring, for 5 minutes, or until no longer pink, incorporating the mushrooms and onion. Add the carrots, flour, thyme, salt, and pepper. Stir for 2 minutes or until the flour is no longer visible.

3. Gradually add the broth, stirring constantly. Bring to a rapid simmer. Reduce the heat. Cover and simmer for 20 minutes, or until the carrots are tender.

4. Meanwhile, prepare the couscous according to package directions. Divide the stew and couscous among 4 bowls.

Down East Clam Chowder

Makes 4 servings

2 slices bacon

1 tablespoons oil

1 onion, chopped

3 ribs celery, chopped

1 teaspoon minced garlic

½ teaspoon dried thyme

3 cans (6½ ounces each) minced clams, drained and added to clam juice

1½ cups clam juice plus juice from drained cans

2 cups chopped Yukon gold potatoes

½ cup water (optional)

2 cups 2% milk, divided

1½ tablespoons all-purpose flour

¼ cup chopped parsley

1. Cook the bacon in the microwave, per package directions, until crisp. Crumble into small pieces and set aside.

2. In a large saucepan, heat the oil over medium heat. Cook the onion, celery, garlic, and thyme for 5 minutes, stirring occasionally, until the onion is softened but not browned. Open the cans of clams and reserve the liquid. Add all of the clam juice and the potatoes to the saucepan. The liquid should just cover the potatoes; add water if necessary. Bring the chowder to a simmer and cook for 10 minutes, or until the potatoes are tender but not mushy.

3. Meanwhile, in a small bowl, whisk ¼ cup of the milk with the flour until smooth. Add to the chowder with the remaining 1¼ cups milk and increase the medium to bring to a simmer, stirring constantly, about 5 minutes, until slightly thickened. Remove the pot from the heat and stir in the clams. Divide among 4 bowls and sprinkle each serving with the crumbled bacon and parsley.

Stir-Fry

PROTEIN (UNCOOKED WEIGHT)	VEGETABLES (CHOOSE 1½ TO 2 CUPS TOTAL)	SAUCE	SIDE
4 oz thinly sliced boneless, skinless chicken breast	½ cup cabbage slaw mix	2 Tbsp bottled teriyaki baste/glaze	½ cup cooked rice noodles
4 oz thinly sliced pork tenderloin	½ bunch baby bok choy	2 Tbsp bottled stir-fry sauce	½ cup cooked brown rice
6 oz peeled and deveined shrimp	¼ cup sliced celery	1½ Tbsp hoisin sauce	½ cup cooked quinoa
3 oz thinly sliced flank steak	½ cup cubed eggplant	2 Tbsp sweet Asian chili sauce	
4 oz thinly sliced boneless, skinless chicken thighs	½ cup sliced mushrooms		
3 oz smoked tofu, cubed	¼ cup sliced onions		
	½ cup sliced zucchini		
	½ cup cut asparagus		
	½ cup sliced bell peppers		
	½ cup cut green beans		
	½ cup snow or snap peas		
	½ cup shredded or sliced carrots		
	¼ cup small fresh pineapple chunks		
	1 cup small broccoli florets		
	1½ to 2 cups frozen Asian vegetable blend		

▶DIRECTIONS

Heat 1 teaspoon vegetable oil in a medium skillet over medium-high heat. Stir in ½ teaspoon minced fresh garlic and/or ginger, if desired, and heat for 30 seconds.

Add protein and cook while stirring until the meat/chicken/pork/shrimp is no longer pink or tofu is browned. Transfer to a plate.

Add another 1 teaspoon oil to the skillet. Add the vegetables and 1 tablespoon water. Cover and steam for 1 to 2 minutes. Uncover and cook while stirring until they're tender yet crisp.

Return the protein to the skillet, stir in the sauce and 2 tablespoons of water, then heat through. Serve on top of the side item.

▶FLAVOR BOOSTERS

Season your stir-fry to taste with:

- Red-pepper flakes
- Fresh basil or cilantro
- Sliced scallions
- Reduced-sodium soy sauce (just a few dashes)

- Chili-garlic sauce or paste
- Sriracha
- ½ teaspoon toasted sesame seeds
- 1 teaspoon chopped peanuts or cashews

▶ SMART SHORTCUTS
FROZEN ASIAN MEALS

PRODUCT	CALORIES	PAIR WITH . . .
Lean Cuisine Spa Collection Szechuan-Style Stir Fry with Shrimp	240	1 cup steamed broccoli + 12 peanuts ½ oz dark chocolate
Lean & Fit Teriyaki Chicken	250	
Kashi Lemongrass Coconut Chicken	300	⅔ cup fresh pineapple chunks + ⅓ cup (half of 5.3-oz container) 0% plain or vanilla Greek yogurt
Lean Cuisine Honestly Good Lemongrass Salmon	320	

Shrimp and Rice Skillet

PREP TIME: 5 MINUTES	TOTAL TIME: 15 MINUTES

Makes 4 servings

½ cup vegetable broth

2 tablespoons reduced sodium soy sauce

2 teaspoons rice wine vinegar

2 teaspoons cornstarch

2 bags (10 ounces each) frozen brown rice

2 tablespoons olive oil

1 bag (16 ounces) peeled and deveined frozen medium shrimp, thawed and drained

1 clove garlic, minced

1 bag (12 ounces) frozen oriental vegetable mix, thawed

2 cups grapes, divided

1. In a measuring cup, whisk together the broth, soy sauce, vinegar, and cornstarch. Set aside.

2. Prepare the brown rice according to package directions.

3. In a large, deep, nonstick skillet or wok over medium-high heat, heat the oil. Cook the shrimp and garlic, stirring, for 3 minutes, or until the shrimp is almost opaque. Whisk the broth mixture and stir into the skillet or wok. Add the vegetables and cook, stirring, for 5 minutes, or until the shrimp is opaque and pink and the sauce thickens.

4. Divide the rice and shrimp mixture among 4 plates. Serve each with ½ cup grapes.

Sweet-and-Sour Chinese Pork

PREP TIME: 15 MINUTES	TOTAL TIME: 30 MINUTES

Makes 4 servings

1 cup chicken broth

2 tablespoons reduced-sodium soy sauce

1 tablespoon white or rice vinegar

1 tablespoon cornstarch

2 tablespoons olive oil

1 pork tenderloin (about 1 pound), cut into 1" cubes

1 small red onion, cut into wedges

2 red or yellow bell peppers, thinly sliced

1 clove garlic, minced

1 cup canned-in-juice pineapple chunks, drained

3 cups cooked brown rice

1. In a measuring cup, whisk the broth, soy sauce, vinegar, and cornstarch until smooth. Set aside.

2. Heat a nonstick wok or large skillet over medium-high heat for 2 minutes. Add 1 tablespoon of the oil. Add the pork. Cook, tossing constantly, for 3 to 4 minutes, or until no longer pink. Transfer to a bowl.

3. Add the remaining 1 tablespoon oil to the pan. Cook the onion, pepper, and garlic, tossing constantly, for 3 minutes, or until tender-crisp. Add the pineapple and the reserved pork to the pan. Stir in the reserved broth mixture. Cook, stirring constantly, for 3 minutes, or until the mixture thickens and is heated through. Serve over the rice.

Orange Chicken and Broccoli

Makes 4 servings

- 1 large bunch broccoli
- ¾ cup orange juice
- 2 tablespoons reduced-sodium soy sauce
- 2 teaspoons cornstarch
- 2 tablespoons orange marmalade
- 2 tablespoons oil

- 1 pound chicken tenders, trimmed and cut into 1" pieces
- 3 large cloves garlic, minced
- 1 tablespoon minced fresh ginger
- ⅓ cup reduced-sodium chicken broth
- 1 red bell pepper, thinly sliced
- 3 cups cooked brown rice

1. Cut the broccoli into small florets. Trim and discard about 2" of the tough broccoli stems. Thinly slice the remaining stems. Set aside.

2. In a small bowl, combine the orange juice, soy sauce, cornstarch, and orange marmalade. Stir until blended and set aside.

3. In a wok or large nonstick skillet, heat the oil over medium-high heat. Cook the chicken, stirring frequently, for 3 minutes, or until no longer pink and the juices run clear. Add the garlic and ginger and stir to combine. With a slotted spoon, remove the chicken to a plate.

4. Add the broth and broccoli to the wok and reduce the heat to medium. Cover and cook for 2 minutes. Increase the heat to medium-high and add the bell pepper. Cook, stirring frequently, for 2 minutes, or until the broth evaporates and the vegetables are crisp-tender. Stir the sauce and add to the wok along with the chicken. Cook, stirring constantly, for 1 to 2 minutes, or until the sauce thickens and the chicken is hot. Serve over the rice.

Tacos

WRAPPER	FILLING	TOPPING	GARNISH (PICK 2)	SIDE
2 soft white corn tortillas (6")	1 cup meatless crumbles	2 Tbsp corn kernels	2 Tbsp cubed Hass avocado	½ cup grapes
2 hard taco shells	5 oz peeled and deveined cooked shrimp	¼ cup salsa	2 Tbsp guacamole	1 cup cubed watermelon or cantaloupe
8" flour tortilla	¾ cup browned 93% lean ground turkey	4 tsp light sour cream	2 Tbsp shredded 2% milk Mexican/ taco cheese blend	8 baby carrots + 1 Tbsp light ranch dressing
	3 oz smoked tofu, cubed or crumbled		2 Tbsp shredded 2% milk Cheddar cheese	1 cup mixed vegetables (from frozen) + 1 tsp butter
	3 oz sliced grilled chicken breast		2 Tbsp shredded 2% milk Jack cheese	
	⅔ cup rinsed and drained canned black beans			
	½ cup vegetarian refried beans			
	⅔ cup browned 90% lean ground beef			

▶DIRECTIONS

Warm the shell or tortilla per package directions.

Heat the filling until warm. Season to taste with a few sprinkles of chili powder or salt-free taco/ Mexican seasoning blend.

Serve the filling in the shell or tortilla with a topping and two garnishes.

Pair with one side.

▶FLAVOR BOOSTERS

Rev up your tacos with these "freebie" toppers:

- Diced fresh tomatoes
- Shredded lettuce
- Chopped onion
- Cabbage slaw mix
- Sliced scallions
- Fresh lime wedge
- Chopped fresh cilantro

▶ SMART SHORTCUTS
FROZEN BURRITOS AND ENCHILADAS

PRODUCT	CALORIES	PAIR WITH...
Glutenfreeda's Gluten-Free Chicken & Cheese Burrito	227	¼ Hass avocado, sliced ½ cup fruit sorbet
Kashi Chicken Enchilada	280	3 cups bagged romaine salad blend + 5 cherry tomatoes + 2 Tbsp light dressing/vinaigrette + 2 Tbsp shredded 2% milk cheese
Amy's Black Bean Burrito	290	½ cup grapes
Evol Cilantro Lime Chicken Burrito	320	¾ cup fresh raspberries
Helen's Kitchen Burrito Bowls Baja Pinto Bean Bowl	340	
Evol Shredded Beef Burrito	360	
CedarLane Three Layer Enchilada Pie	380	

Mexican Shrimp Tacos

Makes 4 servings

- ¾ pound medium shrimp, peeled
- 12 scallions, trimmed, cut in 1" pieces
- 2 teaspoons canola oil
- ½ teaspoon ground cumin
- ¾ cup grape tomatoes, halved
- ½ ripe avocado, sliced
- ¼ cup chopped cilantro
- 2 tablespoon ground flaxseed
- Juice of 1 lime
- Pinch salt
- 8 corn tortillas (6" diameter)
- 4 oranges, each cut into 4 wedges

1. Toss shrimp, scallions, oil, and cumin in a bowl. Let stand 15 minutes.

2. Meanwhile, in a large bowl, combine the tomatoes, avocado, cilantro, flaxseed, lime juice, and salt. Set aside.

3. Coat a perforated grill rack or broiler pan with cooking spray. Preheat the grill rack set over a grill or broiler pan. Place the reserved shrimp and scallions on the grill rack. Cook 4 minutes, tossing twice, or until the shrimp are browned and opaque. Remove to a plate.

4. Place the tortillas directly on the grill or broiler pan. Cook about 1 minute on each side, or until warm and starting to puff.

5. Place 2 tortillas on each of 4 plates. Divide the shrimp and scallions evenly on top of the tortillas. Top with the tomato mixture. Serve with the orange wedges.

Chicken-Taco Salad

PREP TIME: 20 MINUTES   TOTAL TIME: 30 MINUTES

Makes 4 servings

- ⅓ cup ranch dressing
- 2 tablespoons salsa
- 1 tablespoon olive oil
- ¾ pound boneless, skinless chicken breast halves, cut into ½" pieces
- 2 teaspoons fajita seasoning
- 8 cups torn romaine lettuce
- 1 can (15 ounces) pinto beans, rinsed and drained
- 1 avocado, peeled, pitted, and chopped
- 1 large tomato, chopped
- 1 cup crumbled baked tortilla chips
- 1 tablespoon chopped cilantro (optional)

1. In a small bowl, mix the ranch dressing and salsa.

2. In a large nonstick skillet over medium heat, warm the oil. Cook the chicken, stirring frequently, for 10 minutes, or until the chicken is no longer pink in the thickest part. Sprinkle with the fajita seasoning and cook 1 minute longer.

3. In a large bowl, toss the warm chicken mixture with the romaine, pinto beans, avocado, and tomato. Add the salsa dressing and toss to coat. Sprinkle with the tortilla chips and cilantro, if using.

Turkey Tacos with Mango–Corn Salsa

PREP TIME: 10 MINUTES   TOTAL TIME: 20 MINUTES

Makes 6 servings

- 1 firm, ripe avocado, peeled, pitted, and chopped
- 1 mango, peeled, pitted, and chopped
- 1 can (15 ounces) sweet corn kernels, rinsed and drained
- 1 cup cherry tomatoes, halved
- 1 tablespoon lime juice
- 1 package (12) corn taco shells
- 1 pound cooked boneless, skinless turkey breast, sliced into thin strips
- ¾ cup water
- 1 package (1¼ ounces) reduced-sodium taco seasoning mix
- ¾ cup Cheddar cheese

1. In a medium bowl, stir together the avocado, mango, corn, tomatoes, and lime juice. Set aside.

2. Warm the shells in the oven according to the package directions.

3. In a medium skillet, combine the turkey, water, and seasoning. Bring to a boil, reduce heat, and simmer 5 minutes, stirring occasionally, until the water is absorbed.

4. Spoon the turkey mixture into the shells. Top with the salsa and the cheese.

SNACKS

Need a treat, but it's not mealtime? You don't have to deprive yourself while you're losing clutter and weight. For your daily snacks, you can pick from the following lists.

Snacks/Treats

Choose any two items (plus "freebies" as desired) for a 100-calorie snack/treat. Picking from two different sections will help you feel satisfied.

SNACK	PORTION
FRESH	
Apple	1 cup sliced
Applesauce (unsweetened)	½ cup
Apricots	3 whole
Avocado	¼ fruit
Banana	½ medium
Blackberries	¾ cup
Blueberries	⅔ cup
Cantaloupe	1 cup cubes/balls
Cherries (sweet)	10 each
Grapefruit	1 each (4½")
Grapes	15 seedless
Guacamole	2 Tbsp
Honeydew	1 cup cubes/balls
Kiwifruit	½ cup sliced
Mango	½ cup chunks
Orange	1 medium (2⅝")
Papaya	¾ cup chunks
Peach	1 medium (2⅔")
Pear	⅔ cup slices
Pineapple	⅔ cup chunks
Plums	2 medium (2⅛")

SNACK	PORTION
FRESH	
Raspberries	¾ cup
Shelled edamame	¼ cup
Strawberries	1 cup sliced
Tangerine	1 medium (2½")
Tomato salsa	¾ cup
Watermelon	1 cup cubes/balls
SAVORY	
Almonds	7 whole
Black beans	¼ cup
Cashews	4 whole
Deli lean ham	2 oz
Deli roast beef	2 oz
Deli turkey breast	2 oz
Hard-boiled egg	1 large
Hummus	2 Tbsp
Natural almond butter	1½ tsp
Natural peanut butter	1½ tsp
Olives	8 jumbo
Peanuts	12 each
Pecans	5 halves
Pistachios	12 kernels
Pumpkin seed kernels	4 tsp
Shrimp, cooked	4 jumbo
Smoked salmon	1 oz
Smoked tofu	1 oz

(continued)

Snacks/Treats—Continued

SNACK	PORTION
SAVORY	
Sunflower seed kernels	1 Tbsp
Tuna, water-packed	1 pouch
Turkey pepperoni	12 slices
Walnuts	4 halves
CREAMY/SWEET	
0% plain Greek yogurt	⅓ cup (half of 5.3-oz container)
0% vanilla Greek yogurt	⅓ cup (half of 5.3-oz container)
1% cottage cheese	⅓ cup
1% milk	½ cup
100% fruit spread	1½ Tbsp
2% milk Cheddar cheese	1 slice (¾ oz)
2% milk Jack cheese	1 slice (¾ oz)
2% milk provolone cheese	1 slice (¾ oz)
2% milk Swiss cheese	1 slice (¾ oz)
Butter	1½ tsp
Chocolate syrup	1 Tbsp
Chocolate-hazelnut spread	1½ tsp
Dark chocolate (60% to 70% cacao)	⅓ oz
Fat-free vanilla frozen yogurt	¼ cup
Feta cheese crumbles	2 Tbsp
Fig bar	1 cookie
Frozen fruit/juice bar	1 each (2.5 oz)
Fruit sorbet	¼ cup
Honey	2 tsp

SNACK	PORTION
CREAMY/SWEET	
Light blue cheese dressing	1 Tbsp
Light ranch dressing	1 Tbsp
Light sour cream	3 Tbsp
Maple syrup	1 Tbsp
Marshmallows	2 regular
Parmesan cheese	½ oz
Part-skim mozzarella string cheese	1 stick (0.8 oz)
Part-skim ricotta	2 Tbsp
Plain soy milk	½ cup
Raisins	2 Tbsp
Reduced-fat cream cheese	2 Tbsp
Sweetened dried cranberries	2 Tbsp
CRISPY/BREADY	
Air-popped popcorn	2 cups
Baked tortilla chips	6 each
Baked woven whole wheat crackers	3 each
Brown rice cakes	1½ each
Chocolate wafers	2 cookies
English muffin	½ each
Graham crackers	2 squares
Low-fat granola	2 Tbsp
Mini pretzels	12 each
Multigrain crispbread	1½ slices

(continued)

Snacks/Treats—Continued

SNACK	PORTION
CRISPY/BREADY	
Pita chips	4 each
Shredded wheat cereal, plain	⅓ cup bite-size biscuits
Stone-ground wheat crackers, reduced-sodium	6 each
Sweet potato chips	5 chips
Toasted whole grain oat cereal	½ cup
Vanilla wafers	3 cookies
Whole wheat bread, regular slice	½ slice
Whole wheat bread, thin slice	1 slice
Whole wheat pita (6½")	⅓ pita
FREEBIES	
Bell peppers	
Black pepper	
Broccoli	
Carrots	
Cauliflower	
Cucumber	
Fresh herbs	
Hot-pepper sauce	
Lemon juice	
Lettuce	
Cayenne	
Celery	
Chili powder	

SNACK
FREEBIES
Cinnamon
Cocktail sauce (up to 1 Tbsp)
Mustard
Tomato salsa (up to 2 Tbsp)
Vinegar

▶LIQUID GRATIFICATION

Although it's best to avoid "liquid" calories, here's how to splurge smart:

BEVERAGE	100 CALORIES IS . . .
Beer	8 oz
Flavored latte	8 oz fat-free milk + 1 shot flavored syrup
Hard alcohol (80 proof)	1½ oz
Hot cocoa	1 packet classic mix prepared with 6 oz water + 1 marshmallow
Light beer	12 oz
Orange juice	7 oz
Sweetened iced tea	8 to 10 oz
Wine	4 oz

Chapter 7

HOW TO MOVE TO LOSE THE WEIGHT

ere's an essential truth about clutter: It seems to gather on its own without any involvement from you. Thousands of pounds of it can fill the spaces and cover the surfaces within your home, yet you don't recall expending any effort to make it happen.

That's just how it is.

The same tends to be true with weight. A recent study told the story of how roughly 10,000 young men and women changed as they aged into midlife. On average, they gained more than a pound a year. Most expanded into a higher BMI category by middle age, such as moving from a healthy weight to becoming overweight, or advancing from overweight to obese.

It's typical for extra weight to slowly and silently settle upon you. Gaining just 1 pound a year for 20 years can dramatically change your appearance and your quality of life!

That's just how it is.

It's also normal for you to not notice that you've gained weight. Another recent enlightening study involved two large groups of people—each numbering more than 380,000—who were interviewed in back-to-back years. They all reported their height, their weight, and how much their weight had changed in the previous year. If the weight change they reported had been *true*, obesity would have fallen in the United States that year by 2 percent for men and just under 1 percent for women. But the nation's obesity rate actually went up by about one-half of a percentage point during that period. These folks simply weren't very mindful of their weight change.

There are many parallels between the clutter in your home and the clutter on your hips. Both types create a rift between the life you *want* to be living and the life you're *actually* living. Both can interfere with the peace and calm that should fill your mind, and both can impede the way you live day to day.

Neither form of clutter will go away as easily as it was gathered. Getting rid of the excess stuff in your home requires physical effort, mental focus, and deliberate choices. Losing extra pounds demands the same commitment. To lose a meaningful amount of weight and then keep it off for years, you must make a deliberate choice to eat right and stay physically active.

Just doing a bit of exercise here and there isn't going to be enough. Experts now think that losing weight and staying fit require a substantial amount of physical activity—enough that it'll probably require a significant change in your daily schedule.

The American College of Sports Medicine says that doing 2½ hours of moderate-intensity activity each week may help you see *only modest* weight loss. In other words, if you want to lose a lot of weight, moving your body around for 30 minutes a day, Monday through Friday, likely won't be enough. While it'll probably be good for your overall health, it won't necessarily move the needle on your scales. Instead, you may need closer to 4 hours of physical activity per week. That's the equivalent of about 50 minutes of activity 5 days a week.

You can argue with this necessity, or ignore it, or feel like it doesn't apply to you. You can say that you don't have the time to exercise this much or that it's just not fair that you should have to do this.

But again, this is just how it is.

If you want to make major changes to your weight, you have to move around a *lot* more than our society is generally accustomed to doing.

But here's some good news: You can ease into a more physically active lifestyle over time, even if you're completely sedentary now. My program will help you gradually become more active by introducing effective, challenging, and simple activities into your schedule. By the end of 6 weeks, if you follow the physical activity portion of the program, you'll be well on your way to the hour a day that supports meaningful weight loss.

The exercise portion of *Cut the Clutter, Drop the Pounds* has three main components.

Walking. This type of aerobic exercise is a good fit for this program. For starters, it's essentially free to do, and it requires minimal equipment aside from comfortable shoes and clothes, which you probably already have. You don't have to join a gym to do it. And you don't have to learn any new skills.

All you have to do during the first week of the program is walk for 5 minutes 2 or 3 days a week. You'll slowly build up to where you're walking 30 minutes a day for 5 days during the final week.

Walk around your block. Walk on your treadmill. Walk in place in your home if it's raining or your neighborhood isn't safe for walking. You can use your walking time to practice being aware and mindful of what's happening in the present moment. Or you can plan out your next bout of decluttering.

Strength and flexibility training. Doing movements to keep your muscles, bones, and joints strong is an important aspect of a fitness program.

You're especially going to need strength in this program. You'll be venturing deep into your closets, basement, attic, and shed, where you'll wrestle hundreds—or even thousands—of pounds of household items out of your home.

As a result, I'll ask you to do strength-training movements up to 3 days per week. I worked with Liz Davis, MS, who designed a program that you can do around your house without any special exercise equipment. Liz is a mom, a trainer, a competitive bodybuilder, and an exercise physiologist. She came up with simple movements that make use of items you probably already have. These exercises will strengthen your arms, legs, shoulders, abdomen, and back.

Liz also recommended some basic yoga moves to improve your flexibility. These won't force you to bend yourself into any unusual shapes. If you're having trouble just picking your socks up off the floor, these should help.

Decluttering. Simply bagging up old clothes, pulling books off shelves and re-filing the keepers, and climbing up and down into your attic to bring out storage containers burns calories.

However, in general, you shouldn't count easy housekeeping chores toward your weekly quota of physical activity. A recent study from the UK of more than 4,500 people found evidence that housework may not be physically challenging enough to provide all the health benefits of exercise. Experts stress that your activity should be at least *moderate intensity*, which is the equivalent of walking briskly. The most recent physical activity guidelines put out by the federal government don't count housework as an option.

However, in most of the weeks of this program, the type of housework you'll be doing is harder than simply sweeping your entryway or loading the dishwasher. I suspect you'll find that completely decluttering your home in 6 weeks—or even doing a big chunk of it—is a physically challenging endeavor. Like the woman whose story I told in the introduction of this book, I've heard from plenty of people who lost weight after they just added decluttering activities to their normal routines.

Any time you're cleaning your house or carrying out clutter, you're going to be burning more calories than you would if you were sitting down. But I would still urge you to follow the walking plan and do the strength- and flexibility-improving exercises in addition to your daily decluttering tasks.

I want to make sure you're burning enough calories to make a significant improvement in your weight. I also want your body to be strong and limber enough to clear all of that extra stuff out of your home. These exercises will help ensure that happens.

I'd like to make two final points about the physical activity you'll do during the next 6 weeks:

1. Your mindset as you go into the program, especially the exercise component, is critical for success. Many of us have struggled with exercise our whole lives—myself included—but reframing the way you think about physical activity can help enormously.

   This program is a gift that you're giving yourself. You are making an effort to improve your life, your home, and your family because you—and they—are worth it! Please don't consider this exercise program something that you're obliged to do or something that someone is forcing upon you. Instead, accept it like a key that can unlock better functioning and an improved sense of wellness.

2. If you're already following some type of deliberate, planned exercise program on most days of the week, I don't necessarily expect you to abandon it for this one. I simply ask that if you stick to what you're already doing, be sure that you're getting at least as much exercise that improves your aerobic fitness, strength, and flexibility as you would from the *Cut the Clutter, Drop the Pounds* plan.

   If you're following an exercise program that your health care provider wants you to do, then please stick with it. If you're completely sedentary or you have any injuries or chronic health problems, check with your health care provider before starting this plan.

I'll now turn this chapter over to Liz Davis, who will show you how to do the strength-training and yoga movements.

The Moves That Will Help You Become a Lean, Clean, Clutter-Busting Machine

This program is designed to give you a challenge that improves your strength—but you should *not* end each day feeling like you're too worn out to move.

Please perform each exercise either:

▶ Between 8 and 12 times (also known as repetitions or "reps") or

▶ Until you can no longer perform them with the proper form, which I'll show in the following pictures

You'll do one round—or set—of each exercise. As long as you pushed yourself fully, one set should be sufficient to increase your strength. However, if your muscles don't feel fully fatigued after one set of 8 to 12 reps, please do a second set.

As the weeks go on and you find yourself getting stronger, you may need to do two to three sets of 8 to 12 reps in order to fully work your muscles. It's up to you to add these additional sets as you see fit.

Here's the full list of exercises that I'll be suggesting over the next 6 weeks.

Bent-Over Rows

Stand with one foot in front of the other, about 2 feet apart, while holding a milk jug or similar-size object in one hand. Use the other hand to support yourself on your thigh. Keeping your knees slightly bent and your upper body straight, lean forward at the hips roughly 45 degrees. Extend your hand down toward the floor at chest level.

Slowly pull your elbow back behind your body, bringing the object in your hand up to the side of your chest. Squeeze your shoulder blades together during this motion. Lower the object back down and repeat as necessary. Switch sides and perform the exercise on the other side.

Biceps Curls

Fill a duffel bag with objects, clothes, and any other clutter that you wish to get rid of, until it is heavy enough to feel challenging but not impossible to carry. Please note: As the weeks go on, you can fill this bag to make it heavier, if performing the same exercise no longer feels challenging. These instructions apply to all exercises that require a duffel bag or purse.

Stand with your feet close together. Hold the duffel bag in front of you with both hands, with your arms extended toward the floor and your palms facing up and away from you.

Lift your hands upward toward your chest, holding your elbows stationary at the sides of your abdomen. Avoid leaning back as you lift the duffel bag. Lower your hands back down and repeat as necessary. You can also do this exercise holding the duffel bag handles with one hand and curling the bag with one arm.

Bridge Pose

Lie on your back on the floor. Place your feet flat on the floor with your knees bent. Lift your hips up toward the ceiling while you keep your arms extended on the floor alongside your body and your head and shoulders resting on the floor. Your body should form a straight diagonal line from your knees to your upper chest. Hold the pose for 5 to 15 seconds and repeat two or three times or as necessary.

Chair Pose

Stand with your toes pointed forward and your feet touching or slightly apart. Extend your arms over your head, palms facing each other, as you bend your knees and lower yourself down like you're about to sit in a chair. Allow your rear to stick out, but keep your upper body upright as much as possible (rather than bending forward). Hold the pose for 5 to 15 seconds and repeat two or three times or as necessary.

Child's Pose

Kneel on the floor, resting on your knees and the tops of your feet. Your feet should be touching and your knees should be apart. Lean forward, extending your arms in front of you with your palms down and your arms spread shoulder-width apart.

You should end up facing the floor with your ribs resting between your upper thighs and your forehead touching or approaching the floor. You should also be reaching forward far enough with your fingertips that you feel a good stretch in your upper back. Hold the pose for 5 to 15 seconds and repeat two or three times or as necessary.

Close-Grip Triceps Pushups

To do these, stand with your feet several feet away from a countertop or dresser. Place your hands on the dresser, spaced slightly closer than shoulder-width apart. Lower your chest as far as you can toward the dresser while holding your torso straight (in other words, your rear shouldn't be sticking out or sagging down). Your elbows should stay close to your body, as opposed to flaring out. Press your body back up away from the dresser. Repeat as necessary.

Deadlifts

Stand with your feet shoulder-width apart and your toes pointed forward. Hold a weighted duffel bag in front of you with both hands with your arms extended toward the floor.

Bend forward from the hips to a 45- to 90-degree angle, keeping your back flat and your legs slightly bent. Straighten back up to the starting position—squeezing your butt muscle as you stand up—and repeat as necessary.

Kickbacks

Stand facing a countertop, with your feet side by side about a foot from the counter. Place your fingertips on the counter for support. Lift your right leg behind you, keeping your leg straight. The effort to lift your leg should come from your butt muscle. That's one repetition. Repeat as necessary before switching to your other leg.

Jumping Jacks

Stand with your feet together, your toes pointing forward, and your hands raised at either side of your head. Shift one foot out to shoulder width while at the same time raising your hands over your head with your arms extended. Return to the beginning position and repeat on the other side.

Knee Lifts/Crunches While Sitting on Your Office Chair

Sit on the edge of your seat with your feet on the floor and your knees together. Lean back against the back of the chair and hold on to the edges of the seat if you wish.

Keeping your knees together, lift them toward your chest while slightly tilting your shoulders and head toward your knees. Return to the beginning position and repeat as necessary.

Alternate one foot at a time to make the exercise easier.

To make it harder, simply lift your arms from the chair.

Leg Raises—Front

Stand with your feet together, with a chair to your left side. Place your left hand on the back of the chair for support and lift your right leg in front of you. Keep your right leg straight and lift it as high as is comfortable. Repeat as necessary, then turn around and switch to the other side, holding the chair with your right hand for support and lifting your left leg.

Leg Raises—Side

Lie on your right side with your right upper arm and elbow on the floor and your head resting in your right hand. Your legs should be extended, with your left leg stacked on your right leg. Keeping your left leg extended, raise it into the air as far as is comfortable, then lower it back down onto the right leg. Your entire body should be in a straight line throughout the movement. Repeat as necessary, then switch to the other side. Be sure to keep your hips facing forward.

Mountain Climbers

Hold yourself off the floor in a pushup position. You will be facing downward, your hands placed on the floor at shoulder width and arms straight but not locked. Your legs should be straight and extended behind you. All your weight will be on your palms and your toes.

Keeping your back straight, pull your left knee toward your chest. Return your left foot to the starting position and repeat with your right knee. Go back and forth from leg to leg.

To make the
exercise easier,
support yourself
on your knees
and pull in one
at a time.

Standing modification: Raise one knee until your thigh is parallel to the floor, while
extending the opposite arm upward. Pause 2 seconds before alternating sides.

Shoulder Raises

Stand with your feet slightly apart and your toes pointed forward. Hold a weighted duffel bag or purse in each hand with your palms facing your thighs.

As you remain facing forward, raise your arms out to your sides to shoulder level, keeping your arms straight through the entire move. Lower the bags back down to the beginning position, again keeping your arms straight. Repeat as necessary.

Note: This exercise can be done one arm at a time. It can also be done to the front to work the front portion of the shoulders.

Shoulder Presses

Stand upright with your feet shoulder-width apart. Hold a soup can or other object in each hand (you can also do the exercise empty-handed). Begin with your hands up even with your ears, with your elbows bent at roughly 90 degrees. Press your hands up and over your head until your arms are straight up, but your elbows aren't locked.

Lower your hands down until your elbows are once again bent at roughly 90 degrees. As you do so, squeeze your shoulder blades together. Repeat as necessary.

Sit on a Chair and Stand

Stand with your back to a chair or couch, with your feet about a foot in front of the chair, pointed forward, and spread shoulder-width apart. Squat down, with your upper body upright, so that you end up barely resting on the chair. Stand up without touching your hands to the chair. Repeat as necessary.

Squat Kicks

Stand with your toes pointed forward and your feet spread slightly wider than shoulder-width apart. Squat down, keeping your knees forward (but not extending past your toes) and your upper body upright. As you squat down, bring your hands up in front of your upper body.

Now, press yourself back into a standing position, drawing your hands down to your sides. Keep your ab muscles tight throughout the movement. As you stand, gently kick one foot out in front of you. Squat and repeat with your other foot. Go back and forth as necessary.

Stationary Lunges (or Split Squat)

Stand with your feet together and your hands on your hips. Take a step backward with one foot. Bend your front knee, with your back leg extended behind you and the back knee slightly bent, and lower your body. Much of your weight will be on your front foot; allow only the toes of your back foot to touch the floor. Keep your back heel off the floor and both toes pointed forward at all times. This will be less stressful on your knees. Keep your ab muscles pulled in tight throughout the motion.

If you'd like, lower yourself far enough that your front leg is bent at a 90-degree angle and your back knee comes close to the floor. Make sure your front knee doesn't reach forward past your toes.

Press yourself back up to an upright position and repeat. When you're done on that side, switch to the other side.

Stationary Squats
While Holding On to Your Desk

Stand with your toes pointed forward and your feet spread slightly wider than shoulder-width apart. Your desk should be about 2 feet in front of you. Place your hands on the desk for support.

Squat down, keeping your knees forward (but not extending past your toes) and your upper body upright. Now, press yourself back into a standing position. Keep your ab muscles tight throughout the movement. Repeat as necessary.

Sumo Squats

Stand with your feet wider than shoulder width and your toes pointed outward. Hold a weighted duffel bag in front of you with both hands, with your arms extended toward the floor.

Lower yourself straight down, holding your upper body mostly upright but allowing your rear to stick out a bit. Be sure as you squat down that your knees don't extend out past your toes. Press yourself back up and repeat as necessary.

Toe Raises

Stand with both feet together and toes pointing forward. Lift your heels off the floor so that you're rising up on the balls of your feet. You should feel your calf muscles tighten as you rise. Lower your heels back to the floor and repeat as necessary.

Tree Pose

Stand with your feet shoulder-width apart and your toes pointed forward. Using your hands, if necessary, bring your left foot up and place the sole of your foot against your right inner shin (or inner knee or thigh if you can do so). Your left knee will be bent and pointed out to your left. Balance on your right foot for 15 seconds. If you lose your balance, get back into position and finish your time.

Switch to the other side.

Triceps Dips

You can do these on a chair that doesn't swivel, a sturdy coffee table that's not glass-topped, a couch, or a step. Sit on the edge of the chair with your hands also resting on the edge, then walk your feet forward until your legs are extended in front of you with your knees bent. Your rear is slightly in front of the chair, and all your weight is on your palms and your feet.

Lower your rear toward the floor, allowing your elbows to bend behind you. Press yourself back up until your arms are straight but not locked. Repeat as necessary.

Walking Lunges

Stand with your feet together and your hands on your hips. Take a step forward with one foot. Bend your front knee with your back leg extended behind you and the back knee slightly bent, and lower your body. Keep your ab muscles pulled in tight throughout the motion. Keep your back heel off the floor and both toes pointed forward at all times. This will be less stressful on your knees.

When starting out, you don't have to bend your knee or lower your body far. Make sure your front knee doesn't reach forward past your toes.

Press yourself back up to an upright position, step forward with your back foot so your feet are together, and repeat on the other side. You'll end up "walking" forward as you do your lunges.

Walking Lunges with Glute Kickback

Start with your left foot in front of your right with your feet about 2 feet apart and your back heel off the ground. Lower your body so that your front knee is bent at approximately a 90-degree angle and your back leg is slightly bent and moving toward the floor. As you press your body back up, lift your right leg up behind you, using your butt muscle to do so. Keep the back leg extended, pausing for a brief second. Step forward onto your right leg and begin performing the lunge exercise again.

Wall Pushups

To do pushups against a wall, countertop, desk, or stair, stand with your feet several feet away from the object. Place your hands on the object a bit wider than shoulder width. Lower your chest as far as you can toward the object while holding your body straight (in other words, your rear shouldn't be sticking out or sagging down). Press your body back up away from the object. Repeat as necessary.

Warrior 2 Pose

Step forward with your left foot into a deep lunge. Your left knee should not extend past your left toes. Your right leg should be extended behind you, with your toes pointed out toward the right.

Now turn your hips and shoulders so your body is facing the right. Extend your arms widely so that your left arm is extended out over your left knee and your right arm is extended over your right leg. Your hands should be open and your palms facing out. You should be looking down your left arm, and your right leg should be straight and extended in the opposite direction of your left leg. Hold the pose for 5 to 15 seconds and repeat two or three times or as necessary.

Woodchoppers

Stand with your toes pointed forward, your feet spaced about shoulder-width apart, and your knees slightly bent. With both hands, grasp a weighted object with a handle—such as a large Thermos filled with liquid—and extend your arms downward so you're holding the object over your left thigh.

Keeping your arms extended, lift the object up and across your body so you end up holding it over and to the right of your right shoulder. Keep your abdominal muscles tight throughout the movement. Repeat as necessary before switching and performing the exercise on the other side.

Part 3

The Six-Week Program Begins

Chapter 8

MAKE EACH WEEK A SUCCESS

Though the *Cut the Clutter, Drop the Pounds* program is a 6-week activity, in a sense you can also look at it as *1* week's worth of effort that you repeat and expand upon six times.

Each week, you'll engage in a flurry of decluttering activity in a new room or area of your home while following a similar series of steps. Before you begin, I wanted to offer some quick pointers that can help you succeed from the first week to the last and beyond.

Your Blueprint for Each Room

When you prepare to declutter each new part of your home, I understand how daunting the challenge may seem. I've ventured into rooms where I could only see some ceiling, a little of the floor, and none of the wall space. But you could eat an elephant if you had to, and you can do this, too.

Here's how to tackle each area:

Create a vision. We are all programmed to focus on what we want "for" everything. "What do you want *for* your birthday?" "What should we eat *for* dinner?" "What furniture do I want *for* my living room?"

What's wrong with this approach?

▸ It almost always leads you to buy something. You're buying something that you hope will bring you happiness or show that you're feeling love and concern.

▸ It too often focuses on how you can serve objects—"How can I give this room what it needs?"—rather than how objects should serve you.

The word "for" takes you the wrong way. Instead, start with the word "from."

"What do you want *from* your birthday?" (In other words, how do you want to feel at the end of the day?) "What do we want *from* breakfast?" "What do I want *from* my living room?" By framing the question this way with each new room of your house, you describe your vision for the space.

Your vision is your starting point for decluttering the room. This vision sums up how you want the room to suit your needs, what emotion you want the space to evoke, and how you'll feel once the room is doing its job.

It's easy to say, "I want a painting *for* my bedroom" and to find one that's suitable. It's more challenging to say, "I want peace and calm, romance and tranquility *from* my master bedroom" and then work to create that mood in your space.

But doing this first will help you declutter the room more efficiently—and enjoy better results for the effort you put into it.

Follow a list of tasks. How do you eat that elephant? One bite at a time. Each week, I've provided a list of tasks that take you through each room in a deliberate manner. Some rooms require more tasks than others. Some tasks are easy, some take more time and labor.

At the beginning of each week, I'd recommend that you scan the list of tasks and figure out how to divide them evenly over the week so you have enough time for each.

Give yourself plenty of time. You're losing weight and making your home livable again. These are not trivial undertakings. They're huge improvements of utmost importance. Give these activities the time and focus they deserve.

Plan your day around how you'll eat and when you'll do your decluttering tasks. Keep your kitchen stocked with foods on your meal plan so you never order a pizza because your cupboard is empty. Schedule everything else around this program rather than squeezing in the program when you have a few spare minutes.

It's quite possible that after the first 6 weeks, the changes you've made will become second nature, and sticking with them won't require so much time and attention.

Set Yourself Up for Success

A few more steps will help you savor your successes and leap over obstacles when you encounter them.

Remember that it's not just about the decluttering. Be sure not to forget to make time for exercise throughout the week. Stick with it so your body becomes ready for the increasing physical challenges as you progress through the program.

Take photos. Before you start on each area, take a picture of it. By looking at a picture of the clutter, you can view your rooms from another, more detached and less emotional perspective.

Afterward, you'll be able to enjoy your new room even more once you take an "after" photo to do a side-by-side comparison. Down the road when you're in the post-program maintenance phase, you'll also have photographic reminders of how you never want your home to look again.

While you have your camera out, consider taking pictures of mementos that you're going to haul out. Letting go of things is often easier if you have photos that preserve the memory of them.

Get support. The participants on the test panel weren't just keeping in touch with me during the program—they were also supporting each other via a social-media group. Afterward, many of them told me how much the encouragement from the other participants helped them.

Be sure to line up your own forms of support and create ways to broadcast your success (if you enjoy sharing these sorts of events, of course). You might:

▸ Get on Facebook, put your before-and-after pictures on Twitter, or take to the social-media site of your choice. I have a Facebook page with more than 65,000 creative and encouraging followers. If you're stuck on a problem or you feel like celebrating, someone is likely to offer an answer or share your happy moment with you. (I'm often part of these online conversations, too!)

▸ Tell your friends that you're about to start this program and ask them to check in periodically to see how you're doing. This holds you more accountable for sticking to your plan.

▸ Find a mentor who has worked hard to conquer a major challenge. Most of us know someone who's lost a lot of weight, stopped smoking, struggled with an addiction, or learned to manage depression or anxiety. Ask if you can talk about your progress with your home, your weight, and your mindset if things get tough.

Bring your family on board. You'll especially need the support of everyone else who lives in your home. Since you're probably going to be rearranging rooms they use—and you'll likely want to get rid of some of their stuff while

(continued on page 200)

The Clutter Chronicles

Joe Shigo, 51

POUNDS LOST: 21

AMOUNT OF CLUTTER REMOVED:
Seven large bags of trash and three bags filled with items for donation

Joe shed a lot of pounds on the *Cut the Clutter, Drop the Pounds* program by gaining a new vision.

He calls himself "a big guy in general." But when Joe showed up for the program's launch, the 51-year-old telecommunications specialist was surprised by the number on the scale.

He used to keep his weight under control with 45-minute workouts on his lunch hour. But when he injured his already-aching knee in 2011, his exercise time dwindled.

He started the 6-week program carrying 301 pounds.

"I said, 'This ain't happening!' I felt totally unhealthy and unhappy with the sluggishness and tiredness that comes with the weight," he says. He had a more urgent motivation to lose weight, too: He was

Before

scheduled for knee-replacement surgery in a few months, and his doctor told him that if he lost weight, he would put less stress on his new knee.

Physical activity wasn't easy for him during the program, but he found that he could manage his eating choices very well. He stuck to 2,000 calories per day, and he carefully controlled his portion sizes. If he was planning to enjoy a special treat at dinner, he'd cut back on what he ate earlier in the day.

He also learned to find healthy foods that wouldn't break his budget.

"People say that eating healthy is more expensive. It may be if you go to a regular supermarket," he says. Instead, he made regular trips to farmers' markets and a chain of stores in his area that offers reasonably priced fruits and vegetables. For the cost of a trip to a fast-food restaurant, he could buy more produce than he could eat at one sitting.

While his willpower and his ability to track down healthy food bargains helped in his weight loss, he credits a different mental tool for making the real difference.

"The biggest thing I got out of this program, and it really impressed me the most, is to have a vision. If something in a room helps you achieve your vision, that's good. If it doesn't, then get rid of it. It's the same with food."

After the program, Joe discovered that he had shed the most weight of all the test panelists, a whopping 21 pounds in 6 weeks— more than 3 pounds a week! He also lost 6 inches off his waist.

With a new knee (and presumably smaller pants), Joe is spreading the importance of having a vision.

"We're redoing a buddy's shed. It's where we go on the weekend to watch the race or the football game. We have a computer and TV out there, but the place is totally a mess. I told him, 'You have to sit there and think of what your vision is!' We're close to being done with fixing it up, and it absolutely looks fantastic," Joe says.

"I also find myself telling my daughters, 'Will *that* help you achieve your goal? Is this friend helping you to better yourself in life, or is she pulling you in the other direction?' That's what I got out of this program."

you're decluttering—you'll want them to have some appreciation for what you're doing.

Convene a family meeting to outline your plan. Tell them what you'll be doing to each room. Tell them how you're going to be spending your time. As you develop a philosophy that guides your decisions to keep items or get rid of them, tell them how the process works.

Let them know that you take this program seriously and that their support and cooperation are critical for the success you expect. Even better: Have them join you in your decluttering and weight loss activities whenever possible! When your family is involved, they are far more likely to be committed to the changes you hope to achieve.

Chapter 9

WEEK ONE: YOUR COOKING AND DINING AREAS

The kitchen is one of the most important rooms in your home.

More than just an area for preparing food, the kitchen is the place where you pass along values to your children, demonstrate the joy of conversation, and as a family participate in the ancient ritual of sharing a meal.

Your kitchen and your dining areas are also tightly linked to the inner workings of your body and your mind. When you're clearing out an overstuffed life, I believe you have to start here. Your kitchen strongly influences your food choices, so this is also the natural place to begin when decluttering your waistline. It often provides enough space for you to stash away hundreds of thousands of calories' worth of food—healthy or otherwise.

As you declutter and reorganize your kitchen, the key question to ask is "Am I using this space to hold foods that help me create the body I want?" Are the supplies in your kitchen helping you stay lean and strong? Or do you pack your pantry and fridge with foods and drinks that fuel your journey into obesity and poor health?

This week, you'll also give thought to how you use your dining area.

Perhaps your dining room (or whatever area your home provides for eating) is a welcoming space for your loved ones to share their joys and challenges of the day. Perhaps it's where your family comes together to be nourished and grow closer. Maybe you block out the rest of the world, letting it carry on without you while you dine together in your refuge.

Or is a completely different scene playing out in your dining room? Maybe your table is covered with hobby supplies or schoolwork or laundry. Maybe you eat standing up in the kitchen. Maybe everyone in the household eats silently in front of the TV, fork in one hand and smartphone in the other.

Deciding What Your Eating Spaces Mean

For most of us, the kitchen and the dining areas are the places in the home where we connect with our food. By "connect," I mean both eating the food and processing emotions related to it.

These spaces can be a stage for you and your loved ones to maintain your bodies, and even heal them, with good food choices. You can focus your mind on enjoying your dishes, not just with your sense of taste but with all of your senses. Here you can connect with your family, too. You can experiment with new foods with your spouse or partner or relax with old favorites. Kids might become more talkative and accessible during mealtime when they escape their usual distractions.

The warm feelings that your family can generate at mealtimes may help prevent or reduce household stress that builds up at other times of the day.

On the other hand, you may be letting these opportunities for physical and emotional maintenance pass you by, like so many people do nowadays:

▸ You hand over the responsibility for feeding you to restaurants, where the cooks are typically more interested in your business than your health.

▸ You eat whatever's convenient rather than making choices that specifically meet your needs. This goes back to the notion of asking "What do I want *for* dinner?" (something fast, something tasty) rather than "What do I want *from* dinner?" (foods that give me my daily dose of nutrition; a meal that won't provide a bunch of needless calories that will stick around as fat).

▸ You eat without paying a bit of attention to your food. It's on your plate, in your mouth, and gone. You're unable to say exactly how much you ate or what it even tasted like.

▸ You dine alone, with everyone in your home eating at different times and in different spots.

Which version do you choose? The occasions during the day when you eat are extremely important to your physical and emotional health, even if you don't realize it in the moment. Also, the time that any of us has to spend with

One reason why your kitchen and dining room have such a powerful impact on your life is because they can hold a *lot* of food!

- In the typical new home, 19 percent of the space is devoted to the kitchen and dining room. That's bigger than the master bedroom (12 percent) and just a bit less than the family room and living room combined (20.1 percent).

- Most new homes, especially larger ones, have a walk-in pantry. These pantries offer 37 square feet of storage space, on average.

- At nearly 22 cubic feet, new refrigerators are about 11 percent bigger than those sold in 1980. More storage space means more room for food that was prepared and packaged outside the home—with ingredients that you didn't control. It also means more chances to stash choices that keep you unfit and unhealthy.

- Speaking of refrigerators, the number of people using a second fridge has risen substantially over a fairly short time. In 2009, 23 percent of American homes kept a backup stash of food in a second fridge, compared to just 15 percent in 1997.

loved ones—parents, kids, siblings, and spouses—is ultimately limited. If you don't make use of those mealtimes, you don't get them back.

Starting today, which story will you tell in these spaces?

Kitchen Memories Can Linger

Each of us carries into our adult life impressions, attitudes, and behaviors instilled in us in childhood. It's very likely that deep in your mind you have tucked away experiences that took place in the kitchen and dining room that still influence how you think about food today.

Did you memorize family recipes from yellowed, faded cards and learn to take pride in your cooking? Did a loved one feed you ice cream to console you after a bad day at school? Or are your kitchen memories not so happy? Did a parent who survived hard times scold you if you didn't finish your meal? Did you sneak down to the fridge late at night and indulge your cravings in shame?

Did you learn to celebrate with food?

Or that food equals love?

Or that food makes your discomfort go away?

All of these types of old memories can be a factor in your present-day weight. This week, part of the "clutter" you'll be sorting through is your attitude toward food. You're also going to examine the way you use your kitchen and dining room. This includes decluttering these spaces, but your mission goes far beyond that. You'll be making choices that will affect your diet, the way you think about eating, and the way the people in your household interact with each other.

Decluttering and reorganizing your kitchen and dining room will require 11 tasks. You can scatter these evenly across 7 days of the week. Or you can do them all throughout the week and rest on the weekend.

Or, and this might happen, you'll realize that you can't complete the tasks in just 1 week. That's fine, too. It took years for you to accumulate everything you have in your home, and for some people, completely finishing a particular area in a week is too ambitious.

If you're not finished by the end of the week, move on to the next room and come back and finish your kitchen later, either at the end of the program or on a slow day during the program.

Ready to dig down through your clutter to look for the happier home, body, and mind that are waiting under there?

Let's get started!

Task 1:
DEVELOP A VISION FOR WHAT YOU WANT FROM YOUR KITCHEN

This task simply requires you to sit down and do some thinking, ideally with the other people in your home.

I know you're probably excited to throw out some old appliances, and we'll get to that very soon. But please take ample time for Task 1, as it's crucial. Without this vision, you can certainly obtain a clean kitchen and dining room, but you won't make the deeper changes in your habits and behaviors that lead to the improvements in your health that you want.

Determining your vision simply requires asking "What do I want *from* this room?" You have a lot of options.

WEEK ONE TASKS

- ☐ Create your vision.
- ☐ Collect malignant items.
- ☐ Clean out your fridge and freezer.
- ☐ Clean out your pantry.
- ☐ Clear all horizontal surfaces.
- ☐ Tackle your preparation area.
- ☐ Address your countertop command zone.

- ☐ Sort through dishes.
- ☐ Clean up your cleaning area.
- ☐ Take care of your dining room.
- ☐ Get rid of malignant items.

Plus

- ☐ Mindset adjustment
- ☐ Physical activities

▸ I want a relaxing place where I can check in with my family.

▸ I want this to be a place where I take 10 minutes to relax in the morning before I go to work and 30 minutes to decompress in the evening.

▸ I want to be able to focus on what I'm eating in this room and to be able to express gratitude that I once again have enough to eat today.

▸ I want a space that welcomes guests, is fun to cook in and easy to clean, and says "I value sharing meals with family and friends."

▸ I want to explore new styles of cooking, so I want my kitchen to support a lot of experiments.

As you can see, creating a vision requires an idea of how you'll use your kitchen and dining room, how you want to feel in these spaces, and what these areas will look like. These are closely related, and one affects the other. Make sure the *appearance* and *contents* of the room support the activities you're planning to do here.

When you're defining your vision, make sure you cover the specifics. If you want the entire family to eat together in the dining room, do you mean every night? If your kids do their homework in the dining room or kitchen, when do they need to clear out so it becomes an eating area again? I can't tell you what your vision should be, but if it's possible, I would highly recommend that you *only* use these spaces for cooking and eating—and that you *only* do your eating here.

This is also a good time to make sure that your family is on board with the plan. A shared place needs a shared vision, both for creating spaces that work for the family and to provide a sense of shared ownership and responsibility.

Do your kids want to eat in the den while they play video games? Does your spouse plan to keep buying the nacho chips, ice cream, and beer that you're going to have trouble resisting while you're trying to lose weight? If you or a household member uses the dining area for crafts or puzzles, those need to be minimized. If you're eating gingerly so you don't disrupt a 1,000-piece jigsaw puzzle, your focus is not going to be on your food. Get agreement on what everyone in your home is willing to do, and seek compromises that keep them happy but also help you succeed during the next 6 weeks and beyond.

I want you to be mindful of what you eat, because this is a secret weapon against body fat that too few people know how to use. You're not going to be truly mindful of what goes into your mouth if:

▶ You're cooking or eating during other activities. For that reason, I'd recommend that you rid your kitchen and dining room of televisions and computers. Ban smartphones from the dining room unless someone's expecting a life-or-death call.

▶ You're distracted by other stuff that doesn't belong. Kitchens become a catchall for household debris: piles of bills, unread magazines, homework, and stuff that doesn't seem to have any other home. During the next week, move all this stuff out of your kitchen.

With all this in mind, please take some time to create your vision for your kitchen and dining room.

KITCHEN VISION

This is what I want *from* my kitchen:_____

_____

_____

_____

_____

How I want to *feel* in this space:_____

_____

_____

_____

This is what I want *from* my dining area:_____

_____

_____

_____

How I want to *feel* in this space:_____

_____

_____

_____

Task 2:
SEPARATE THE "BENIGN" FROM THE "MALIGNANT" ITEMS

Every week, once you've established your vision for the space we're focused on, the next step will be to identify all the "malignant" clutter in that space.

The stuff you own has power—the power to take you to another place and time, to remind you of events long past, to overwhelm or depress you. Malignant clutter poisons your point of view, your habits, and your behaviors. It makes you feel bad about the decisions you've made. It makes you think less of yourself. It makes you second-guess yourself. It gets in your face, undermines your confidence, and calls you a failure. It reminds you of lost love, missed opportunities, or times past that you wish you could move on from. It's harmful, and rooting it out must be your priority.

Task 2 is to carefully inspect your kitchen and dining areas and list all the malignant items—or better still, gather them in one pile. These things can bring up all kinds of emotions. The idea of throwing them out might be hard, even when you can see they're bad for you.

So you don't have to get rid of them right now, if you don't want. You have all week to first get used to the idea. Right now, I just want you to identify these items and set them somewhere unobtrusive. Our goal over the week is for you to become aware of the malignant clutter, to reflect on its place in your life, and to prepare to deal with it in a way that helps you wrestle back the power that it holds over you.

It's up to you to decide what's benign and malignant in your household. But I'd suspect that the kitchen and dining room items that might make your malignant list include the following:

Junk food. A small amount of snacks might be okay. But if your kitchen is stuffed with cakes, candy, and ice-cream bars—and it's all making you fat, and you can't stop eating it—it needs to go! Ideally, you'll develop the ability over the next 6 weeks to enjoy these foods sparingly. But for right now, I suspect that if it's there, you'll eat it. So the less junk food you keep in your home, the better.

Processed foods. Get rid of boxes of salty, shrink-wrapped, premade meals. For the next 6 weeks, I'd like for you to put a little more time and attention into preparing food for yourself and your loved ones.

Unhealthy cooking tools. Toss out deep-fat fryers and any other cooking implements that require heavy doses of fat, and devices that you only use to prepare a food or snack that contributes to your excess pounds. Does your cake ball maker beg you to make doughnut holes every day? Perhaps it needs a new home.

Plates, cooking gadgets, and utensils that represent some type of failure. Perhaps it's the set of dishes that you thought would help you become a beloved kitchen diva like the one on TV (but didn't). Maybe it's the kitchen items you purchased during a previous marriage or during a particularly difficult period of your life. Odds are high that anything you bought from the TV after midnight is not something that makes you feel good about yourself.

Objects that cause you pain. These may come from a place of love, but they hurt you. Perhaps they're empty chairs around the dining room table now that your kids have gone to college. Maybe it's a stack of inherited cookbooks that you never use but feel too guilty to give away. Now is a good time to pull these out and set them aside so you can figure out what to do with them.

For each piece of malignant clutter, ask yourself:

▸ How did this get here?

▸ What power does this item have over me?

▸ Is this item helping me create the vision I have for the space?

▸ Is this item serving any purpose or helping me in some positive way?

▸ What feelings linked to this object have kept me from throwing it out?

▸ How would I feel if this item disappeared on its own right now?

▸ Could this item that's a source of pain or disappointment to me become a wonderful addition to someone else's life?

Task 3:
CLEAN OUT YOUR FRIDGE AND FREEZER

When decluttering your home, it's critical to think of each room as a collection of zones. A zone is an area where you keep similar items or where a particular activity takes place. By dividing a room into zones, you:

▸ Establish a home for things that will live in each space

▸ Define how the space will be used

▸ Create a limit for the amount of stuff that you'll permit in each zone

When it comes to your health, your refrigerator/freezer area is one of the most important kitchen zones.

For this and every zone in your home, I want you to first ask yourself:

What do I want *from* this area? Someone who grew up in a financially strapped household where having enough to eat wasn't guaranteed might want a fully stocked fridge at all times. Someone with low willpower might want only healthy foods. Decide which needs you want your refrigerator/freezer to meet. Keep in mind that the *Cut the Clutter, Drop the Pounds* program's meal plans are designed to lead to weight loss. To get the full benefit of this program, please be sure that your fridge and freezer (and other food storage areas) hold the kinds of foods that will carry you to success.

How much space do I want to allow for each type of item? Spend a few moments sketching out a mental map of your refrigerator. Determine how

Refrigerators and freezers run best when they have open space in the bins and shelves. An overstuffed unit may not stay cool enough and may be more likely to require costly repairs. That's another reason why what you *don't* put into your fridge is as important as what you do put in it.

much space you'll devote to fruits and vegetables, milk and other dairy, condiments, and other contents.

Once you settle on these criteria, get to work. Ask yourself whether each item helps your refrigerator perform the function you want from it. If it doesn't, toss it. If you realize you have way too much bottled water or salad dressings, get rid of them.

As I discussed earlier in the book, many people hold on to items they don't need because they feel it would be wasteful to discard them. Sometimes that's a valid concern, like with food, since we do live in a world where many people don't have enough to eat. If you don't want to keep food or drinks that are unopened and unexpired, consider offering them to friends, family members, food banks, or homeless shelters.

As you're cleaning and decluttering, give all the shelves and bins a good scrubbing and sanitizing.

When you finish, if you have a second refrigerator in your garage or another room, clean it out, too.

Task 4:
CLEAN OUT YOUR PANTRY

Give your pantry the same treatment that you gave the fridge/freezer. Before you decide what will go into the pantry, decide what you want this zone to provide for you. (You're the boss, and each zone works for *you*, not vice versa.)

Are you trying to get more whole grains into your diet? Make sure your pantry keeps plenty of those available. Do you live a long way from the supermarket, and you'd like to reduce the unnecessary trips that cut into time you'd rather spend elsewhere? Then make sure the pantry is well stocked with the items you use often.

Decide how much space should be available for each type of item (such as canned goods, cereal, pasta, boxes of teabags, etc.). The pantry often attracts all sorts of nonfood items, such as pet supplies and grocery bags. If possible, keep nonfood items to a minimum in your pantry, so this zone's primary function remains keeping you nourished.

Clean out your entire pantry, wipe up any dust and crumbs, and haul out stuff that's old or expired. If any type of item exceeds the space you're giving it, figure out how to use it quickly, give it away, or throw it out.

Task 5:
CLEAR OFF ALL HORIZONTAL SURFACES

Given enough time, dust will accumulate on every horizontal surface in your home: shelves, countertops, end tables, coffee tables, and desktops. It's simply gravity at work.

But due to another, less-investigated law of nature, clutter gathers on all these surfaces, too. These cluttered surfaces become a highly visible contributor to household messiness. That creates two problems:

▶ When these areas are cluttered, your home is cluttered.

▶ When items pile up on these spaces, you can't use them for their intended purpose.

▶ WHAT'S YOUR FRIDGE TELLING YOU?

When clearing the horizontal surfaces in your kitchen, make sure to confront the big vertical surface looming over the room, too. Namely, your refrigerator.

Personally, I don't think anything should go on the refrigerator. If you must put kids' artwork, report cards, novelty magnets, and a calendar on the fridge, I urge you to keep them to a minimum, and only put them up after you first try to find a more logical home for them.

Jeanne Arnold (the household archae-ologist you met in Chapter 1) and her colleagues found a link between the number of objects on the fridge and the degree of clutter in the rest of the home. They wrote that the surface of your refrigerator may act like a thermometer of sorts, giving a measurement of how much purchasing your family does and how much "stuff" you hold on to over time.

In other words, if you can't keep clutter off your fridge, you probably aren't doing any better in the rest of your home.

So a fundamental rule in home organization is that you have to keep flat surfaces clear and uncluttered. This will immediately create a more open and welcoming space.

Your kitchen has a high density of horizontal spaces—your countertops, the top of your refrigerator and microwave, your kitchen island, and so forth. Your first step in decluttering them is to ask yourself "How do I want these horizontal surfaces to make my life easier?" (Rather than "What do I want to put here?")

In any space, especially the kitchen, it's important to remember that flat surfaces are *not* for storage—they're for preparing and serving.

If your vision for your kitchen is something like "I want to be able to easily prepare and serve food in my kitchen," then look at whether the items on your countertops and shelves *help* you or *hinder* you. Anything that gets in your way or adds to your cleanup time needs to go. Clear out all the piles of mail, instruction manuals, work materials, knickknacks, collectibles, computers, food wrappers, and any other debris that doesn't belong.

If your horizontal kitchen spaces look like clean, functional workspaces, your kitchen will look larger and more inviting, and you'll be more likely to cook and less tempted to just load the family into the car and eat elsewhere.

Task 6:
ADDRESS THE PREPARATION AREA

Kitchens function most smoothly when the zones are clearly defined. The preparation area is the space where you assemble the ingredients for a meal. This zone should allow you to pull meals together in the most efficient way possible.

The only items in this space should be the things that help you prepare your meals. This includes:

▸ Pots and pans

▸ Knives

▸ Kitchen utensils like ladles and stirring spoons

▸ Colanders

▸ Herbs and spices

Step back and consider the space in your kitchen that's devoted to meal preparation. Look at the places where you keep your pots, pans, cutting boards, utensils, and storage containers. Are these items conveniently located?

How much space will you allow these items to take up? Which items do you regularly use, and which are just consuming precious space?

Grab a box and systematically go through all the drawers and cupboards that hold food preparation items. Get rid of the worn-out, unused, damaged, or just plain ugly stuff that no longer has a place in your home. If you find items that are not used for food preparation, decide where they belong or whether you should simply toss them. Pots and pans unused for more than 12 months can probably go. If you have duplicates of any items, some of them can go. Any plastic storage container without a lid must definitely go!

Task 7:
CONQUER THE COUNTERTOP COMMAND ZONE

This is the area where you put food on plates just before you serve your meals. This area should be clear, clutter-free, and functional, with handy access to platters, serving utensils, and flatware. Any other items that don't serve this purpose should go elsewhere.

Carefully examine this zone. Does it currently help you do this task, or is it cluttered with kitchen- and non-kitchen-related items? Whatever objects are currently getting in the way of an efficient serving space need to go. Decorative items that clutter the space—no matter how pretty—need to find a new home.

Check your platters and serving dishes. Do you have a reasonable number, or are many of them long unused? Remove all your utensils and kitchen gizmos from their drawers. Decide which items you really need and use, and get rid of the ones you don't.

Task 8:
CLEAN UP YOUR DISHES

In most kitchens, dishes and glassware tend to fill up the cupboards that are available to them, whether or not the owners use them regularly.

For this task, bring out all dishes, cups, and glassware from your cupboards. Get rid of any items that are chipped or damaged, as well as those you simply don't use. Take this opportunity to toss out all of those free and souvenir plastic cups that seemed useful when you brought them home but now just take up space. If you have unmatched items, decide if you want to keep the irregular pieces or simply discard the partial set.

Now decide how much space you're willing to provide for your dishes. Put the items you're going to keep back into these spaces, making sure to keep like items together. Discard any items that don't fit into the spaces you've allocated.

Task 9:
ASSEMBLE YOUR CLEANING PRODUCTS

Kitchens can go from sanitary to grimy in a hurry! For this reason, it's crucial to keep the right cleaning products close at hand so you can quickly and easily clear a mess, remove a spill, or just wipe the countertops clean at the end of an evening.

In most kitchens, the cleaning products stay under the sink. People often find that venturing into this dark, spooky place is one of their least-liked tasks in the kitchen, but I promise that this step can be one of the most rewarding.

First, remove everything from under the sink and place it on your kitchen counter. Discard any old, unused, empty, or just plain odd products and items. I guarantee you'll find multiples of some cleaning products (like partially filled bottles of the same spray cleaner)—if so, merge them into single containers. (However, don't mix different types of cleaners in one container.)

Odds are good that you'll be able to toss out several nearly empty containers of cleaning products. In most cases, it's okay to just pour small amounts of household cleaners down the drain, then recycle the container. If you have larger quantities, be sure to dispose of them responsibly.

While the under-sink area is empty, thoroughly clean it. Finally, reload the space with only those items that you need and use regularly. Consider using plastic storage bins to keep similar items together. This will help keep the space tidy and enable you to quickly and easily find what you're seeking— which you'll be grateful for the next time you're fumbling around for the right bottle in this dark, spidery area.

Be sure not to overload the space. If you have extra items that you want to

---

▶ STREAMLINE YOUR CLEANERS

You don't need to stuff cleaners made for every type of surface in your home under the sink. In fact, this short list of cleaners should cover most of your needs:

- An all-purpose surface cleaner

- Glass/window cleaner

- Surface scrub for difficult stains

- Furniture polish and polishing wipes

- Shower/bathroom cleaner

Keep your products in a plastic caddy so they're easy to find, store, and transport around your home. (That way you won't need to keep multiple bottles in different locations.)

keep but don't need in the kitchen, relocate them to the garage or basement with other surplus cleaning supplies.

Task 10:
TAME YOUR DINING ROOM

The next zone you'll tackle is your dining room. If you don't have a formal dining room, then turn your attention to the area where your family gathers to eat. If you eat in front of the television, I strongly advise you to move your meals to a place that's free of distractions, a place solely for sharing meals together.

Creating and maintaining a welcoming dining space is a key component of the *Cut the Clutter, Drop the Pounds* plan. Having a place dedicated only to eating and sharing food as a family will greatly improve how you view your food and how you consume it. Taking your food to a place where you can focus on it will help you pay more attention to what's going into your mouth—and whether it's going to help you lose weight, or whether it's yet another food that will keep you overweight and unhappy.

You'll also be able to pay more attention to your body's signals: Are you actually hungry? Can you feel satisfied with smaller portions?

So think about the way you want your dining area to function for your health and your family's happiness. Anything that doesn't help you realize your vision for this space—anything that's interfering with that goal—has no place in this room.

To be realistic, the room may also need to serve double duty as a homework or hobby area. If this is the case, talk with family members and figure out together how you'll keep those uses from interfering with a relaxed and mindful dining atmosphere at mealtimes.

Task 11:
TAKE OUT YOUR MALIGNANT ITEMS

Now is the time to turn your attention back to your malignant kitchen items: the stuff that makes you feel guilty, or sad, or like you've failed as a cook or as a provider for your family.

As bad as this stuff is, I know it's often difficult to "break up" with it. It's just like addressing a relationship that's bad for you or that has run its course. Even when you know you need to do it, making that break can be incredibly painful.

I have dealt with all kinds of malignant clutter over the years. I know how crippling some items can be, how they can crush your spirit and, without warning, bring up memories of times or events that send you into sadness, anger, and despair.

I also know that the only way *over* a problem is *through* it. By dealing with malignant clutter, you remove hurdles that are keeping you from your best life. A few years ago, I worked with a family that had endured the father's battle with lymphoma. Every member of the family was left shaken by the experience.

Fortunately he was in remission, and his odds for continued good health were great. But in one corner of the living room, I found an upper-body and head cast that held him completely still during his extensive radiation treatments. The whole family blanched when I lifted the cast aloft. They hated what the cast represented. Still, they couldn't let it go.

Your malignant clutter may have been tormenting you for years. But you're getting a fresh start, and this harmful clutter is presenting obstacles to your growth and success. Now's the time to get rid of your first batch of malignant clutter. If you simply must have a reminder that this stuff was part of your life, take a picture of it, then tuck away the physical photo in a desk or stick the digital version deep into the belly of your computer.

It's time to give this clutter to the world outside your home. Gather up the pile and:

- ▶ Distribute items to friends or family.

- ▶ Sell things on Craigslist or on consignment.

- ▶ Donate it to Goodwill.

- ▶ Set things out on your curb with a sign that reads "FREE."

- ▶ Recycle whatever you can.

- ▶ Accept that some items are worthless and throw them in the trash.

After a long conversation, the family I was just telling you about agreed to my suggestion that we *burn* the cast as a way of saying good-bye to the cancer and signaling a new beginning. This was one of the most emotional moments I have ever had as a professional organizer. Everyone was in tears as flames reduced the cast to ashes. But in that moment, there was also a great sense of joy and release. By letting go of this piece of malignant clutter (the worst kind of malignant clutter, in fact), the whole family was free of the destructive power that it held over them.

Week One
Mindset Adjustment

This program is about clearing away the unwanted stuff that's been building up in your body, home, and mind for years or decades. A powerful tool for making these changes is to practice mindfulness meditation for just 5 minutes every day, starting this week.

This is not a difficult or complex task, but it's one that some people in the test panel found especially challenging. Somehow those 5 minutes were the ones they had trouble sparing.

Set aside this time and set a timer for yourself. It's just 5 minutes. Consider it a little space in the day for treating yourself. It may feel like you're not doing anything, but you are.

This exercise simply requires that you sit in a quiet environment and focus on your breath moving in and out of your body. If any other thoughts pop up in your mind, just let them pass through without paying them any attention. Don't argue with them or get mired in them or allow them to upset you. Let them slip away and return your focus to your breathing.

This exercise helps you recognize that your thoughts aren't your boss. You don't have to do what they say. You'll also learn that *you* are not your thoughts. Instead, your thoughts are these little things—often clutter!—that merely pop up in your head, and they don't have to define your identity.

If you don't think sitting still for 5 minutes is a good use of your time, consider this: How many minutes a day do you spend worrying? Or daydreaming? Or being angry? How does that time make your day better?

Week One
Fitness Activities

It's time to start clearing out clutter from your body, too: the extra fat, the fatigue, and the inability to function at your best that can result from lack of exercise. It's time to make an easy start toward becoming active. Please make time to do the following activities.

(continued on page 220)

The Clutter Chronicles

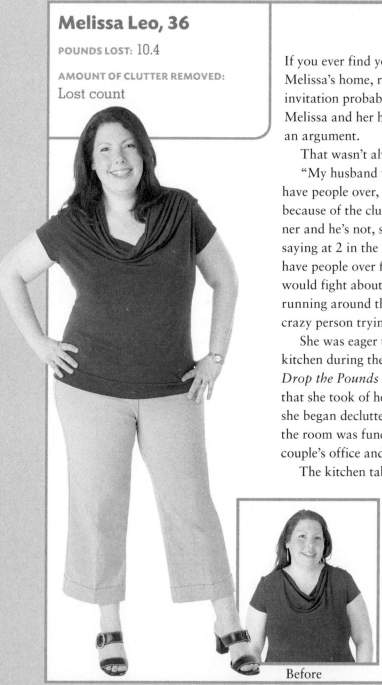

Melissa Leo, 36

POUNDS LOST: 10.4

AMOUNT OF CLUTTER REMOVED:
Lost count

If you ever find yourself visiting Melissa's home, rest assured: Your invitation probably didn't cause Melissa and her husband to have an argument.

That wasn't always the case.

"My husband would want to have people over, and I wouldn't because of the clutter. I'm a planner and he's not, so he was always saying at 2 in the afternoon, 'Let's have people over for dinner.' We would fight about it, and I'd be running around the kitchen like a crazy person trying to clean."

She was eager to tackle that kitchen during the *Cut the Clutter, Drop the Pounds* program. Photos that she took of her kitchen before she began decluttering showed that the room was functioning as the couple's office and catchall area.

The kitchen table was a mess.

Before

Two countertops held laptop computers. Another was strewn with stacks of papers and a grocery bag stuffed with what appeared to be Thomas the Tank Engine toys. A bottle of spray cleaner stood at the ready, though none of the spray would even be able to land on the counter surfaces.

Now, however, she can tidy up her kitchen in a few minutes, so having company over "is not a big deal," she says. "The clutter was affecting our relationship. This program made me realize how much of an issue we were having."

She made another kitchen-related change that led to a big improvement: She stopped stocking it with junk food that she'd eat mindlessly in the evenings.

"Once the kids were in bed, it was my time to decompress and watch TV. That was also when I would eat, because my hands were free while I was watching TV," she says. Not only did she stop buying chips and junk food, she also started using her television time for more useful tasks.

"I didn't have time at night to sit and eat, because that's when I would do my decluttering. I realized when I was decluttering, I wasn't hungry. I had been mindlessly eating before."

She faced some tough challenges, like the pile of keepsakes her dying mother left her when Melissa was 21.

"She said to me, 'I want you to take stuff even if you don't like it right now, because your tastes are going to change.' So I took stuff I didn't want," she says. "It's now been almost 15 years, and there are still things I'm not using. She collected dolls, which I have in a box in my basement, but I'll be passing some off to family members and selling the rest."

She had good teammates helping her through the 6-week experiment. Her 3-year-old daughter joined her on trips to drop off donations at Goodwill, and her husband was happy to let her set the vision for each room—with one catch.

"He just wanted to get rid of the piles of stuff in the kitchen!" Melissa says. He got his wish, as their dinner guests can attest.

WALKING

Two or 3 days this week, take a 5-minute walk around your block, your neighborhood, a park, or if you have one, on a treadmill. Walking in place while watching TV or listening to music works as well. While you're walking, plan out your decluttering tasks for the day (or tomorrow if you're walking in the evening).

ACTIVITIES TO IMPROVE YOUR BODY'S ABILITIES

In addition, perform these movements described in Chapter 7 on 1 or 2 nonconsecutive days after your muscles are nice and warm from walking or decluttering.

- ▸ Enough Walking Lunges (page 187) to carry you from your living room to your kitchen
- ▸ 10 Wall Pushups (page 189) with your hands on the edge of your kitchen counter after you've finished clearing it
- ▸ 10 Shoulder Presses (page 178) with equal-size canned goods
- ▸ 10 Bent-Over Rows (page 162) with a full milk jug or gallon of water
- ▸ March in place for 3 minutes before finishing for the day

---

This brings us to the end of Week One. If your kitchen and dining areas aren't thoroughly decluttered and organized, they should be well on their way.

Now take a good look at what you've accomplished. Put a checkmark in the "win" column in your mind. Take a photo and post it to Facebook. As you move on to the next room, use these food-related areas as a clean, wide-open space for fueling your future health and fitness.

Chapter 10

WEEK TWO: YOUR BEDROOM

I've come to realize that the single most important room in any home is the master bedroom. I know that's a huge statement, and I'd invite you to take a couple of moments to ponder the significance of what I'm saying.

The master bedroom is the room that sets the emotional tone of your household. It is the central place where you build and maintain a healthy, strong relationship with your spouse or partner—which has a huge impact on your overall happiness. It's where you're most intimate and it's also where you engage in the mysterious process of sleep.

I honestly believe that the master bedroom should be treated as sacred space in a home. It should be respected, honored, and cared for in a reverent way.

The master bedroom has only *two* proper functions:

▶ It's the space where you focus on the intimate elements of your relationship.

▶ It's a space where you replenish your body and spirit with rest and sleep.

That's it. That's the ideal function of your bedroom. Unfortunately, my experience has taught me that many people seem determined to use this room for everything else.

The master bedroom's proper role is not to be your home theater, communications center, or child's play area. Plenty of other rooms are better suited for those purposes.

It should not serve as your home office or the hub for checking your electronic devices. Or your dining room.

Your bedroom should not resemble a workout center. Even a single treadmill with pants hanging from it doesn't belong there.

Speaking of clothes, your bedroom should not serve as a room-size clothes hamper for all your dirty clothes or as a storage area for your clean laundry that you haven't put away.

Finally, your bedroom is not the place to store weird stuff, like car parts stacked up in the corner, which I was once puzzled to see in a home.

In many homes, the master bedroom acts as a catchall for clutter and activities that flow into it from elsewhere in the home. Unfortunately, when these take root in the bedroom, they can harm your physical and emotional health.

When you take steps to set up a bedroom with only two very specific purposes, you'll make a profound change to the foundation of your well-being. The fixes you make to your bedroom this week can improve your:

▸ Mental health and focus

▸ Energy levels

▸ Weight

▸ Family relationships

But first, you'll probably have to rethink how you've been using your bedroom for your entire adult life (and possibly even in your childhood).

Permissible Use for Your Bedroom #1: A Quiet Space to Focus on Yourself and Your Partner

Your master bedroom is typically the one place in your home where you can truly be yourself without interruption. Even if you derive a lot of your identity from the gardening you do outside or the cooking you do in the kitchen or the woodworking you do in the garage, these are things you *do*, not who you *are*.

In your bedroom you share your most intimate self. You can gaze at the ceiling and ponder your place in the universe. As you sleep, you become completely vulnerable, shielded from the outside world by the safety of your bedroom walls.

In the rest of the home, you have many other roles. In your bedroom, you can simply be yourself, both as an individual and—if you're married or partnered—as one part of the relationship at the center of your household.

In the bedroom, you completely expose yourself to this other person, both literally and metaphorically. You connect on a deep level. You retreat to this room to develop plans that affect the rest of the family, without interruption. The bedroom is the quiet, unhurried space where you do the things that feed your relationship. I strongly believe that how you treat your bedroom is a good metaphor for how you treat yourself and your relationship with your partner.

Stress is running high among married couples, and this stress creates a heavy burden in an already overstuffed life. The American Psychological Association's 2014 *Stress in America* report noted that relationships (whether with a spouse, romantic partner, or kids) were a "somewhat" or "very significant" source of stress for 56 percent of respondents.

An earlier survey from the organization found that:

▸ 32 percent had argued with their spouse or partner in the previous month (a number that seems comically low to me!).

▸ For 45 percent, stress had a negative effect on their relationship with their spouse or partner.

▸ Close to half—43 percent—said they'd eaten too much or had eaten unhealthy foods during the previous month due to stress.

Your bedroom can be a reliable—and unbeatable—refuge for addressing concerns with your spouse before they become a source of stress, or simply for escaping life's challenges if you're the sole occupant of your bedroom.

However, judging from the bedrooms I typically see, most people aren't using this room as a quiet space for improving their emotional health or their relationships.

When I visit homes with kids under 12 or so, it's often hard to distinguish between the parents' bedroom and the kids' bedrooms. The master bedroom will have toy cars and plastic building blocks underfoot and stuffed animals on the bed. DVDs of animated movies orbit the parents' television, and neon-colored snack food wrappers peek out from under the pillows (both of which are a problem for another reason, as we'll soon see).

Reasonable people can disagree on whether kids should use their parents' bedroom as a hangout area. I strongly vote "no." I grew up with six siblings in a home where space was tight. We certainly would have enjoyed adding our parents' bedroom to our roaming-around territory, but we knew that it was off-limits to us.

MAKE YOUR BED—IT'S IMPORTANT!

I often say that old wisdom is good wisdom. If your mother reminded you to make your bed, it was for a good reason. Whether you sleep alone or with someone else, making your bed is the first step in an uncluttered day.

- Making your bed is a way to honor the place that holds you safe, warm, and protected overnight.

- When it's the first thing you do in the morning, making your bed is a statement that you're going to go through your day in a thoughtful, deliberate manner.

- If your bedroom, and especially your bed, is a reflection of the relationship you share with the other person in the bed, then straightening the sheets and comforter shows that you're respecting the relationship by taking care of the little details.

- When it's time to go to bed again, pulling back the sheets and sliding into this well-kept cocoon is your sign that your brain can now rest.

No matter the size of your home, I urge you to set aside your bedroom as a special place for the one or two adults who are in charge of your household. This sends a strong and unmistakable message to your children: The master bedroom is a special place for parents. It's a space that needs to be respected, since it is not like the other rooms in the house. It's a room with a purpose and mystique like no other. This is a positive message to send to your children. Your relationship is special, and everyone in the family can honor it by establishing a place for it!

Create other bedrooms, playrooms, and family areas that meet your kids' needs for connection, learning, and entertainment. Let them know they're welcome to have the run of the rest of the house. Be firm when you say that their toys, books, gadgets, and other clutter must stay in these areas—and not in your room. Sorting through your thoughts, maintaining a relationship with your partner, and recuperating from the challenges of a grown-up life all require a room that's calm and free of distractions. Demand nothing less.

You must also demand of yourself that you're going to keep your room free of *grown-up* toys and distractions. These disturb the other vital use of your bedroom.

Permissible Use for Your Bedroom #2: Rest and Sleep

In 2013, the National Association of Home Builders reported a survey finding that seems both obvious and surprising: "The only type of room . . . present in the typical new home 100 percent of the time is a master bedroom." This is a room important enough to put in *every single new home* and the vast majority of older homes, as well. So why are people spending so little time actually sleeping in them?

A 2013 Gallup poll found that American adults sleep an average of 6.8 hours per night, which is less than the 7 to 9 hours that health experts recommend. The number of those who sleep 6 hours or less nightly—40 percent—hasn't changed much in the past 25 years. The Centers for Disease Control and Prevention calls our national sleep deprivation a "public health epidemic." It has found that many adults have trouble concentrating or remembering things because they're sleepy.

Maintaining a healthy weight and a clean household requires that you remain awake and aware during the day. Your mind needs to be focused on what you're eating, what you're buying, and how you're hanging on to stuff. If you can't think straight due to fatigue, you're not going to make your best choices.

Poor sleep has also been linked to the following:

Obesity. Lack of sleep may increase your appetite and thus the likelihood that you'll eat. Research has found that when you're sleep-deprived, levels of a hormone called ghrelin tend to go up. This hormone increases your appetite.

In a small German study, nine men spent three nights in a sleep lab, with at least 2 weeks between each overnight visit. One night they slept for 7 hours, one night they slept for 4½ hours, and one night they didn't sleep at all. (On their sleepless nights, they stayed up reading and watching movies in a well-lit room.) Just one night of shorter sleep led to more feelings of hunger and higher ghrelin levels. Both were especially pronounced after the completely sleepless night. In the long run, the researchers noted, these changes "may result in weight gain and obesity."

Depression and anxiety. Insufficient sleep can also make you more likely to become depressed or anxious (the inverse is true, too—if you're depressed or anxious, you may have more trouble falling asleep). A study that followed more than 9,600 young Australian women found that those who often had sleeping problems at the beginning of the study were more than four times more likely to have depression 9 years later. They were also nearly three times more likely to have anxiety!

Chronic health problems. Poor sleep can raise your risk of a variety of health issues that would definitely act as a type of burdensome clutter in your life. These include diabetes, high blood pressure, and cancer. Obesity related to the sleep loss doesn't always explain the appearance of these diseases, by the way.

In addition, getting too little sleep may raise your risk of Alzheimer's disease. A study that put 70 adults into a high-tech scanner found that those who slept less had higher levels of a substance called beta-amyloid in their brains. This stuff is composed of bits of sticky protein that collect into clumps called "plaques." These plaques—which you could call a kind of clutter that doesn't belong in the brain—are more common in people with Alzheimer's.

Getting good sleep isn't one of those general niceties that's good for you, that you can take or leave without harm. Sleep maintains a lot of important chemical processes in your brain and your body. You need it to sustain a strong, fit figure and a smoothly operating mind, which are two of the main goals of the *Cut the Clutter, Drop the Pounds* program.

So *please* use this week to fix any problems in your bedroom that are keeping you from getting the sleep you require.

Sleeping with the Enemy?

If you're reading this book, then you're likely struggling with your weight, your sense of serenity, and the state of your home. I'd wager that poor sleep is playing some role in all of these issues—and that better sleep would help relieve you of these burdens.

That's why in the coming week, I want you to remove any of the obstacles in your bedroom that are preventing you from creating a restful, relaxing, and nurturing space. (While you're at it, remove anything that hinders your romantic relationship with your partner.) A good place to start is with electronics.

In its 2014 survey, the National Sleep Foundation found that parents' and kids' bedrooms are brimming with light- and noise-making electronic devices (see "Electronics in Adults' Bedrooms"). In many of these bedrooms, these devices sometimes stay "awake" after the humans go to sleep, ranging from 10 percent of parents' computers to 34 percent of televisions. Even more alarm-

▶ ELECTRONICS IN ADULTS' BEDROOMS

- 62 percent have a television
- 45 percent have a tablet or smart-phone
- 26 percent have a computer
- 13 percent have video games

Source: National Sleep Foundation

ing—more than one-quarter of adults in the survey said that in the previous week they'd gotten up to read or send a text or e-mail after they'd already gone to sleep!

Electronics can blatantly distract you from going to sleep or staying asleep. But the specific type of light they produce can have an even sneakier effect on your sleep.

Your eyes don't just allow you to read, look at your kids, and keep your car on the road. They also serve as sensors that affect your cycle of sleepiness and alertness, without you even knowing it. During the evening and night, when artificial light hits the retinas that line the inside of your eyes, it prevents nerve cells in your brain that encourage sleep from doing their job. At the same time, it stimulates cells in your brain that keep you awake. This light also puts the brakes on your natural flow of melatonin. Normally, your melatonin levels rise in the evening. This hormone, made by a structure in your brain, helps you feel sleepier as bedtime approaches. The sum effect of all those brain changes is that you feel more awake later into the night.

Many of today's entertainment devices, from TVs to tablets to smartphones, use LEDs to create light. Cells in your retinas that send wakefulness-related messages to your brain are especially sensitive to the light from LEDs. So when you're playing games on your smartphone or e-mailing co-workers at 11 p.m., you're also staring directly into a stoplight telling your brain DON'T GO TO SLEEP.

The National Sleep Foundation suggests that you darken your surroundings in the hours before you go to bed. Use low-wattage bulbs in your bedroom, and even turn your alarm clock away from your bed or block any light it makes. It also recommends that if you have trouble falling asleep or staying asleep, keep electronics out of your bedroom and stop using them at least an hour before bed.

I agree with these recommendations wholeheartedly. TVs, tablets, smartphones, and computers have no place in your bedroom. I understand if you feel some resistance to this idea, as it's quite possible that you've had a television in your bedroom for most of your life.

However, ask yourself this question: "Do these electronics help me obtain what I want *from* my bedroom, which is to focus on myself, connect with my partner, or sleep?"

You could argue that watching movies with your significant other is a pleasant way to spend time, but you can shift this to the living room. And if you're a doctor on call or your child is at a sleepover, I understand the need for a phone in your room. But otherwise it most likely can wait until morning—outside of the bedroom.

Along with your electronics, I strongly recommend that you find new homes for your:

Food. Remember: Whenever you eat, you should be aware of what you're eating. You're tasting your food, smelling it, and appreciating it. You're not driving your car, talking on the phone, or working.

If you're in bed, I don't think you're likely to be doing mindful eating. Odds are you're sleepy. You're also probably watching TV or goofing around on the Internet if you haven't yet barred your devices from the bedroom.

There's reason to believe that late-night calories aren't good for your waistline. After tracking 52 volunteers' sleep and diets for a week, researchers found that taking in calories after 8 p.m. is associated with a higher body mass index. They concluded that calorie consumption after this time may raise your risk of obesity.

Pets. I suspect that you may be horrified at the thought of turning your pet away from your bedroom. But this is *your* room, not your pet's. Does having your dog or cat in the bedroom help you sleep better? Does it bring you and your partner closer together? Perhaps you can make a case for it. But please give this some attention before you make your decision.

If your pet is keeping you awake by scratching, yipping, or staring in your face—or its presence is leading to arguments with your spouse—then consider finding a new sleeping arrangement for it.

Work. Almost 15 million Americans are self-employed, and many others with an outside job sometimes work at home. I understand the reasons why you'd have work materials in your bedroom, whether you run your own business or merely bring some work home from the office occasionally. Maybe your bedroom offers the only free space for a desk. Maybe you

▶ WEEK TWO TASKS

☐ Create your vision.

☐ Identify malignant items.

☐ Clean off your bed and the space underneath it.

☐ Clear bedside tables.

☐ Clear tops of dressers.

☐ Un-stuff your dresser.

☐ Clear the floor.

☐ Declutter the bedroom.

☐ Clean dust and cobwebs.

☐ Organize your linen area.

☐ Get rid of malignant items.

Plus

☐ Mindset adjustment

☐ Physical activities

feel most creative at night, and it's easier to keep your notebooks near your bed.

But you're simply not going to sleep as well if the last thing you see before you turn out the light is your pile of work papers. Thoughts of deadlines may keep you awake, and work-related problems may invade your dreams. Your occupational equipment is also bound to decrease your bedmate's contentment with the bedroom.

Your work supplies must go somewhere else in your home. If you don't have a corner in another room to set up a desk, perhaps you could work at your local coffee shop that offers free Wi-Fi. Or you may be able to find a small, inexpensive office space to set up shop near your home. (You may find these advertised online as "co-working spaces." Sharedesk.net is a site that may list workspaces in your area).

As you begin to tame your overstuffed bedroom, your first few steps will be similar to how you began with your kitchen and dining areas last week. The ultimate goal will be to create a quiet, protective oasis in the home for yourself or for connecting with your spouse or partner, and to start enjoying better sleep.

Please note that you don't need to tackle your clothes closet this week. The closet and your bathroom play a large role in how you see yourself. As a result, you'll un-stuff those areas together later in the program.

However, I do ask that you give attention this week to the closet, chest, or drawers that contain your bed linens.

Task 1:
DEVELOP A VISION FOR WHAT YOU WANT FROM YOUR BEDROOM

I've tasked you with creating a place for intimacy and sleep. But you'll still need to come up with a more specific vision for your bedroom. I love working on master bedrooms, and over the years I've found that some words surface again and again when talking about a vision for this space:

- Haven
- Kid-free
- Sanctuary
- Relaxing
- Romantic
- Sexy
- Getaway
- Resort-like
- Spa-like
- Retreat

Think about the words that reflect what you most want from this space. Also consider the specific flavors you might want within that larger goal.

Do you imagine a sparsely decorated, easy-to-clean room? Do you live in the city and need heavy blinds to block out lights and sounds at night? Do you live out in the country and enjoy letting the dawn sunlight gradually brighten your room before you wake?

Spend some time to decide on the "feel" you want in the room, in terms of its function and your emotional response to it.

MASTER BEDROOM VISION

This is what I want *from* my master bedroom: _____

_____

_____

_____

How I want to *feel* in this space:_____

_____

_____

_____

_____

Task 2:
IDENTIFY THE MALIGNANT ITEMS IN YOUR BEDROOM

Bedrooms can harbor quite a few malignant items that, up until a few pages ago, you may not have realized were so harmful to your emotional and physical health.

These are the objects in your bedroom that keep you awake at night. They spur arguments with your spouse. They create distractions in a room that should be peaceful to the eyes. Or they bring out strong emotions that disturb your sense of tranquility.

Look around your room and identify these objects. Tuck them into a storage space in your home (if you have room), get rid of them, or if you can't quite force yourself to relocate them yet, stack them in a corner of your bedroom for later.

Your bedroom might be harboring malignant objects such as:

▸ An excessive number of reminders of your or your spouse's earlier life (such as childhood photos with beloved relatives who are now departed)

▸ Exercise equipment, especially gear that you haven't used as often as you'd planned. This brings out feelings of failure in the very room where you want to feel content with yourself—not threatened with negative self-talk.

▸ Bedding or furniture you bought or used in a previous relationship. The memories that these items dredge up can distract you from your present moment. They're not likely to bring up happy thoughts for a spouse or partner who's aware of their significance, either!

▸ Other items that I already mentioned, such as work-related equipment (especially reminders of a failed business), food, electronics, and stuff that simply belongs elsewhere in the home

Task 3:
CLEAN OFF YOUR BED (AND UNDER IT, TOO)

If you share your bedroom, come to an agreement with your bedmate on the type of environment that your bed will provide. Should it hold lots of designer pillows and decorative bedding, or a much less elaborate setup? A heavy comforter or a light blanket? Be ready to compromise, and review the sidebar on page 285 on how to work together to reach an outcome that makes everyone happy.

Now summon up all the courage you have, put on gloves and a dust mask if you feel the need, and drag out everything that's under your bed. I think it's perfectly reasonable to store stuff under your bed, so long as you meet these four criteria:

1. You don't have enough storage space elsewhere in your home.

2. You truly need or want to keep these items (rather than just kicking clutter under the bed so you don't have to decide what to do with it).

3. These objects don't prevent you from keeping the area under your bed clean and dust-free.

▶ WHAT'S *THAT* DOING UNDER THERE?

I recently asked a group of Facebook followers to clean under their beds and report the weirdest item they found. If you clear out any discoveries like these, your bedroom will be a healthier and saner place to rest your head:

- Two cases of spaghetti sauce

- A scooter—in pretty wrapping paper—that the parent forgot to pull out and give to the child at Christmas

- Sleeping cats

- Husband's skateboards

- Ferrets and the household items they, well, ferret away

- 21-year-old wedding bouquet

- Elderly aunt's photo albums from her trip to Europe in the 1950s

- Multiple instances of pet vomit and feces

- A bottle containing rotten milk

- A mouse nest in a shoe

- Computer accessories that a wife didn't want her husband to know she'd bought

- An expensive set of kitchen knives that the owner felt guilty about buying, so she hid them

- A live frog

4. The objects don't disrupt the good vibes, the atmosphere, the feng shui, or whatever you want to call the psychological climate of your bedroom. This is the space where you spend about one-quarter to one-third of your day. This is where you are intimate with your spouse. If something weird or disgusting (see the box on the opposite page) or just inappropriate (a wedding dress from a previous marriage) is lurking under the bed, I strongly believe it's going to contaminate everything that goes on in your bedroom.

Haul out any objects that you no longer wish to store, and for the rest, consider organizing like items together into dust-proof, under-the-bed storage containers before you return them to their spot. This will make cleaning under your bed an easier task, and it keeps these items clean and fresh.

If an object you pull out is covered in dust, ask yourself whether you really need it. In general, if something has been unused for 12 months—and that dust is certainly evidence of this—you should let it go.

Periodically check back under your bed to see if you're ready to part with anything you've stashed under there.

Task 4:
CLEAR OFF YOUR BEDSIDE TABLES

The flat surfaces in your bedroom, like all those throughout your home, tend to attract dust, clutter, and unnecessary decorations. This chaos makes rooms *look* smaller and *feel* less peaceful. This is especially true in the bedroom.

Just before you turn out the light, the last thing you see shouldn't be a mess on the bedside table just inches from your face. For this task, clear off everything from your bedside tables. Only keep items that have a purpose for being on display in your bedroom. That includes:

▸ Lamps

▸ A book and a magazine that you're currently reading

▸ An alarm clock

▸ A small number of deliberately chosen mementos

Find a better place for your:

▸ Books and magazines you've already read or plan to read after the current one. If you have a collection of books that you intend to read, keep the to-be-read titles on a bookshelf in your home, not here.

▸ Keys

- ▸ Pocket change
- ▸ Jewelry
- ▸ Makeup
- ▸ Creams and lotions
- ▸ The day's receipts

Discard any items that you don't need or use, and give your bedside table a good dusting.

Task 5:
CLEAR OFF THE TOPS OF YOUR DRESSERS

This is another flat-surface task. Put away or get rid of the usual clutter like:

- ▸ Jewelry
- ▸ Cosmetics
- ▸ Phone and other communications devices
- ▸ Fragrances

Only keep out items that you use regularly and that you need to see. Consider using small plastic bins or decorative totes to store the other items. Put them where they can easily be accessed: a bedroom dresser or drawer, a shelf in your closet, or even in a bathroom cupboard close to where you dress. When you're finished decluttering, dust those flat surfaces.

Task 6:
CLEAR THE FLOOR

Your floor is the largest flat surface in your bedroom, and as such, it deserves plenty of attention (and *you* deserve to be able to vacuum it easily). Remove any items that don't fit your vision for the space, and put all items where they belong. That means:

- ▸ Clothes in the laundry hamper in the closet or other out-of-the-way spot
- ▸ Shoes in the shoe rack in the closet
- ▸ Paperwork in your office
- ▸ Food utensils in the kitchen

This is a great opportunity to identify permanent homes for the items that you usually just drop on the floor of your bedroom.

Task 7:
CLEAN OUT YOUR DRESSER

Your dresser is another "zone" in your bedroom. It should only contain clothes that you wear regularly. Decide how much of each type of clothing (socks, underwear, workout clothes, etc.) you'll store in your dresser.

Empty all your drawers and inspect each item of clothing. Discard anything with holes, worn-out waistbands, or stains. Get rid of stuff that doesn't fit. Toss socks without mates and garments you haven't worn in the past year.

If you have clothes with sentimental value that you don't plan on wearing again, decide whether you really need to keep them. If so, store them somewhere else so they're not taking up space for clothes you're actually using.

Sort everything neatly into its proper drawer. Each drawer should be easy to open and close. If it won't close, pull out your least-favorite items and get rid of them. Remember: A closed drawer is more important than 20 pairs of underwear you never wear!

Task 8:
DECLUTTER THE REST OF THE ROOM

Go through any zones I haven't mentioned yet, such as inside your bedside tables, trunks, and decorative tables (but not your clothes closet—you'll get to that later). Remember that bedside tables are not meant to be used primarily as storage. Begin by emptying everything onto your bed.

Be strict in deciding what should live in your bedside table. Things that were randomly dumped here sometime in the past have no place in your bedside table or in your bedroom. Say good-bye to old tissues, pieces of Lego, the takeout menu from your local pizzeria, foreign coins from your overseas vacation, movie tickets, the earring without a match, the pocketknife you got when you were 12, and the beaded whatever-that-thing-is that your child made at summer camp. It may sound silly, but I promise that a decluttered, clean, and well-organized bedside table will bring you joy you hadn't imagined!

Scour the remaining areas in your bedroom. Get rid of anything that doesn't support a simple, quiet, relaxing environment. Should every item support the two goals of your bedroom (togetherness and sleep)? Yes. Should every item fit the more specific vision you established for the room? Yes. Does everything in your room do so? Unlikely. If you do decide to keep them, should they go somewhere else? Certainly.

Task 9:
CLEAN DUST AND COBWEBS FROM THE ROOM

There is nothing like the feeling of clean, crisp sheets and a spotless bedroom. It makes you feel like you're checking into a relaxing resort every night. Think about stepping into a hotel or resort room for the first time: Just seeing a bit of clutter or dirt will greatly reduce the enjoyment you'll feel about staying there. Why expect less from your own home?

Now is the time to rotate or flip your mattress and give it an airing. Move your furniture and give the room a thorough dusting and vacuuming. You might even consider deep-cleaning your carpets with a rental unit available at many supermarkets and hardware stores. Consider rearranging the furniture so that you take maximum advantage of the space and natural light. You might even want to purchase new bed linens to really set the room off.

Wash your curtains, clean the rugs, dust the baseboards—and enjoy what a decluttered, spotless, welcoming haven feels like. Welcome to your new sanctuary!

Task 10:
CLEAR OUT UNWANTED LINENS

Even if you store your bedding in a non-bedroom location (such as your laundry room or a closet in your spare bedroom), it *is* bedroom-related, so now is a good time to sort through these items.

I recommend that you keep no more than two extra sets of bedding per bed. Perhaps you'll want one set of lightweight sheets for summer and a set of flannel sheets for winter. What you *don't* want is a jumble of mismatched sheets from half-discarded old sets, sheets with holes or embarrassing stains, or fitted sheets with stretched-out or torn elastic in the corners.

Sort through the pile of bedding and make separate piles of each complete set you own. Decide on the two you'll keep for each bed. Fold these neatly and slip each set into its matching pillowcase. You'll now have several pillowcases that each contain a full set of bedding, which is the foundation for a well-kept linen area.

Go through your blankets and comforters at this time. I also recommend that you keep no more than two of these per bed. Many people have a pile of blankets and homemade quilts that they received as gifts stashed away in their linen closet. Pull these out and evaluate whether they help you attain your vision for the room or whether they've become clutter.

If you truly wish to keep a blanket, then use it. If you have a giant stack of inherited quilts that your grandmother made, and you've kept them solely out of a sense of quilt guilt (yes, that is a thing!), go through the collection and pick out the one or two that are the best crafted or that best match the décor of your bedroom. Offer the rest to other family members, friends, or Goodwill—and take satisfaction in knowing that the fruits of grandma's time and skill are actually being appreciated, rather than hiding unseen in a dark closet.

Also, keep this in mind: Sheets and towels that are no longer usable are always welcomed at animal shelters for use as bedding for pets.

Task 11:
GET RID OF YOUR MALIGNANT ITEMS

If you piled up any items during your first task of the week that make you feel guilty or sad or nostalgic or angry, and you know they don't belong in the peaceful environment of your bedroom, it's time to do something with them.

This can be particularly hard with malignant clutter in the bedroom, as this stuff often represents your most intimate relationships, whether current or past. Take a moment to honor the importance of what you're doing when you move this stuff out of your bedroom. Think about the person you've become since you bought or received these items as gifts.

Throw them away and take note of whether you feel a little lightening of your spirit as they vanish. If someone else can use these items, give them away. Or sell them and use the proceeds to fund a day trip or a longer vacation.

Sleep easier tonight knowing they're out of your bedroom.

▶ **A SATISFIED TEST PANELIST SPEAKS:**

Kristen says: "One shocking discovery— The quilt I wanted on my bed (a wedding gift from my mother) had been in a dry-cleaning bag out of sight for nearly a year! I'm so happy it's back where it belongs."

Week Two
Mindset Adjustment

This week's mindset adjustment builds upon last week's exercise. For the past week, I invited you to simply spend 5 minutes a day quietly focusing on your breath and observing the thoughts that pop up in your mind. Experts recommend this activity as a primary way to develop greater mindfulness, which heightens your awareness of what's going on in your life.

This week, I ask you to become more mindful of the food you're about to eat by incorporating these steps into your day:

▶ Decide what you want your food to do *for* you. Do you want it to provide nourishment? Help you lose weight? Meet the criteria for a heart-healthy diet? Whenever you get the urge to eat or drink anything—and I mean *anything*, whether it's a beverage while you're refilling your car or a full meal— stop to assess whether the food or drink will help you meet your goal.

▶ Remember that just because your mind gets the impulse to eat something, you don't have to obey it.

▶ Really savor the flavor and aroma of the food you're eating. Consistently ask yourself whether you're still hungry or whether you truly need to eat more.

Week Two
Fitness Activities

Walking frequency: With your increased energy, build up to walking 3 days this week.

Duration: Take a 10-minute walk around your block, the neighborhood, the park, or on a treadmill if you have one. Walking in place while watching TV or listening to music works, as well. As you walk, plan out your decluttering strategy for the day (or the following day if you're exercising in the evening).

In addition, perform the following movements on 2 or 3 nonconsecutive days after your muscles are nice and warm from walking or decluttering.

Grab one or two duffel bags and fill them with bedding and items that you will either donate or give away. While holding the full duffel bag or bags, perform:

- 10 Sumo Squats (page 183)
- 10 Deadlifts (page 168)
- 10 Biceps Curls (page 163)
- 10 Shoulder Raises (page 176)

Put the bags down and perform:

- 10 to 15 Close-Grip Triceps Pushups (page 167) against your (cleared-off) dresser
- 10 to 15 Mountain Climbers (page 174)
- Marching in place for 5 minutes

You've definitely earned your rest over the course of this week, and you should now have a bedroom that provides it.

The Clutter Chronicles

Tiffany Rehrig-Schaeffer, 40

POUNDS LOST: 10.2

AMOUNT OF CLUTTER REMOVED: 10 to 15 bags

When it comes to taming her home's clutter and managing her weight, Tiffany tells a very common story.

"I've started so many times to try to get my house in order, and I'd do real well for a while and then the motivation would just go away. It was the same thing with, like, running a 5K. A couple of times I started it, and I just didn't follow through with it," she says.

"I thought this was a chance to combine the two things I've been unsuccessfully starting and stopping, so I could work on both at the same time."

Her biggest challenge was clearing out her four kids' clutter, both because of the sheer volume of it and the emotions she felt when she sorted through it. Getting rid of the excess wasn't always

Before

easy. Tiffany felt a connection to toys that her three daughters—ages 6 to 12—and her son had played with over the years. But she worked through her feelings, and the outgrown playthings went to the local charitable donation store.

"We get a lot of hand-me-downs, since I have a cousin who has a daughter and friends with daughters. Lots of the stuff is really nice, but in all truthfulness my kids could probably go a month without wearing the same clothes twice because of all the hand-me-downs we get.

"That contributed to a lot of our clutter upstairs. The clothing didn't fit into the closets or the drawers. Something that stuck with me through the whole program is that you have to find a place for everything. You have to determine how much your home will hold. Anything above and beyond that is excess that you don't need. I went to each closet and each space, and said, 'This is what will fit.'"

Tiffany also struggled with the feeling that, despite her efforts, she could be doing *more*.

"There were times when I got stressed and would think, 'I'm not where I should be.' Then I would use a mindfulness technique. I would sit and calm myself down. It wasn't something that I did every day, but I used it when I felt that stress creeping in."

Even weeks after the program finished, Tiffany was still making trips to the donation center. She wasn't finished decluttering, and that was okay. Unlike some of her earlier experiences, her motivation was still working for her.

"I'll admit that I would feel at times like I was not living up to my end of what I was supposed to be doing in the program. But if you do that, you can get into a downward spiral. You have to say, 'You know what? Tomorrow's a new day,' and just look at what you've accomplished so far!

"I think all of us set out with very good intentions and goals, but life just gets in your way sometimes. I didn't allow those times that I felt bad about what I *didn't* accomplish to overshadow what I *did* accomplish."

Chapter 11

WEEK THREE: YOUR BEDROOM CLOSET AND YOUR BATHROOM

s we stood side by side, staring into the closet, I knew we were about to have an emotionally charged conversation.

The closet told me a few things about the lady of the house: She was much larger than she used to be, which she wasn't happy about. And the request I was preparing to make would force her to give up a daydream that was giving her temporary comfort.

Oh, and a camera crew standing by would capture the following moments for a TV show. (Your activities this week might not be easy, but at least you have some privacy while you do them!)

The Hidden Truths about Your Closet

Whenever someone asks me to declutter a home, I know with 100 percent certainty that at some stage in the process, I'll be sorting through an excess of clothes and clothing accessories. For some reason, clothing is at the top of the list of items that we buy in excessive amounts, hold on to for far too long, and invest more of ourselves into than we reasonably should.

It's no wonder that "the closet" has come to be a euphemism for the place where people hide their secret selves. Many people do the same thing with their actual closets, hiding many different versions of themselves that they would like to present to the world.

The clothes we own are more than just fabric that covers our bodies. Instead, our clothes:

▸ Send a very clear message of who we believe ourselves to be

▸ Provide the very first impression that we give to others

▸ Convey a great deal of our feeling about style and fashion

The old saying is that "clothes make the man" (or woman). It's probably even truer that the closets holding our clothes tell the tale of who we truly are.

Based on what I've found while digging through strangers' closets, I suspect that you have two kinds of clothes in yours.

Clothing you wear frequently, portraying who you are now. These are the clothes that are more or less the correct size for your present body shape. They're generally age-appropriate, and they reflect your occupation and your current interests.

The clothes that actually fit you are usually not props for an unrealistic version of yourself that doesn't exist, nor are they usually items that recall sad times or evoke bad memories. In general, these are not the clothes that are going to take a lot of your time this week . . . so long as you actually wear them.

However, most of us regularly wear only 20 percent of the clothing in our closets. The rest hangs unworn, gathering dust and taking up space. If your closet is bursting with clothing that might fit you but you never wear, then this is the week to address it.

That said, it's the *next* category that may require even more of your focus.

Clothes that represent the way you wish you were. Some of these items are clothes that have specific memories, dreams, or wishes attached to them. It's the fraternity T-shirt. Your favorite jeans from when you were 20 pounds lighter. The running clothes you wore in your marathon phase 10 years ago. They're symbols of unique times in your life that still exert a hold on you.

These memories aren't tucked back in a special place where you have to go out of your way to access them, like your photo album or your college alumni newsletter. They're hanging in your closet, right next to the clothes you rummage through every day. Every time you get dressed, you can't help but see these clothes, and then you experience a flood of memories that distract you from the present moment and may even sour your mood for the day.

Other types of clothes can be even more disruptive to the mindful, authentic life that I hope you start creating during this program. These are the too-small clothes that you can't currently wear but that you hope will fit you on some wonderful future day.

I'm not talking about clothing that's a single size smaller than what you currently wear. I mean those clothes that you haven't fit into for years and—if you were honest with yourself—you'd admit you're never going to fit into again. (Even if you could wear them, they're probably out of style now!) These clothes serve no purpose other than to mock you; to reinforce the idea that you cannot succeed at weight loss; and to drain you of motivation and the necessary enthusiasm for change.

Being physically and emotionally healthy, with a streamlined and organized home around you, requires that you remain grounded in reality and aware of the present moment. Many of the tasks that I'm asking you to do can hold you secure in this kind of life.

But if you have a closet full of "wish clothes," these pose a real and ongoing threat to the mindful, authentic life that you could attain. I have seen the debilitating effect that these garments can have on a person's spirit.

If you have to face these clothes every day, when you should be excited by the choices in your closet and pleased to be picking out the outfit you're going to wear, you're likely to:

▸ Get sidetracked by memories

▸ Become lost in a daydream in which you're finally wearing that cute blouse that hasn't fit you since the day you bought it. Everyone's complimenting you! The guy behind the counter can't even focus on making your coffee because he's too busy checking you out!

▸ Rake yourself over the coals for not losing the weight that's keeping you from fitting into all of those jeans. You've barely woken up this morning and you're already unhappy with yourself.

While taping that TV show I mentioned earlier, I could clearly see that this woman's closet held an abundance of these hurtful wish clothes. To demonstrate my point, I asked her to join me in pulling all the clothes out of her closet and arranging them by size.

When we were finished, the piles covered the spectrum of sizes from 6 to 20. My client in this decluttering task was a size 18—she kept some larger clothes to accommodate weight fluctuations—but her clothing could easily have accommodated 20 women with all sorts of shapes.

▶ ARE YOU BUYING THIS MYTH?

People often feel that having more clothes in their closet makes getting dressed easier. That might sound reasonable, but it's not true.

In many overstuffed closets, a large portion of the clothes don't fit. If you're in a hurry in the morning and have to try on five garments that are too small, your fruitless quest reminds you that you haven't gotten around to addressing your weight. Rather than help you, your closet has insulted you and wasted your time.

An overabundance of clothes that actually fit can raise your stress levels, too. Spinning your wheels as you pick through clothes that you no longer enjoy, that looked better in the store than when you brought them home, or that resemble other items you like better is not a good use of your precious time.

Instead, stock your closet with fewer clothes of higher quality. Only buy clothes that you love and keep them only as long as you love them.

Every single time I help people turn their closets into a space that helps them efficiently and easily show their best self to the world, we can both feel their stress rapidly dissipate.

Let's be honest. Clothing and weight are two taboo subjects with women—and often men—who are heavier than they wish to be. There is simply no easy way to navigate these waters. If you've seen me at work on TV, you know that my style is not to embarrass or humiliate the people I work with . . . but it's also not my style to sugarcoat the obvious. I believe that people welcome direct talk, even if it stings.

My words came without emotion or judgment as I honestly told her, "Look, you're going to have to accept this fact. You're over 40 and have been your current size for more than 15 years. In your heart, do you see yourself ever being a size 6 again?"

I wasn't trying to hurt her feelings. Or give her the idea that she would never lose weight.

I merely wanted her to reframe how she was thinking about her weight, her clothing, and her life. It was time to wake up to a few realizations: She could be beautiful and happy and more physically fit in ways that were true to where she was in the current moment. She very well could lose weight. People do it every day. I'm hoping *you're* doing it today. But the goal of fitting into those clothes was not going to motivate her to make it happen. In fact, those size 6 clothes were making her feel worse about herself rather than inspired.

I have seen this many times: People set a totally unrealistic "goal," in this case, hoping to drop from a size 18 to a size 6 without a plan to make it happen. When they don't make significant progress toward that goal, they reinforce the idea that they're a failure. And those size 6 clothes that they see every day (or in the case of guys, let's say size 32 jeans) ram that feeling home!

Your closet should be a place for clothes that you love and wear, for garments that emphasize the best parts of who you are right now. It should *not* be:

▸ A souvenir collection

▸ A dieting reminder that hounds you to lose weight (this doesn't work!)

▸ A storage area for non-clothes-related odds and ends

This week, I want you to return your closet to its rightful role in your home. Turn it into a space that you enjoy stepping into, which helps you quickly and efficiently get ready in the morning. Create a clothing collection that sends you out into the world feeling confident and self-assured.

After you clean your closet, your other assignment for the week is to tame the other room in your home that should reflect who you really are but too often sabotages your self-image.

▸ USE THE POWER OF LAUGHTER TO LET GO

A little humor is a great way to cope with the attachment we have to our stuff.

The stuff we own has power over us—the power to make us sad, the power to remind us of wasted money or opportunity, the power to replay the dream that we never followed.

How do you take power away from the forces that want to control your life? Laugh at them! Can't let go of your high school cheerleader outfit 25 years later? Smile at your silliness. Is it impossible to part with any of the 150 rolls of paper towels you have? Picture yourself covering several tennis courts with your paper towels (which you could do), then giggle about it.

Do you absolutely have to hold on to a pair of skinny jeans that you can barely get one leg into? Imagine what you'd look like if you actually squeezed yourself into them and have a deep laugh! We're all a little crazy when it comes to our stuff. Own it. Laugh about it. Let it go!

There's a Problem in the Bathroom

The bathroom is not just the place where you clean yourself and prepare for the day. It's also where you change from who you are to who you *want* to be. It's where you conceal the faults you perceive in your appearance and look for new ones that have escaped your notice.

In many homes, the bathroom is also the showcase for the vast range of ingenious products from our planet's cosmetics, hygiene, and pharmaceutical companies (and the marketers who work for them).

Is your skin dry? Do you have gray hair? Acne? Zits? Worry lines? Age spots? Crow's-feet? Laugh lines? Does your lipstick wear off too fast or not sparkle enough? Have you had coffee stains on your teeth for too long? What other appearance problems can you find? Your nearest pharmacy, supermarket, or department store is almost guaranteed to offer not just one possible solution for each of them, but many. Television, magazines, and billboards assure us there's a lotion, potion, powder, cream, or gel for every blemish, wrinkle, crease, or spot you can possibly find (and a few you haven't yet!).

By next year, or even next month, you can add to your collection new and improved options that promise to work even better!

If you're unhappy with how you look, I'd be willing to bet that I would know it simply by peering in your bathroom, just as I found insight into my size-6-through-20 acquaintance from her closet.

That's because much of the stuff you keep on your bathroom's shelves and counters has the same purpose as many of the clothes in your closet. You buy these products not just because you want to cover up a blemish. At some level, you want to be like the people in the commercial or on the package: smiling, attractive, and without cares. You want your life to be just a tiny bit happier or easier, and this product offers that promise, even if it doesn't fulfill it.

You may feel that somehow merely having the right products on your counter—like keeping smaller clothes in your closet—will magically transport you to this new life. Because the bathroom is such a private place, where you can have some expectation of not being disturbed, it's easy to get caught up in a make-believe world when you're in here.

But look around your bathroom and ask yourself how well your cosmetics and hair treatments and hygiene products actually deliver on their promises. Have the products provided a good return on the financial and emotional

▶ WEEK THREE TASKS

- ☐ Create your vision.
- ☐ Collect malignant items.
- ☐ Clean out your closet.
- ☐ Clean out your bathroom's medicine cabinet.
- ☐ Clear off flat bathroom surfaces.
- ☐ Clear out your under-sink area, other cabinets, and drawers in your bathroom.

- ☐ Bring in organizational tools.
- ☐ Get rid of malignant items.

Plus

- ☐ Mindset adjustment
- ☐ Physical activities

investment that you've made in them? How many of these products altered your life in any meaningful way? How many provided true happiness?

My guess is that few, if any, did. Aside from a core group of personal care products and basic cosmetics, you could probably toss out most of the items in your bathroom and your life would go on unchanged.

This week, take a better look at yourself than the view your mirror provides. Look deeper. I'd like you to develop a realistic plan for how you portray yourself when you leave your house. Could you be happier if you accepted more of the details of your appearance that you try to hide? Are you trying to look like yourself or the people in the commercials? Are you content to look your age, or are you desperately trying to reverse time while you're in the bathroom with the door closed?

A sense of mindfulness goes a long way in helping you answer these questions. During the first week of this program, I asked you to start paying attention to the constant stream of messages and images that your mind is sending you. In the second week, I offered suggestions for how to use mindfulness to gain insight into what you eat and why you eat it.

The same strategies—observing the way you talk to yourself, identifying why you choose one option over the other, and pausing before you make a purchase—will help you create a closet and bathroom where you can work with the appearance that you have, instead of chasing an image you'll never attain.

Task 1:
DEVELOP A VISION FOR YOURSELF

In the previous weeks, I asked you to start with a vision for specific rooms. We're going to start this week a little differently. I want you instead to create a vision for how you want to look, from your clothes to your face to your hair. Starting at this point will help you to decide more easily how your closet and your bathroom will support these goals.

So, when it comes to how you want to look, do you want to appear vigorous and energetic? Fashionable? Professional? Virile? Self-assured? Sophisticated? Do you prefer a more casual disheveled look, or would you rather pattern yourself on the models in the monthly glamour magazines?

While you're doing this, I recommend that your vision achieve these three As. Be sure that your goals are:

Age-appropriate. No one should have to put effort into presenting themselves like they're in their twenties! You're either actually in your twenties and you naturally look like it, or you're older and you should use your true age as your starting point. You can find examples of men and women who look terrific in every decade of life. You can look confident, modern, sexy, and *alive* at any age.

You don't have to maintain the hair color you had when you felt that you were at your peak attractiveness. Your arms and chest don't have to fill out your T-shirt like they did when you were on the football team. After a certain age, if that's your vision, you're going to make yourself miserable trying to attain it—and you'll probably come up short anyway. Instead, create a vision that builds on what you have to offer right now and capitalizes on your best attributes, at whatever age you actually are.

Authentic. Avoid trying to put together an image that's not true to who you are. Your efforts are going to come at a cost to your bank account or your happiness if you have to:

▸ Spend money you don't have in order to look wealthier than you really are

▸ Dress a certain way to try to connect with a crowd where you still aren't going to fit in

▸ Suck in your belly to fit into your clothes

Honesty, integrity, and authenticity are hugely attractive traits in any person.

Attainable. Whatever look you're going for, you shouldn't have to do a lot of work to obtain it. Your natural gifts should take you most of the way to your vision, then the right clothes and products can carry you that last little bit.

Once you establish your vision, everything in your closet and bathroom should support it. Any items that don't help you should not stay.

Task 2:
IDENTIFY YOUR MALIGNANT ITEMS

You probably have a lot of malignant clutter tucked away in these areas, but it may be hard to recognize. It could include:

▶ Clothing that represents an unhappy time in your life or a good time that ended badly (such as clothes that remind you of a past relationship, or something you bought out of anger or spite)

▶ Items in your closet that you just haven't had the energy or willpower to deal with—particularly items that might have belonged to someone else or that you've inherited and are now holding on to out of a sense of guilt

▸ Miracle cures that wasted your money. If you bought a serum "proven" to reduce dark circles under your eyes but it didn't work, you're going to feel aggravated about the wasted expense every time you look at the bottle. You may feel that your dark circles must be especially severe if this stuff works for everyone but you. But ultimately, you're going to be reminded: "I still have these damned dark circles under my eyes!"

Gather all your malignant items into a big box and set them in the corner of your bedroom. Since you cleaned so well in here last week, the box should stand out like an ugly troll that you chased out of your closet and bathroom cabinet. If you're not yet ready to part with these items, you don't have to do so today.

Task 3:
CLEAN YOUR CLOSET

It may not be the biggest area in your home size-wise, but the density of stuff in your closet can make it a surprisingly time-consuming place to declutter. (I have a picture of me climbing into a client's closet by wedging myself through a small space at the top of the door. Going through the mountain of clutter underneath me was, unsurprisingly, a big job.)

So I'm going to break up this task into smaller steps. You may want to tackle these steps back-to-back or take a break in between.

Step 1: Do the quick and easy pass. Grab a trash bag, take a deep breath, and bravely step—or climb—into your closet.

Start at one end of your hanging items and quickly move down the rack, throwing everything that you know you don't want to wear into the trash bag.

▸ SOMETIMES YOU JUST NEED A HAND

If you're stuck making a decision, call for help. Invite a close friend or friends you know well, who have opinions you trust. Open a bottle of good wine, or sparkling water if that's your preference, and ask for feedback on what looks good and what doesn't. Stage a fashion show if nec-essary. Honest opinions, a few laughs, and the realization that you've made some not-so-fashion-forward choices will go a long way toward deciding which clothes make you look great and which would look better on a mannequin at your local Goodwill.

▶ WHAT HAPPENS IF I THROW SOMETHING AWAY, AND THEN I NEED IT?

Often someone will tell me, "Hey, Peter, I threw away that cruddy old umbrella, and a week later it rained and I got wet! Why did you make me think I should throw that umbrella away?"

I get this a lot. Here's my answer.

You will without a doubt discard one item or another that you later discover you need. It's just the way of the universe and it should never be an excuse to not let go of anything. Often people will use this fear to justify not throwing or giving anything away. I'd rather that you need to repurchase one item than use this fear as an excuse to keep 1,000 other pieces of clutter.

Yes, you might get invited to an '80s theme party next week and realize you just got rid of the perfect 30-year-old shirt. That's a small price to pay for the stress-free closet you've created.

Just start moving, without overthinking. Throw any empty clothes hangers on the floor to be collected later. Move quickly and be decisive. If you're not sure, leave the item hanging and keep going. This first step is about speed and showing your closet who's boss.

At the end of the exercise, take the trash bag(s) straight to the trunk of your car. Drop them at a donation center on your next trip out of the house. Repeat this exercise on a number of successive days, each time being a little more critical and paring your hanging clothes down a little further. Arrange like items together as you open more space so that you can decide which duplicates are unnecessary and can go.

I firmly believe that you should only have three types of clothes in your closet.

Clothes that fit you now. You can make some allowances for items that are *close* to fitting you, especially since you're currently involved in a weight loss effort that could put you into these clothes in the near future. But if they're more than two sizes too small, get rid of them. If you have any clothing that's significantly too large, just in case your weight ever gets away from you, get rid of it, too. Believe in yourself. Why make it easier to gain weight? Commit to the change that you want for yourself and mold the spaces around you to support those goals.

If you wind up losing 30 pounds and need to replace a bunch of clothes you tossed out, so be it. I can almost *hear* a protest forming in your mind right now, so I went ahead and addressed it in the box above.

▶ TIME REPEATS ITSELF

We all have a tendency to buy clothes of a recurring type. For women it's often a cute black dress, and for men it's often light-blue button-down shirts with a subtle pattern.

I remember working with one woman to declutter her closet, where there was no order in the space and no logic to where things were hung or stored. Once we pulled everything out of the closet to arrange like items together, we discovered 23 black cashmere cardigans. TWENTY-THREE!

She sheepishly told me that her mother had commented that a black cardigan is indispensable in every woman's wardrobe. Since she could never find one in her closet, she simply bought another whenever she saw one in a department store.

Don't laugh—we all do it! Check how many dresses, shirts, or T-shirts you have that look exactly the same, and next time you're tempted to buy another of that style, smile knowingly and walk away.

There is always a tension between what you have today and what you might need tomorrow—and changing this balance requires making a best guess. Make a reasonable decision about the clothes that should stay, focusing on those items that fit you now. When you get to the desired weight you're aiming for, if you have to invest in some new clothing, make that a gift to yourself. (Do you really want your reward for weight loss to be a bunch of old, perhaps dated-looking clothing anyway?) For now, commit to today and let all those wrong-size clothes go.

Clothes you feel great in. Maybe it's a comfortable pair of jeans. Maybe it's the top that magically accentuates your waist like no other blouse can do. Maybe it's the suit that makes you feel 3 inches taller.

When you establish your vision for how you want to look, these are likely the kinds of clothes that make your vision real. Keep these clothes. Give them a place of honor in your closet where you'll see them and want to wear them again and again.

Clothes that bring you compliments when you wear them. I'm not encouraging you to seek all your validation from other people. But it certainly feels great when we're complimented on our clothing choices.

So keep the clothes that get positive attention (making sure to stay age-appropriate and authentic to who you are). Since we so often speak more harshly to ourselves than the people around us do, this kind of good feedback may distract you away from negative self-talk: "Wait a minute—I'm not unfashionable. Someone just asked me the other day where I got this jacket!"

Step 2: Do another quick and easy pass. Grab another trash bag. Just as you did with the hanging items, move through your closet to discard items on shelves or in drawers that you can quickly and easily decide have no place in your home. Make a second pass if you're feeling empowered.

▶ THE CLOTHES THAT *DON'T* BELONG

So those are the three categories of clothes that I recommend you keep. You should strongly consider getting rid of everything else, especially:

- **Clothes with tags.** I often see unworn clothes in people's closets with the tags still hanging from them. Maybe you only bought them because they were a bargain. Maybe they looked great in the dressing room but not so appealing in your bedroom mirror. I can guarantee that if the price was the best thing about an article of clothing that you bought, then it doesn't deserve to be in your closet. If you've had ample chances to wear these clothes but didn't, today's the day to toss them.

- **Mementos.** You may have had a great time on your company softball team. Maybe you take pride that you put yourself through college working as a magician. But if you're only keeping your softball uniform or your top hat around for the memories, they don't need to be in your closet. Consider parting with them. After all, you will still have the memory even if the object is gone. Or, if a keepsake is so important to you, find a special place of honor in your home to display it. (I'm guessing you'll suddenly realize it's not so important after all.)

- **Collectibles.** If you have 100 commemorative baseball caps in your closet, that's at least 95 too many! If they're important enough to keep, they're important enough to not hide. Pick out a few—I'd say no more than five—that represent your favorites or that best display the essence of why you wanted to start this collection. Set them out on a shelf or cabinet so you can enjoy them. Lose the rest. It's quite possible you'll be doing a lot more of this in Week 6, so parting with this stuff now will give you more practice.

The more you practice this exercise, the better you'll be able to quickly judge what stays and what goes.

Revel in the increased open space in your closet. It's already starting to breathe just a little more easily!

Step 3: Move through your closet and place every item of the same kind on your bed. That includes sweaters, T-shirts, dress shirts, dresses, blouses, and jeans. Discard any items that no longer fit you, that are torn or stained, or that you don't wear. These should already be pared down from Steps 1 and 2, but this gives you another way to see the clothing that doesn't belong in your closet. Place duplicates together so that you see what you're prone to buying repeatedly.

Identify the space where you're going to put each group of like items and assess how many clothing items will reasonably fit there. Your space now determines how many you can keep.

Step 4: Clean out everything that's not clothes. I often see closets filled with tennis rackets, books, unwanted gifts, toys, paperwork, and all manner of stuff that wouldn't fit under the bed.

Grab another trash bag. If you find anything that doesn't help you present yourself to the world, it needs to go somewhere else or you need to get rid of it.

Step 5: Shoo away your extra shoes. The record for the largest number of pairs of shoes I've found in one house is . . . 3,500. And no, this wasn't Mariah Carey's huge collection!

Perhaps you might respond like some women who looked at me with a mischievous grin and asked, "So what's the problem?"

Shoes can be hard to part with, but you're on a roll and they're next up.

First, grab any shoes that are covered in dust—signifying that you haven't worn them in many months—and any others that don't fit you or that you don't wear. Put them immediately into a trash bag and into the trunk of your car.

Next, collect all the remaining footwear in an open space in your bedroom. Put like shoes (boots, pumps, sneakers, flip-flops, etc.) together and line them up in pairs. Check the space you are assigning to shoes in your closet and

▶ CLEAR STACKS FROM THE BOTTOM UP

If you keep any clothes in stacks in your closet, odds are good that you can get rid of the bottom one-third of any stack without noticing the difference. Dig down to the bottom of these stacks and part with the items that you just don't wear.

tally the number of pairs that will reasonably fit there. Now move down your line of shoes and make the tough decisions you know you must make!

Remember one of our golden rules: You only have the space you have. If stuff won't fit, it's not because you don't have enough space. It's because you have too much stuff. Cull the shoes so they fit into the space you've assigned to them.

That said, if you're lucky enough to have extra space high on your closet shelves, in a spare bedroom, or in your basement, you might consider storing shoes that you don't wear frequently—like snow boots or super-dressy heels—in one of these locations.

Task 4:
GIVE YOUR MEDICINE CABINET A NEW FACE

You'll now shift your attention to your bathroom. Empty out your medicine cabinet. Place all items on the bathroom counter and group like items together. Toss out items that are outdated or no longer useful. That includes old beauty products, expired prescription or over-the-counter medications, and quick-fix products that didn't give you the results you wanted. If you haven't used a product in 12 months, pitch it.

Decide on the types of products you'll keep in your medicine cabinet and establish areas where each type will go. Set clear limits for how much you'll keep. Only purchase new items in quantities that will fit within their allotted space. As you buy new products, try to find items that can multitask, such as a lotion you can use on your face and body.

Remember to keep items that you use regularly—like toothbrushes and razors—on the most accessible shelf so you can quickly and easily get to them.

▶ PRODUCTS CAN AGE QUICKLY

Cosmetics have a relatively short useful life span. If you keep them stashed away for too long, they can actually be harmful. The closer to your eyes the product goes, the shorter its shelf life. Throw out any products that you've had for longer than these time limits.

Mascara: 3 months

Liquid eyeliner and eye shadow: 3 to 6 months

Compact powder: 8 months

Creams and lotions: About a year

Perfume: 3 years

Consider keeping your medications somewhere outside your bathroom. Despite the name, your bathroom's medicine cabinet is actually a poor choice for these products. The heat and steam in the room can cause them to break down, lose their potency, or go bad more quickly. A better choice may be a high cabinet in your kitchen that's out of children's reach and away from your sink and stove.

Now is also a good time to reconsider your beauty routine and makeup choices. If you discover that you have more makeup or beauty products than you will ever need, or that you have overstocked on items that you thought you would use, consider adopting a simpler style that requires less effort, stress, and daily product usage.

Task 5:
CLEAN OFF ALL HORIZONTAL SURFACES

Every horizontal space in your home is prone to collecting clutter. But the accumulation in the bathroom tends to be acute, given the small size of the room and the high number of small objects it contains.

In your bathroom, this clutter can prevent you from cleaning up the splashes and puddles that also gather on flat surfaces here. This, in turn, promotes mold and mildew. Again, a basic rule of organizing: Flat surfaces are *not* storage areas! Clear off everything but the basic essentials from your sink area and countertops, such as a soap dispenser or bar of soap in a dish. Everything else needs a better home to ensure that the space stays clean, open, and uncluttered.

Keep the top of your toilet tank cleared off, too. This isn't a storage area, either. Items on this flat surface are likely to fall into the toilet. If you have to go after them, it's gross. If the plumber has to go after them, it's expensive. Also keep the floor of your shower or sides of your tub free of containers, razors, and stray objects. These are a safety hazard and they make cleaning more difficult.

If you have a child in the home, it's okay to have a few toys in the tub. But keep it to a half dozen or fewer.

Task 6:
CLEAN CABINETS, DRAWERS, AND UNDER THE SINK

It's amazing how much can accumulate under a sink in a normal-size bathroom. Take a deep breath and start making this space work for you. First, pull everything out from under the sink and also from your drawers and cabinets. As you do so, throw away anything that's out of date, ignored, or just plain nasty! Arrange like items together and, after you've wiped out the drawers, cabinets, and under-sink area, make a decision about what will now reside there.

Make sure that the items you use most frequently are placed closest to you in the easiest-to-access drawer or cabinet. Again, decide how much space you'll allow for each type of item (such as cleaning products, bars of soap, rolls of toilet paper) and move out anything that exceeds your limits.

Space is generally limited in any bathroom. Make wise choices so that this room is now a pleasant and useful place that helps you get ready for your day and, later, settle in before you go to sleep.

Task 7:
BRING IN ORGANIZATIONAL TOOLS

A simple but effective strategy, in your bathroom and throughout your home, is to always keep like items together. This approach makes it easy to find anything you're looking for, saves you money by avoiding repurchasing items you already have, and helps ensure that every space stays uncluttered and organized.

Consider buying small plastic storage containers, caddies, or sectioned trays to hold:

▸ Products for your lips

▸ Products for your skin

▸ Products for your hair

▸ Gadgets for holding your hair, such as barrettes and scrunchies

▸ First-aid supplies

Create new storage spaces in areas that are going unused. For example, your bathroom is filled with empty vertical spaces that could hold items. Consider:

▸ A clip with a magnet to hold your tweezers on the corner of your mirror or on the inside of your medicine cabinet door

▸ A caddy that hangs from your showerhead to hold bathing products

▸ Shelves on a wall with open space

▸ Racks that hang on the inside of your cabinet doors

Task 8:
GET RID OF ALL YOUR MALIGNANT ITEMS

Go back and take one last look at the malignant objects you pulled out of your closet and bathroom earlier in the week. Sell them, share them, or donate them. Enjoy the freedom you feel without them under your roof.

Week Three
Mindset Adjustment

You're probably the harshest critic of your looks. That's because you likely care more about your weight and appearance than anyone else does. You definitely have greater access to harass yourself—in bed, in the bathroom, in the car—than anyone else does.

And odds are good that you direct a level of critical, harsh comments to yourself that you wouldn't tolerate from anyone else. As you learned in Chapter 4 from Kristin Neff, PhD, the self-compassion expert, critical self-talk doesn't encourage you to make self-improvements. It actually holds you back.

If you give yourself a hard time about your weight when you try on clothes or about your appearance as you stand before your bathroom mirror, it's time to adopt a kinder tone. Sometime this week, I'd like for you to do this self-compassion exercise that Dr. Neff recommends.

1. Take out a blank sheet of paper.

2. Write down what you'd do and say if a close friend were feeling bad about himself or herself. What would your tone of voice be like?

3. Now consider what you tell yourself when you are feeling bad or facing a challenging situation. What kind of tone do you take with yourself? Write this down.

4. How are these approaches different? What factors cause you to talk to yourself differently than you would with someone else you care about?

5. Write down how your life might become different if you talked to yourself in the way that you'd talk to a close friend who was in need.

The next time you're dissatisfied with your weight or your hair or your complexion or your posture, try to modify the internal comments you direct toward yourself. Speak to yourself like a good friend would. If you can change the tone of your inner conversation, it will become a powerful force that helps to propel you to better health, fitness, and organization.

Week Three Fitness Activities

Walking frequency: Go 4 days.

Duration: Take a 15-minute walk around your block, the neighborhood, the park, or on a treadmill if you have one. Walking in place while watching TV or listening to music works as well. While you walk, plan out your decluttering strategy for the day (or the following day, if you're exercising in the evening).

In addition, perform the following movements on 2 or 3 nonconsecutive days after your muscles are nice and warm from walking or decluttering.

While cleaning out your closet, go into your bedroom and perform:

- ▸ 10 Kickbacks (page 169)
- ▸ 10 Leg Raises—Front (page 172)
- ▸ 10 Leg Raises—Side (page 173)
- ▸ 10 Wall Pushups (page 189)
- ▸ 10 Shoulder Raises (page 176) on each arm with a gallon jug of water or a duffel bag of clothes (whichever provides enough resistance)
- ▸ 10 Biceps Curls (page 163)
- ▸ 10 Toe Raises (page 184)

As this week draws to a close, you should find that your closet and your bathroom present an image of tidiness. As you lose weight and develop new attitudes over the course of this program, the image you show in public is likely to change as well. Now's a good time to reflect on the way you've carried yourself—and how you want to present yourself to the world as you start the second half of this program.

Chapter 12

WEEK FOUR: YOUR FINANCIAL HOUSE

I n horror movies, the scariest place is usually the basement. The heroes can hear muffled noises down there, and they can sense that some unseen menace lurks just out of sight.

In real life, most Americans also share a common worry, but the scary whispers are coming from their purses and wallets.

In 2013, the average American felt a higher-than-healthy level of stress, according to a survey from the American Psychological Association. For most people, money played some type of role in their worries. About 70 percent said that money was a significant source of stress. Presumably they didn't have enough of it, or they had trouble managing the money they did have. About two-thirds were struggling with stress related to the thing they do to *get* money: work. And 61 percent were stressed-out about the economy at large.

Like the characters in scary movies, people don't always cope with financial problems in a way that actually leads to a solution. Instead, they're likely to make their problems worse (like the horror movie characters who trip over a root or don't check the gas gauge before they drive into the dark forest). For example, some evidence suggests that many Americans are managing their household finances in a way that *promotes* stress rather than relieves it (see the box on page 264).

If you try to manage your finances at a cluttered desk where you can't find a pen, let alone your bills, your home office space is not going to help you make well-reasoned financial decisions in a timely manner. In fact, a messy office area could literally cost you money every month.

It might even contribute to your weight! In a 2014 study, researchers looked at surveys that Australians filled out each year for 3 years. Those who said they had financial stress during the first 2 years were 20 percent more likely to be obese in the third year compared to those with no financial stress.

I know that financial stress can come at you from many directions, including unemployment, stock market swings, and costly medical emergencies—and you often can't do a lot about these. But if some of your financial stress has grown out of your disorganized records and processes, you can most definitely do something about it now.

This week we're going to focus on the space where you conduct the "business" of your home: the place where you sort through your mail, pay your bills, and generally deal with the endless flow of paper into your home. I'd like for you to put your paperwork in order. I want you to confront the bills you try not to think about and start doing what you can to relieve any financial stress that you're carrying.

I want you to be the hero who walks out of the horror movie unscathed at the end.

Remember that stress affects your mood, your relationships, your general outlook on life, your job, your eating habits, and your overall health. If you're lugging around extra pounds, some of that weight may be due to stress. In addition, if you're feeling anxious, that anxiety may also encourage you to bring more clutter into your home.

▶ WHERE FINANCES ARE AN ISSUE, STRESS FOLLOWS

When it comes to money, there's a lot of unnecessary spending—and resulting stress—going on out there.

- A 2012 survey found that 56 percent of adults don't keep a budget.

- The same survey found that 33 percent don't pay all their bills on time. Paying bills late often results in added fees, and this wasted expense can become substantial.

- About $1 billion worth of gift cards went unused in 2014. (However, this is a great improvement—more than $8 billion in gift cards was wasted in 2007.)

- A 2012 survey found that more than half of adults with a spouse or partner don't regularly set aside time to discuss finances. The same survey found that financial arguments often center on unexpected expenses and inadequate savings.

- In 2012, Americans ran up $32 billion in overdraft fees when they spent more than their checking accounts could cover.

☐ Create your vision.   ☐ Organize Zone 3.

☐ Collect malignant items.   ☐ Get rid of malignant items.

☐ Set up zones.   **Plus**

☐ Clean off horizontal surfaces.   ☐ Mindset adjustment

☐ Organize Zone 2.   ☐ Physical activities

When I've worked with clients to straighten up their home offices and establish systems to manage their paperwork and their money issues, their finances usually improved *immediately*. That's because often for the first time:

▶ They feel a sense of control over their finances.

▶ They can quickly find documents they need.

▶ Fees for late payments disappear.

▶ They frequently find a gift card they've overlooked or a little cash or even a check they haven't deposited.

Without an organized office and a system in place to manage the business of your home, it's easy to lose necessary bits of paperwork or other documents that are important for you and your family.

The same decluttering tasks you'll complete this week hold true whether you handle your household finances from a desk in the corner of your living room or you have an entire office where you operate both your business and your household.

Task 1:
DEVELOP A VISION FOR YOUR OFFICE SPACE

As always, your first task is to establish your vision for what you want this space to do for you. This will vary based on how much work you do from here. If you live in an apartment and work outside the home, you probably won't use this space as much as if you run a business from your home office.

Do you often talk to clients or colleagues via video conferencing? If so, you might want your office to look professional (at least within the spot behind you that the camera sees). Do you want to spend as little time as possible dealing with the details of running a household? If so, you might want to make a priority of keeping this space highly efficient so you can do your work quickly.

I would recommend that your vision include:

▶ Keeping this area *extremely* well organized in order to quickly get your hands on any information you need without wasting time searching

▶ Setting up easy-to-maintain systems in your home office in order to pay all your bills, taxes, and other charges promptly so you don't generate late fees

▶ Dedicating a self-contained space for your office if it's currently just a free-floating pile of papers and checkbooks without a home

OFFICE VISION

This is what I want *from* my office space:_____

_____

_____

_____

_____

How I want to *feel* in this space:_____

_____

_____

_____

Task 2:
SORT OUT YOUR MALIGNANT ITEMS

For a space that tends to be relatively small, your office area may have a *lot* of malignant materials. That's because finances can be stressful and upsetting, and you may have stashed away paperwork from numerous unpleasant life events in this area.

Go through your office area and collect paperwork and other reminders of stressful times. These may include:

▶ Bankruptcy filings

▶ Divorce decrees

▶ Paperwork from legal proceedings

▶ Medical bills

▶ Paperwork or inventory from a failed business

▶ Statements from investments that lost money

▶ Exit materials from a job you lost

You may need to keep some of this stuff in your files, but you don't have to see it every day. It's important to put any paperwork that reminds you of a loss or makes you feel like you've failed someplace where it's not in your face.

If any of this stuff summarizes ancient history and you're sure you'll never need it, then pitch it. But if there's a chance you might need it someday, or your heirs might need or want it, then put it into deep storage, such as in secure bins in your attic or basement.

Task 3:
ESTABLISH ZONES

During this task, you'll start arranging your office space like the layout of your car. The items you use often while you sit in your office chair are akin to the steering wheel and turn signal lever in your car. You want them close. Items you seldom use—like the spare tire and jack—go in the trunk of your car, and along those lines you'll stash less-useful office items farther away from your chair. To begin, I want you to imagine your office space as three distinct zones.

Zone 1: This is the area closest to you within arm's reach as you sit in your chair. Zone 1 is the place where you'll be doing most of your bill-paying and other chores to keep your household running. This may be a desk or even a table where you set up your laptop computer.

This area contains only items that you use regularly and that enable you to operate in the space efficiently and well. These are what I call your *current* or *active* items. They likely include:

▶ A file tray to hold all incoming mail and other paperwork that needs your attention, such as bills and credit card statements. (Better yet, cancel the

▶ A CLEAN OFFICE NEEDS THESE TWO THINGS

The two biggest pitfalls I encounter in home offices are:

- A lack of clear and simple systems

- A *complete* lack of limits

What are systems? Here's an example: By placing all mail that comes into your home into a file tray that stays on a desk or counter, you have established a simple system that will serve you well. If you know exactly where your mail goes, where to find a piece of correspondence at a moment's notice, and what items need your attention at the end of the month, you make huge strides toward saving yourself headaches and reducing your stress.

In terms of limits, you only have the space you have. The moment you start overloading a space, you've begun to lose the clutter battle. If you designated one drawer for office supplies, then that's the only place your office supplies should live. Once the drawer is full, you've reached the limit you set. Don't buy any more office supplies until you deplete your stock!

paper versions whenever possible and get these statements online.) Be sure that everyone in the house knows exactly where the mail goes immediately when it arrives.

▶ A file tray to hold items such as invitations, upcoming school events, or family commitments. You might choose to invest in a notice board to hold these items instead. As you declutter and organize your office, decide what tools work best for you and your family.

▶ Information about active projects such as work being done on your home or upcoming medical treatments. A vertical file holder, with individual folders labeled for quick and easy filing and access, is great for this purpose.

▶ Your computer and phone

▶ Shredder and trash can

▶ A reasonable (this means minimum!) supply of pens, pencils, and other office necessities

You should only put items here if you're going to use them on a day-to-day basis. Remember, Zone 1 equals your car's dashboard.

Sit in your chair and stretch your arms out in front of you. Decide which items you'll need to keep here in order for your office space to function in a way that's true to your vision. Whatever you decide to place here, be sure that Zone 1 can comfortably hold it. Avoid overloading this space, since it's key to helping you quickly and easily manage any day-to-day "business" challenges of your home.

These activities tend to not be the most enjoyable use of your time (unless you truly find satisfaction in balancing your checkbook), so be sure that clutter doesn't give you an excuse to ignore them.

Zone 2: This is the area just a little further away. It should contain items that you use *regularly but infrequently.* Assess the space that's available for items that you'll store in this zone. This is the equivalent of your car's console, glove box, drink holders, and the little storage space in the driver's side door. Where will you put the items that you use occasionally or will be likely to use in the next month? Set limits for what type of objects you'll put here and how much this space can hold.

Items that live in Zone 2 are likely to include:

▸ Books

▸ Research materials and paperwork

▸ Semi-active files such as school reports for earlier semesters or projects that aren't very active but not yet finished

▸ USE THE MAGIC AT YOUR FINGERTIPS

Your smartphone is a great organizing tool that will help:

- Eliminate paperwork

- Keep your life in better order

- Give your memory a jog when it needs it

I no longer keep lists of books I want to read, business cards that I need to remember, or information on products I see in stores that I'm considering purchasing. I either take a photo of the card, use an app to keep lists of things I need to remember, or enter items immediately into my phone (which syncs with my desktop).

Stop thinking of your phone as a phone—it's really a personal digital assistant that's ready to work for you 24 hours a day (minus, of course, the 8 hours when you're sleeping). If you have the technology at your fingertips, use it!

▸ Files for ongoing medical issues that you need to check on regularly but infrequently

▸ Paperwork that you'll need for the preparation of your tax filings at the end of each financial year

Zone 3: Finally, decide where you'll put the paperwork and other objects that you seldom need and that don't belong in either of your first two zones but may be useful someday. This is the equivalent of your car's trunk. This zone might hold:

▸ Electronics accessories like USB cables

▸ Copies of past tax returns

▸ Documents that you need to retain for legal or personal reasons

Give thought to the type of storage containers you will use for holding these items, since they're essentially archived materials that you'll want to ensure aren't damaged through poor storage or lack of attention. Will you put these containers in a closet? In the basement? How much space are you willing to devote to this stuff?

Thinking of your office space in terms of zones will help you assign homes for like items and determine clear limits for how much space you'll assign to different things.

Do you need everything that's currently in your office space? For example, if you have a bookcase filled with clutter, will you even need to keep the bookcase once the clutter is gone? Do you need to *add* anything? Perhaps now's the time for a bigger file cabinet. Or maybe you need some small organizational trays and a pencil cup for your stapler, scissors, mail, and writing implements.

Once you've envisioned each zone, the next step is to start organizing them and getting rid of excess stuff. Now's the time to decide which items will live in each designated area and what supplies, if any, you need to make the different zones work well for you.

Task 4:
CLEAN OFF ALL HORIZONTAL SURFACES
IN ALL YOUR ZONES

Remove everything from Zone 1 that doesn't belong there. Take all this stuff off your desk and move it to Zone 2 for now.

While you're at it, remove all the clutter from the top of your file cabinet and any other storage areas. All these spaces should stay free of knickknacks, stray paperwork, and random objects, and you should refrain from using these areas as storage space.

Offices are notorious for gathering clutter on flat surfaces. That's because a lot of paperwork funnels into the office space from the rest of the home. So do a lot of other objects that don't have a specific place where they belong.

If you only sit down and use this area on occasion, it might seem wasteful to keep these spaces unfilled. Still, maintain these flat surfaces like you would any others in your home: empty and clean. If you don't, when you sit down to pay your bills or organize your finances, clutter is going to get in the way and distract you from your tasks.

Task 5:
ORGANIZE FILE CABINETS AND
OTHER STORAGE SPOTS IN ZONE 2

Now move on to Zone 2, your medium-term storage area for items you use occasionally. If you took anything out of Zone 1, consider whether it should stay here.

A lot of your paperwork is going to go here, such as manuals for your home's appliances (although most of these can now be accessed online, thus eliminating the need for paper copies) and records you'll need for the coming tax season. I would recommend a file cabinet, which can hold a lot of well-organized material but look neat and tidy from the outside. (That's in contrast to a bookshelf, which is going to look very messy even if you neatly stand up rows of file folders and stacks of paper on it.)

As you're organizing your paperwork in Zone 2, I would strongly recommend this philosophy: Good enough is fine. You don't have to aim for perfect.

I have never believed that striving for perfection is a commendable habit. It just sets you up to fail before you even begin. I've lost count of the number of

▶ BUT WHAT ABOUT *VIRTUAL* CLUTTER?

Whenever I'm discussing how to set up an organized, streamlined office, people will invariably ask me how much time and effort they should put toward arranging all those digital documents, music files, and photos on their computer.

Frankly, I just can't make myself get too worked up about electronic files on devices. Unlike physical items, when it comes to the digital world, you're more concerned about *access* than quantity. For starters, having 10,000 documents you don't really need on your computer isn't like having stacks of printed documents on your desk. You're not going to trip over computer files. You're not going to lose the file you really want just because you have so much stored in your computer (assuming you have a basic knowledge of how to use your computer). Within reason, it's pretty hard for you to run out of space to put your electronic files, which is a major reason why we need to avoid clutter in the real world.

These days, you can store vast amounts of pictures and documents fairly inexpensively, either on a backup hard drive or in the cloud. Personally, I keep every e-mail I ever send or receive, since it's inexpensive and easy to store them, and I can easily find specific e-mails with an automated search for key words and phrases that I know are contained in the document or e-mail.

I would simply recommend a few commonsense pieces of advice when it comes to maintaining your computer programs and files:

- Don't pack so much in that your computer begins to work slowly or unreliably.

- Protect your information (especially e-mails, financial figures, and work documents) with passwords that would be hard for a hacker to guess. That means something a little more clever than "password," "123456," or your first name. It's a good idea to use a different password for each application and to keep all of your passwords in a safe place. Some apps and Web sites are available for securely storing your passwords in one place, or you can go old-school and write them on a piece of paper, then place it somewhere secure in your home where you can readily find it.

- It's essential to back up all your files, either to a hard drive that you hook up to your computer or to a cloud-based service that will automatically do the work for you. Hackers are getting increasingly sophisticated in their ability to ruin your files—they can even lock them up, then demand money before they'll give them back to you. Storage is cheap and easy to access, so there's no excuse for lost documents or files that can't be recovered.

times I've seen a wish for perfection totally paralyze a person who dwells on the idea that "If I can't do it perfectly, I can't do it at all."

"Good enough" is a target that's, well, good enough. Having a welcoming, comfortable home is a wonderful thing, even if you have a little clutter here and there. It says that your home is loved and lived in. When you reach "good enough," relax and enjoy the view.

It's possible to get carried away with carefully filing your receipts by month and arranging older paperwork by date. This is generally a waste of time that doesn't improve the appearance or the functionality of your office area. You can use that time much better elsewhere.

Just sort your paperwork into a reasonable-enough degree of organization so that you can later find what you're looking for relatively quickly. Use clear and simple labels and be sure to date files so that when you come back to purge your filing cabinet in the future, you can quickly see how old items are.

Finally, make a note in your calendar one year from today to remind yourself to go through your files and discard any that you no longer need—or move into deep storage the expendable documents that you can't let go of but that are cluttering up precious space in your filing cabinet.

▸ IGNORING YOUR MAIL IS NOT A STRATEGY

I've worked with many couples whose despair over paperwork had gotten to the point where they simply threw their unopened mail—including their bills—into a box or drawer and hoped they'd go away.

This "out of sight, out of mind" strategy may provide some temporary comfort, but it will actually lead you to a much worse place than where you are now. Living in denial is not a long-term solution. It will only compound your problems. By getting your office into shape now, paperwork may become less scary.

As one of the test panelists, Kristen, noted: "Yesterday, as I was standing on the threshold peering in, I kept thinking, I don't even want this room to be an office anymore, so perhaps I can avoid it for another week! But I know that's not the answer. I become really paralyzed in this room. I'm thinking about tackling it with a timer and a very small section at a time!"

Starting today, establish a place for your mail and your bills to live. As it comes in, open it all in a timely manner. This small action will alleviate a lot of stress and serve as a major step toward getting your paperwork (and finances) under control.

▶ HOW LONG SHOULD I KEEP IT?

Experts recommend that you preserve these documents for the following lengths of time:

Marriage licenses, divorce decrees, birth certificates, adoption papers, life insurance information	Forever—and it's wise to keep this sort of paperwork in a lockbox, safe, or safe-deposit box
Vehicle titles, receipts for large purchases, user manuals, real estate deeds	As long as you own the object or property
Tax records	Seven years from the filing date
Contracts	Until you update them
Insurance for your car, home, or other property	Until the policy is renewed
Bank statements	For a year, unless you need them for later tax reasons

Check online or with your personal financial advisor for any legal requirements in your area that may influence which documents you need to keep and for how long.

Keep in mind that in this day and age, when we have immediate online access to so many businesses and organizations, there is little need to keep reams of paper statements. Check with your financial institution to see what they make available online, and do the same for your utility companies and anything else that has traditionally mailed you statements. Embrace the digital age and free up the space that once held years' worth of musty paper.

Task 6:
ORGANIZE ZONE 3

This is your deep storage area. Maybe it's the lowest drawer in your file cabinet. Maybe it's a big plastic container in your attic. The items you keep here are things you'll only rarely need to see, if ever.

That doesn't mean Zone 3 should serve as a dumping ground for a bunch of clutter you don't actually need to keep. If you know for a fact that you'll never, ever need the receipt for your dog's veterinary checkup 2 years ago, throw it away. Don't store it.

But if you do anticipate that you could need an item of paperwork someday—

and when that day comes, you won't be able to find a copy online—then keep it. Deciding whether to keep each item is a judgment call you'll have to make.

Finish sorting through all the items that didn't make the cut for Zones 1 and 2, and evaluate all your paperwork that you won't need anytime soon. Sort it into folders and place it in a container, an out-of-the-way cabinet, or a safe for especially important items.

If items don't make the cut to include in your first, second, or third zones, then throw them away (shredding any sensitive paperwork first is a good idea).

Task 7:
DEAL WITH THE MALIGNANT ITEMS

If you haven't either said good-bye to your malignant items or tucked them away into deep storage, now's the time to do so. We do a lot of paperwork over the course of our lives, and it doesn't always provide a record of happy times.

As you run this stuff through your shredder, then dump it into the recycling bin, try to release the painful memories that are noted on the paper. People are entitled to second chances after all sorts of financial problems, and you deserve to be free from any malignant clutter in your office.

Week Four
Mindset Adjustment

Being present, aware, and mindful whenever you purchase items is our focus this week. Too often we buy things on a whim because we're bored or because they seem like such a bargain we'd be foolish to pass them up!

This week, start practicing mindfulness before you buy any object. Here's how it works. Before you buy *anything*, whether you're in the mall or a convenience store, stop, take a deep breath, and ask yourself *why* you want it. Take a moment to ponder these questions: Why do I want this object? Will the item move me closer to the life I want? Will it help put me into the financial position I want? Do I legitimately need it? Or is it something that I just want in the moment to take my mind off boredom, sadness, or stress?

If it's the latter, put it back on the shelf and walk away.

(continued on page 278)

The Clutter Chronicles

Leah Zerbe, 33

POUNDS LOST: 11.4

AMOUNT OF CLUTTER REMOVED:
10 bags for donation, 5 bags
of trash

Leah's experience isn't just a story of what she lost over 6 weeks. She can also measure her success by what she *found*.

Leah's a busy woman. During the day, the 33-year-old works as a health journalist. After hours, she grows vegetables and strawberries and tends to the flock of egg-laying chickens on the sustainable farm that she and her husband operate.

Until she went through the *Cut the Clutter, Drop the Pounds* program, Leah spent much of her spare time shifting around clutter, over and over, in a never-ending attempt to clean her house.

"Before, I was just spinning my wheels, wasting a lot of time cleaning, but it didn't really look like I was cleaning. It still looked

Before

cluttered," she says. "Since I work from home a lot, one of my biggest clutter sources was the work material that was everywhere in every room. I didn't realize how stressed that made me feel. I think it kept me from ever getting my mind off work, even when I wasn't working."

The most profound message she took away from the program is that everything in her home needs to have a place—and if it doesn't have a place, it needs to go. She donated many of her books to the library, and if she ever wants to enjoy them again, she can just check them out.

"I was actually giving things a place, so they stayed permanently cleaned up," she says. "Since I work really long days, this has been a lifesaver."

One of the treasures she found once she lightened her household burden was *time*. She doesn't have to spend so many hours cleaning now. Plus, with her work materials kept in order, she's a much more efficient worker.

She also found new reservoirs of energy. Like the other test participants, Leah estimated her energy level on a scale of 1 to 10 before the program and again after it ended. Hers soared by 3 points.

With these new gifts of time and energy, she could run more often. She stayed more active than the program required, and she found herself running farther and faster and participating in races on weekends. (Perhaps this contributed to her improved self-esteem, which rose by 3 points on a 10-point scale.)

Leah also found an improved sense of peace, thanks in part to the mindfulness exercises. Her score on the anxiety quiz dropped steeply over the course of the program.

"I'm still practicing mindfulness every day, trying to focus on the moment," she says. "I had a lot more anxiety than I had realized. I still have work to do, but once the rooms started clearing up, I just felt a lot less anxious."

I know this is not as easy as it sounds! We are so conditioned to buy items on autopilot that you'll be surprised by the emotions that this mindfulness exercise evokes. (For a more specific approach to use in these moments, review the STOP exercise on page 61.)

Week Four
Fitness Activities

Walking frequency: Go 4 days.

Duration: Take a 20-minute walk around your block, the neighborhood, the park, or on a treadmill if you have one. Walking in place while watching TV or listening to music works as well. As you walk, plan out your decluttering strategy for the day (or the following day if you're exercising in the evening).

In addition, perform the following movements on 2 or 3 nonconsecutive days after your muscles are nice and warm from walking or decluttering.

▸ 10 Kickbacks (page 169)

▸ 10 Stationary Lunges (page 181)

▸ 10 Stationary Squats While Holding On to Your Desk (page 182)

▸ 10 Knee Lift/Crunches While Sitting on Your Office Chair (page 171)

▸ 10 Triceps Dips (page 186) (use a stationary chair, not a swiveling office chair)

▸ 10 Wall Pushups (page 189)

In addition, while you're deciding whether to keep documents or toss them out, remain standing (or march in place) instead of sitting down.

Today you finished decluttering the place where you work hard to keep your household running. Now it's time to take on something completely different—the areas of your home where you enjoy your leisure time. While this week the tasks were intended to make your life easier, next week the idea is to adjust some rooms of your house so they give your life a healthy challenge.

Chapter 13

WEEK FIVE: YOUR LIVING AREAS (FAMILY ROOM, LIVING ROOM, DEN)

ately, news headlines have been proclaiming that "Sitting Is the New Smoking." In the sense that they're both linked to a lot of health threats, and health experts are very concerned about both, then yes, sitting and smoking *do* have a lot in common.

Here's where they *aren't* alike: Smoking is much less widespread. More than 80 percent of American homeowners now refuse to allow smoking in their home. But sitting is far more acceptable. You can go do that anywhere. In fact, it's become the new national pastime.

And that's a problem.

No matter where we go, it's extremely easy for us to sit. In many places, we *have* to take a seat, like at work. A 2011 study found that today's workers are much less likely to do even moderate exertion at their jobs compared to how our parents and grandparents worked 50 years ago.

Back then, jobs that burned a lot of calories through manual labor were more common, like logging, manufacturing, and mining. Nowadays, most jobs either require workers to do just a little standing, lifting, and walking around, or to park themselves at a desk for 8 or more hours a day.

As a result, compared to workers in 1960, men now burn an average of 140 fewer calories each day at work, and women burn 124 fewer. That's the equivalent of about two chocolate chip cookies a day or a Big Mac and a few fries every workweek.

After a long day of work, surveys show that many people just want to come home and sit some more.

▶ Adults watch about 2 hours and 45 minutes of television every day, according to 2013 data from the US Department of Labor. That's the biggest single use of their time after sleeping and working. (The *fourth* most time-consuming activity of the day? Eating and drinking. That takes another hour or so, generally sitting down.) On average, people reported just 18 minutes a day of sports, exercise, and recreation.

▶ In another poll from 2013, Americans reported their favorite leisure-time activities. For 42 percent, watching television topped their list. Watching TV is one of the most inactive, least calorie-burning things you can do aside from sleeping. A 185-pound person will burn a little *more* than 1 calorie a minute while watching TV and a little *less* than 1 calorie a minute sleeping.

▶ A sizable 36 percent of adults reported doing *no* physical activity during their leisure time in 2008. None. If upward of one person out of three is refusing to get up and move around for the fun of it, please make sure *you're* not that one person.

All this sitting seems to be playing a very active role in the nation's poor health and fitness. Spending too much time on your backside may make you more likely to encounter:

Obesity. Australian researchers found that adults who spent more time sitting had a higher body mass index and waist size. The same was true when they looked at TV habits. More watching equaled a bigger belly.

Another recent study followed a group of more than 158,000 older adults. Those who spent more time sitting down at the beginning of the study—or more time watching TV—had a bigger increase in their BMI over the next 9 years.

One reason why you may gain weight from sitting too long is because you're missing out on big stretches of the day when you could be burning the calories you've taken in that your body doesn't need.

Here's another reason: People tend to eat while they're sitting. But it's not just *any* food. When you're idly watching TV, you're more likely to be eating junk food rather than healthier alternatives. Eating salty, greasy snacks in front of the TV may be a habit you've been developing for decades. You may not fully realize how many calories you're taking in during your TV time.

Serious diseases. Each additional hour that women watch TV each day has been linked to a 26 percent higher chance of having metabolic syndrome. This is a collection of problems like high blood sugar, high blood pressure, and a big belly, which can make you more likely to develop diabetes and heart disease.

Too much sitting may also raise your risk of cancer. German researchers reviewed 43 earlier studies that looked at people's cancer risk in relation to the time they spent sitting. Those who passed the most time watching TV or sitting down had a higher risk of several cancers, including colon cancer and lung cancer.

An early death. Another study followed more than 120,000 men and women for 14 years. All were healthy at the beginning. Those who sat for 6 hours or more daily were more likely to die than the participants who spent less than 3 hours seated. Even if those people who sat for 6-plus hours were physically active during other times of the day, they had a higher risk of dying.

Did you catch that last part? Even if you exercise every day, sitting around too much can still be harmful to your health and your waistline. Researchers noticed this while tracking a group of more than 4,000 Australian adults who exercised for the often-recommended 150 minutes per week. Even though they were physically active for 30 minutes on most days, as their time in front of the TV went up, so did their waist size and blood pressure. In women, more television time was also linked to potentially harmful changes in their cholesterol.

This is a lot of worrisome information—especially if you were expecting this chapter to just show you what to do with all those magazines piled up on your coffee table. I will get to that soon enough. But since this book is devoted to both improving your health and changing the way you use your home, we have to talk about what you're doing with the rooms you devote to leisure— namely, your living room, family room, den, home theater, or "man cave."

It's a little odd to me that we've come to regard the term "sitting room" as a quaint idea from the past, something we'd hear today only on *Downton Abbey*. We now have *living* rooms, correct? But is that really true? While we refer to the space in our home where we spend most of our free time as the "living room," the truth is that it has become little more than a sitting-down room (or even a "lying down" room).

You only have so many hours per day to give your body the thing it *must have* in order to run properly at an optimal weight. That's physical activity. Subtract 8 hours, give or take, for sleep. Take away another 8 hours if you work. That leaves you with 8 hours per day, and part of that's spent sitting down in your car, at your dining room table, reading to your kids, in the movie theater, on a date, or what have you.

That only leaves you with a few hours a day to be physically active—and those are the hours you likely spend in the rooms of your home that you've set up for relaxing. I encourage you to use the next week for not just decluttering but also giving thought to how you can better use these spaces for *moving*, rather than just sitting.

Even if you exercise for an hour every day, that only adds up to a relatively brief window in which you're moving. You still need to spend more time on your feet being physically active for the rest of the day.

Task 1:
CREATE YOUR VISION

The living room (the term I'll use, though in your home it could be a den or family room or several of these rooms) tends to be one of the areas of the home that's cluttered with the widest variety of stuff. That's because everyone, whether parents or kids or pets, tends to have an equal right to use the room, and it's usually the room where families spend the most time together. The room also has no particular function, like the kitchen or bedroom, so all the residents of the home tend to use it for a variety of activities.

In your home, you might see hundreds of books, a TV, a laptop computer or tablet, board games, puzzles, exercise equipment, and hobby supplies in this room. These are all reasonable items to keep in the living room. However, if *everyone* is contributing a limitless pile of his or her own possessions here, the living room is going to become unlivable—very quickly.

It's particularly important to define your vision for your living room. Do you want to use it for entertaining guests? Is it important for you to bring your family together here? Do you want to have fun in this room? Or do you want to relax? Or do you want to use the room for *all* of these things?

Now's the time to figure it out, preferably together as a family. You will need to balance out competing demands. If you share your home with a spouse, partner, or children, it's quite likely that you'll need to make some compromises about who gets to do what with the living room.

LIVING ROOM VISION

This is what I want *from* my living room: _____

_____

_____

_____

_____

How I want to *feel* in this space: _____

_____

_____

_____

Task 2:
START IDENTIFYING MALIGNANT ITEMS

Remember that malignant items make you feel sad, upset, or guilty when you look at them. Based on homes I've been in, I would encourage you to evaluate the following sorts of objects for any negative effects they have on you.

Memorabilia. Do you have any photos on display in your living room—

even of happy times—that stir up feelings of sadness when you look at them? Do your shelves hold heirlooms that you never particularly wanted? Now may be the time to move this stuff elsewhere or get rid of it.

Exercise equipment. Treadmills, elliptical trainers, home gyms, and free weights often wind up in the living room. As long as you've deliberately decided to put this gear in your living room—and it isn't overflowing out of the space you allotted for it—that's fine. What *isn't* okay is to keep exercise equipment here that you've stopped using.

If you're able to safely use your exercise equipment while you're watching TV or reading a book, I would recommend you start doing so. But if you're never going to use it again, get it out of your living room. It represents a missed opportunity to improve your fitness, and I don't want you to feel like you failed by not sticking with it.

Sell this stuff. Now that you're finding other ways to exercise, you might be able to use the proceeds to buy some fitness gear that you *will* keep enjoying.

Collectibles. The living room tends to gather collections. Whether we're talking about music boxes, figurine dolls, holiday decorations, or record albums, collectibles have a habit of growing in number and taking up more room than they deserve.

Another problem: All the members of the household seldom share the same passion for these collectibles. If your spouse has a giant collection of *anything* that's crowding everything else out of the living room, and you're tired of looking at it, it's malignant. It's also disrespectful to you and can harm your relationship.

The same holds true if it's *your* collection and your spouse has complained that it's taking up too much space or too much of your attention. If your spouse is suffering from having to live with malignant clutter, it's going to affect your entire household.

Miscellaneous stuff. Do you have a piece of furniture that you tried to refinish or re-cover, but you were never pleased with the results? That, too, might be malignant. If so, get rid of it (or give it another makeover). Did you or a family member have to convalesce in the living room after an injury because the bedroom was inconvenient? (Remember the story from earlier in the book about the family keeping part of dad's cancer-treatment equipment around? That's not an uncommon occurrence.) It's time to get rid of any left-over evidence that's still lying around.

You don't have to get this stuff out of the living room right now, but you do have to identify it and start coming up with a solution that moves it out of your

Malignant clutter doesn't have to be harmful; it may be stuff that's simply stupid.

I remember one family that had around 80 empty electronics boxes stacked on shelves and in the corners of their living room. It turned out that the husband saved the packaging from every electronic item they purchased just in case they needed to return the product or move to a new home.

His wife, to put it mildly, was not amused.

They had been arguing about this for 5 years when I started working with them. I asked the wife how many boxes she thought would be reasonable. She said, "Zero!" I looked calmly at her and replied, "Come on, be reasonable. How many do you think is a fair number?" She paused and said, "Ten." When I asked the husband, he said, "Twenty." Exercising the power vested in me as an organizing authority, I said, "Okay, it's settled—you can keep 15 boxes." Problem solved.

Remember, they had been fighting about this for 5 years! That's a lot of unrest poisoning their household for no reason whatsoever.

home or somewhere out of sight. As with each previous space, you'll return to this malignant clutter at the end of the week and decide what to do with it.

Task 3:
CLEAR OFF FLAT SURFACES

The living room is filled with flat surfaces—including shelves, tables, cabinets, and seats—and these tend to become covered with stuff. In general, I think flat surfaces should stay clear of all objects. However, that standard can be relaxed a bit in the living room. It's okay, from a clutter standpoint, to keep some knickknacks and photos and entertainment materials on display in the living room, as long as you follow a few rules:

▸ You have to mindfully look at each item and decide whether it *really* needs to be there.

▸ You have to set limits for the amount of stuff you'll put on each table or shelf, or in each area of the living room, and be sure to keep your items from exceeding these limits.

▸ Each area within your living room has to look tidy and well-organized.

So take a look at each space within your living room. Examine the entertainment center, each shelf, and each table. Take a fresh look at each wall and inspect the artwork and other wall hangings. How many DVDs will you keep on your TV stand? Will you ever actually watch them again (especially movies you can stream for free or for $3)? Do you still need to keep your '90s-era CD collection on a shelf now that you have either outgrown the music or have it stored on your MP3 player or computer?

If it's on a flat surface and you can't make a case for it to stay there, it needs to go away or, if you have room, into storage.

Task 4:
GET RID OF BENIGN ITEMS

You've now accounted for the malignant items and cleaned off the flat surfaces. Now do a sweep of the whole room and stow away, move, or get rid of everything else that doesn't belong out in the open.

All items that are hanging out in the living room that don't belong need to go. It's okay to keep a golf putter and a little putting green in the living room, if you've made a conscious decision to keep them there. But if you're simply too distracted (or lazy) to carry your bag of clubs to the garage where they belong, do so now.

If you enjoy crocheting in the living room and that's where you've decided to do it, that's fine. If your sewing basket has been untouched in the corner for weeks, overflowing with needles and thread, it's time to put it elsewhere. If you regularly use your gaming system in the living room, make sure the device, the games, and all wiring are tucked neatly out of sight when you're not playing with it.

Task 5:
COME UP WITH A NEW WAY OF LOOKING AT THE LEISURE AREAS OF YOUR HOME

If you're overweight, many of those extra pounds likely built up on your frame due to not moving your body enough. A recent study found that since 1988, people have been eating about the same number of calories daily, but the number of adults getting *no* leisure-time physical activity skyrocketed.

As you look around your living room, ask yourself: Is the way I use this room encouraging me to look and feel my best? Or is it the place where the calories I eat get turned into fat?

Let the Joneses next door sit nearly motionless in *their* living room for 4 hours per evening. This is definitely one of the areas where you don't want to keep up with them. Instead, refashion your living room from a place where you sit to a place where you burn calories. How you do this is up to you. One simple approach is to just spend less time in this room.

▶ Decide that one night a week, you'll build your evening around an active family outing. Go to a park in your neighborhood or drive to a state park in a neighboring community, and have fun outdoors. Or go ice skating. Or make a family trip to the gym together.

▶ Buy a pedometer or download a pedometer app for your phone and look at *it* instead of your TV. Instead of seeing how many episodes you can binge-watch from a streaming service in one night, make a goal of how many steps you can take in one evening. Try to beat it the following night.

Turn your back on labor-saving devices and celebrate the fact that the extra time you have to spend on tasks will help keep you fit. Instead of a leaf blower, clear your yard with a rake. Sell your riding mower and buy a push mower. Turn down the neighbor kid's offer of clearing the snow from your driveway and do it yourself (or tackle it as a team). You can find things to do year-round that improve your body and your home's appearance at the same time.

Or you can become more physically active while you're hanging out in the living room. You've already been doing exercises around your home for the past 4 weeks. Why not step it up? Use some of the money from selling your stuff (or a gift card if you found one in your office last week) to buy a few inexpensive workout videos. Vow that for every hour you watch TV, you'll spend 30 minutes working out. (You might also find an exercise video to watch on your TV for free on Netflix or Hulu, or one on YouTube to play on your computer. Remember, that's *in addition* to your usual exercise.)

You could also make at least one night each week a "no electronics" night. During this evening, no one watches TV or plays games on the phone or tablet. Play board games, talk, look at old family pictures, and take a little break to remind your brain that it can live without electronic stimulation.

Here are some other suggestions:

▶ Have everyone in the family pile every single book in your home on the floor of the living room and sort them. For every four you keep, you have to take one to Goodwill or the used-book store. (Or more if you really want to weed out your collection!) After you box up the non-keepers and take them to your car, you'll have gotten several minutes of walking and lifting.

- Play a game of hide-and-seek with the kids in and around your house, or put together a scavenger hunt in your home.

- Bring in one box from the basement/attic/garage and go through it while you're listening to music or watching TV. Trust me, you'll be glad next week that you got a head start!

- Rearrange all the furniture in a room or all the artwork in your home. If it doesn't look good, rearrange it again.

Task 6:
TOSS OUT YOUR MALIGNANT ITEMS

If you've been mentally working your way up to shedding the malignant items from your living areas, now's the time to haul them out of your house or, if you have room in a storage space, put them there.

Frequently the malignant clutter I find in living rooms is more annoying than anything else. It might be dad's dusty high school swimming trophies from 1985 or mom's perpetually unfinished (but super messy) craft project that's been sitting on the TV tray in the corner of the room for the last 3 years. (The conflict these items can create between couples is what makes them malignant.)

Remember, the things you own should help you create the life you want. Any items—no matter how they came into your home—that don't help you create the vision you want for your space need to leave. Whether an item causes you minor annoyance or major distress, today is the day it has to go.

Week Five
Mindset Adjustment

Become more aware of how you're using your body. If you realize that you've been sitting still for too long—say, 30 minutes or more—get up and move around. Set an alarm on your phone to go off every 30 minutes, if you must. Stand up and stretch. Find a reason to walk around for a few minutes. Whatever you do, avoid being motionless for long periods.

Your body simply isn't designed to work properly when you're sitting down for too long. Your blood doesn't flow as smoothly through your circulatory system. Muscles in your back, abdomen, and legs get out of balance. Your bones don't get the physical challenge they need to stay strong. Fluid can accumulate in your lower legs. Even your brain may become sluggish.

Week Five Fitness Activities

Walking frequency: Go 5 days.

Duration: Take a 25-minute walk around your block, your neighborhood, the park, or on a treadmill if you have one. Walking in place while watching TV or listening to music works as well. As you walk, plan out your decluttering strategy for the day (or the following day if you're exercising in the evening).

In addition, perform the following movements on 2 or 3 nonconsecutive days after your muscles are nice and warm from walking or decluttering. While working on your living room, put on some of your favorite music; during the chorus of each song, choose one exercise and perform it for the length of the chorus before going back to organizing.

- Dance around the room
- Squat Kicks (page 180)
- Triceps Dips—on the couch or a coffee table that can safely support your weight; no glass-topped tables! (page 186)
- Mountain Climbers (page 174)
- Jumping Jacks (page 170)
- Sit on the couch and stand back up

The whole purpose of this program is for you to squeeze more *life* out of your life. No one in their final days says "I wish I'd sat around the house more, watching TV." (At least, it seems unlikely.) After 5 weeks of decluttering and becoming more physically fit, I hope your energy levels and your mood are riding high.

Once this program is over and you're not decluttering so much, I hope you continue to stay physically active, since that's a crucial component to keeping your weight off. I also hope you come to see your living room as a place where you get a little relaxation after a day with lots of motion.

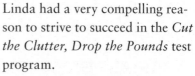

Linda Hayes, 58

POUNDS LOST: 7.6

AMOUNT OF CLUTTER REMOVED:
Roughly 7 bags

Linda had a very compelling reason to strive to succeed in the *Cut the Clutter, Drop the Pounds* test program.

Several months before she started, her son had offered to pay for a cleaning service as a gift. She was thrilled by the thought of housekeepers making her home sparkle every other week—but ironically, she had to declutter her home before her son would start the service. The maids, you see, will clean *around* the clutter, but they won't move it.

"One of the things my son was trying to do was get my home to where I can have people over," she says.

The Allentown, Pennsylvania, teacher sent me a photo of her living room before I first met her, and I could see a lot of clutter (given that it also functioned as a

Before

work area). A laptop computer and stacks of papers covered the coffee table. The couch was loaded with more papers and office supplies.

Linda was determined that she wouldn't miss out on her son's offer, so she dived into the program as a way to hold herself accountable. At the time, she faced a special decluttering challenge, one that many parents of adult children have been dealing with in recent years. Her daughter had moved back home for a time, filling Linda's ranch house with a *lot* more stuff.

The two decluttering principles Linda found most useful were to create a vision for every room in the home and to always remember that *clutter is decisions delayed*.

One decision she made was to change her newspaper subscription, since newspapers were stacking up unread. She switched to three newspapers a week and read the rest online. She tackled the stacks of paperwork, throwing away some and filing the rest. She tamed her closet by tossing out old swimsuits but keeping her 22-year-old "I Survived Hurricane Andrew" T-shirt, a memento of her earlier life in Florida.

She even talked about the importance of a clutter-free lifestyle with her middle school students during a lesson on stress. She pointed out that they could place their handouts in their folders where they belonged. Or they could delay the decision to put their stuff in the right place and just shove it into their backpacks, creating more clutter—and stress when they couldn't find their assignments.

When I talked to Linda after the program ended, contractors were remodeling her bathroom, which had introduced a certain amount of chaos into her home. But "other than that temporary transition, yes, it *definitely* looks decluttered."

Her son was also planning to have a landscaping company give Linda's yard a complete makeover. She was going to extend her new philosophy, which worked so well in her home, to her yard, too: She didn't want fancy features around her house that would require a lot of upkeep. "Instead, my word is *simplify!* I want to have less yard work so I have more time available to invite friends over."

Chapter 14

WEEK SIX: YOUR STORAGE AREAS (BASEMENT, GARAGE, ATTIC, SHED)

"US families have trouble getting rid of their possessions, even those they box up and move to . . . spaces such as garages and basements. Whether they cannot break sentimental attachments to certain objects, do not have the time to sort through and make decisions, or believe objects have value and could be sold on eBay, most families struggle to cope with stored clutter."

That's an observation from archaeologist Jeanne Arnold and her coauthors in *Life at Home in the Twenty-First Century.* Her project—which I discussed at the beginning of this book—provided a snapshot of the clutter in typical modern American homes.

This little passage summarizes the lives of the people I often encounter. Odds are good that it describes how *you* found yourself not so long ago, at the point where you needed to change your relationship with the contents of your home, too.

Throughout this book, I've discussed the three issues that contribute to a clutter problem:

1. An excessive urge to get more stuff. Our society encourages us to seek fulfillment from our material possessions. The ads we see, the stores we visit, and many of the cultural rituals we share teach us to cope with our worries and celebrate our happy moments by buying *stuff*.

Since you see people every day who are so pleased to be buying cars, furniture, appliances, dishes, and toys, it seemed perfectly normal to have a fondness for possessions. Similarly, accumulating more stuff over time also seemed like a normal way to show how well you're living: An expanding pile of belongings was like the line in a thermometer climbing upward, providing a measurement of greater comfort and abundance.

On the other hand, many people celebrate thriftiness as a virtue. So you may have gotten a thrill when you found decorative baskets for 30 percent off; kitchenware at a low, low price during a closeout sale; or a mountain of hand-me-down kids' clothes for free. But what you didn't realize was that you *didn't even need this stuff in the first place*.

The businesses in your community, the retailers selling through the catalogs in your mailbox, and the merchants around the world whom you can find with a computer click offer a vast, deep sea of items you can buy. In comparison, the space in your home is tiny! It's very easy to bring in more treasures from the outside world than your home can hold. Even if you carry just a little more into your home than you take out, eventually you're going to have a problem.

2. Reluctance to throw stuff out. If you were too emotionally attached to throw away, give away, or sell possessions you didn't really need, I completely understand how you would develop these feelings.

Again, we grew up in a society that puts a value on possessions. The messages we all receive throughout our waking hours is that owning stuff is good and that owning more stuff is better! Furthermore, society tells you that the stuff you own solves problems, provides happiness, and makes you more attractive to other people. Why get rid of something that could be useful someday?

In addition, our loved ones show that they care for us when they give us gifts. We also tend to fasten memories to objects. You may have held on to many of your possessions because they felt like souvenirs of wonderful times you've shared with people you loved.

For the most part, no one encourages you to get rid of stuff, unless it's broken, threadbare, or obsolete (like last year's athletic shoes or tablet computers that have been replaced with newer, better versions). In general, people don't understand why you would throw away something that could have sentimental value.

But just as an urge to buy stuff can cross over from being a socially acceptable value to a problem that interferes with your life, so can a desire to hang on to stuff. Most people I work with have overly cluttered homes for both reasons, to a varying degree.

3. Lack of organization. This is the jumble of papers that should be neatly filed in a cabinet or the pile of knickknacks crammed onto a bookshelf. It's the stuff that's out of place, like the laundry basket of shoes in the corner or the jumbo box of crayons scattered under the coffee table.

When people simply own so much stuff that organizing it neatly requires great effort, it's inevitable that clutter will creep in. Even if they have a *large*

▶ STORAGE FACILITIES—YES OR NO?

Off-site storage facilities are a great resource—but only as a short-term solution. Let's say you're relocating, you're remodeling your home, or you've inherited items that are too difficult to sort through in the immediate aftermath of your loss.

In any of these situations, I'd completely understand renting a storage unit for a month or two. Beyond that, I think that storage facilities perpetuate the notion of "out of sight = out of mind."

With rental fees automatically charged to your credit card every month, it's easy to lose track of the costs you're incurring. Storage facilities too easily enable you to lock stuff away and never deal with it—and that's not a good thing. All too often, the items in storage are not worth the fees you've incurred to stash them away. It's

not living mindfully, either, because you're not really paying attention to your possessions or your expenses.

If you have a storage unit, I'd challenge you to calculate how much you've spent on rental fees. Are you shocked?

If you have items in storage, this is your opportunity to deal with them. Arrange to have the contents of your storage unit delivered to your front yard next weekend. Rent a Dumpster. On Saturday, go through the items together with your family. Anything you no longer need or want, just leave it in your driveway with a sign that says "FREE!"

If anything is still left in your driveway on Sunday afternoon, place it in the Dumpster and have it hauled away. You'll eventually recoup the cost by not having a monthly storage bill.

home, I don't see the benefit in maintaining a bunch of stuff that they don't need in the first place.

If you own things, you have to take care of them. You have to clean them, dust them, and store them. Constantly tidying a mountain of possessions you don't really want or need is a major waste of your time, energy, and attention. Getting rid of the excess creates physical space around you, mental space in your head, and time in your schedule. I hope you've come to discover that for yourself.

For the past 5 weeks, you've been developing a new relationship with your possessions.

Before you started this program, *they* had too much control over *you*. But you've been learning to look at the stuff you own differently. You've gained an understanding of why you brought it all into your home and why you've been reluctant to part with it.

Hopefully, you've gotten to the point where you're only going to buy things that will help you attain the vision you've set for your life. And if you're going to keep each item that you already own, it's because it has a good reason to stay in your home. I hope you now know that it's not a good reason to keep something because you'd feel wasteful or guilty if you got rid of it.

I hope that *you* now have control over your possessions.

At the same time, you've been following an exercise program designed to help you get stronger and leaner. You may be carrying fewer unnecessary pounds that were hanging from your body like extra luggage. You may feel lighter when you move around. You may be able to carry heavy loads without becoming winded and sore.

All these discoveries you've made and all these challenges you've faced in the past 5 weeks of this program have been building up to this week's tasks. The entire program has led to this: It's time for you to tackle the clutter in your garage, attic, basement, shed, and any other storage areas.

Saving the Biggest Jobs for the End

These are usually the toughest areas, so I left them until now for a good reason. I hope you've been able to strengthen your body and your mind sufficiently to tackle these areas.

These tend to be the most densely packed spaces in and around the home.

You don't spend time in them every day. When you invite company over, you don't hang out in these rooms. Typically, their sole purpose—with the exception of any living areas in the basement and parking space in your garage, if you still have room for your car—is to store your stuff. So they may be even more overcluttered than the rest of your home.

When you address these areas, you're not just going to be deciding what to do with a few possessions. No, you'll likely be uncovering *hundreds* of items that will require one verdict after another: Do I keep this, do I donate it, do I give it to a friend or family member, or do I throw it out?

The stuff here tends to be big and heavy. It's often dusty and hard to carry. These are the trunks in the attic that were so hard to carry up that your back aches at the mere thought of moving them again. It's the massive mountain of boxes in the garage. It's the broken drill press in your workshop and the lawn edger in your shed.

You'll need to be strong and limber to handle these objects. You may need extra determination to make well-reasoned choices in an environment that's cramped, poorly lit, and scorching hot (or bone-chillingly cold and damp).

Another particular challenge you may face this week is that the possessions you keep in storage often have greater emotional weight. Again, clutter represents delayed decisions, and that's especially true for the stuff in storage. You may have stuck items in here not because you really wanted them, but because you weren't able to throw them out. These may be things that were just too painful to look at or address, and seeing them again is going to come as a blow.

The coming week may be hard, but the work you do will leave you in a better place going forward. Having storage spaces that are harboring these

▶ KNOW YOUR LIMITATIONS

If you sense that any boxes, furniture, appliances, or other heavy items will push the limits of your lifting and moving ability, recruit someone to help you.

Share some of your newfound decluttering philosophy with your helper and offer to return the favor when he or she tackles a basement-cleaning project someday.

Once you're finished with this program and doing long-term maintenance, it might be helpful to have a companion who supports your efforts to keep clutter away.

WEEK SIX TASKS

☐ Create your vision.

☐ Collect malignant items.

☐ Declutter each zone in each storage room.

☐ Get rid of malignant items.

Plus

☐ Mindset adjustment

☐ Physical activities

kinds of possessions isn't good for the physical state of your home or your emotional health.

I often use this analogy: If you're in a relationship with someone, and that person doesn't honor and respect you, then it's no surprise that the relationship quickly sours. It's exactly the same with the space in your home. If your home is holding on to things that you find upsetting, they act like old resentments and grudges buried in a relationship. Even though they're not out in the open, you know they're in there. Somewhere in your mind, you're waiting for them to spring out and upset you. You'll never feel comfortable, relaxed, and motivated in that space. Whether it's with another person or your living space, without honor and respect you can't have a nurturing, satisfying relationship.

You're so close to having a space that fully supports your physical and mental health. I'm confident that the skills you've been developing will carry you the final distance in creating it.

Task 1:
CREATE YOUR VISION OF THESE AREAS

Take a close look at all the storage areas you'll be tackling. Aside from being places to stash a large volume of possessions, what else might you want these areas to do *for* you? Other considerations you might want to keep in mind include whether you'd like to:

▸ Make room for a living area in your basement or attic

▸ Provide more open space so you can get in and around these areas easily

▸ Ensure that these areas don't pose health hazards or create threats to your home's value (like dampness in a basement or animal infestations in piles of stored items in your attic or garage)

- Create space for valuable items (How much sense does it make to keep your garage or shed filled with junk that you don't really want, while a $3,000 riding lawn mower or a $25,000 car sits outside in the elements?)

- Get rid of some of your possessions so you can display and appreciate a smaller number of treasured items

Ideally, would you like to be using your storage spaces differently? Now's the time to make it happen. While you're surveying your storage areas, break each of the rooms down into zones. Each zone could be a corner of the room, a stretch of wall, a space on the floor, a stack of storage shelves, or a cabinet.

Make a note of how you want to use each of these zones and what you'll keep or store in them. Mentally, envision like items in each zone. The physical limit of that zone determines the volume of items that you can place there. If the volume of stuff intended for a zone exceeds the space assigned for it, you know that there's only one thing you can do: Discard enough items so that what's left fits comfortably into the space.

STORAGE AREA VISION

This is what I want *from* my basement: _____

_____

_____

_____

This is what I want *from* my attic: _____

_____

_____

_____

This is what I want *from* my garage: _____

_____

_____

_____

This is what I want *from* my shed: _____

_____

_____

_____

How I want to *feel* in these spaces: _____

_____

_____

_____

Task 2:
SORT OUT YOUR MALIGNANT ITEMS

Don't be surprised if your storage areas turn out to be high-malignancy spaces. The stuff you unearth from deep in your piles of possessions is likely to contain things you've avoided dealing with for a long time, which may trigger particularly painful memories.

If you come across belongings that upset you, remind you of hard times, or make you feel like a person you don't want to be anymore, *now*'s the time to get rid of them. You're hopefully well on your way to being a healthier, more organized, more mentally awake person. Why keep this stuff around if it's going to interfere with the terrific progress you have going?

If you can't manage to throw away malignant items just yet, set them aside and do it as your final task of the program.

Task 3:
DECLUTTER ONE ZONE AT A TIME
UNTIL YOU'RE FINISHED

Pick a box, a corner, a portion of a storage area, or any other defined space that you can work through in one session, and get busy sorting and tossing stuff out. I like the idea of getting into the routine of pulling out one box of stuff each night before you eat dinner, then spending the evening doing a bigger sweep.

The usual rules you've been following elsewhere in your home apply here. In general, only keep items that:

- Are useful to you or that you know will be useful in the near future. The likelihood that you'll use stuff in storage is probably lower than for the stuff you found in the living spaces of your home. For example, if you encounter a box of Christmas decorations, keep the ones you actually use and let go of the ones you know you won't put up again. If a $5 string of lights doesn't work when you plug it in, discard it.

- Help you reach your current goals. Even if something was important to you a year ago, your needs and expectations may have shifted during this program. Is this still something you want?

Clearly label anything you're holding on to. Once you put an item into a box and put that box into the attic or basement, you'll quickly forget what's in it without a very descriptive label.

Special items warrant special consideration, such as:

Heirlooms. I can hear it already: "Peter, I can't get rid of *any* of this stuff my mother gave me. All of it represents the legacy she left behind." Here's the response I give people when they tell me that: "When you think that *everything's* important, then *nothing* becomes important." You have a sea of objects in which nothing stands out as meaningful.

In these situations, shift your task to finding the four treasures that are hidden among all this stuff you inherited. Find the four things that make your heart sing. Perhaps it's the four:

- Nicest collectible figurines your grandmother gave you over your lifetime

- Pieces of jewelry your mother wore the most often

- Paintings your father made that have the most artistic value

Give those four favorite items a place of special honor in your home. Frame them. Display them. Wear them. When you look at them, savor the emotional

▶ THINGS AREN'T PEOPLE

So you're digging around in your basement and you find, let's say, an ugly sweater that your mother gave you years ago. Don't get confused: This thing is *not* your mother. It's an ugly sweater.

When you get rid of it, you're not laughing in your mother's face or rejecting her love or wasting her money. All you're doing is taking a thing you own out of your house because you don't need it.

The things that people give you are *not* those people. You can keep loving these people even as you pass along the things they give you.

response you get. Those feelings may be stronger because they're not watered down by the not-so-great stuff you kept. Now give yourself permission to let the rest of the items go.

Of course, if you scan this pile of hand-me-downs and realize "I don't really see anything here I'd actually want to use or display in my home," then that's a good sign that it's time to pass these possessions on to someone else.

Mementos of your life. The same is true here. Pick out small, meaningful items like your yearbooks or your class ring and put them somewhere in your home where you can look at them more easily.

If you have a box of newspaper clippings of your high school sports career, pick out the best ones, frame them, put them on display or put them into a scrapbook, and let the rest go. If you're too embarrassed to make a big deal of your teenage athletic accomplishments, that's another sign that this stuff isn't worth saving.

If you still have an old wedding dress, do you really need to save it? Yes, it was likely expensive and commemorates a big day in your life. But are you planning on wearing it if you get married again? That's maybe *not* the best way to start a new marriage. Are you saving it for your daughter? What if she doesn't want it years from now? Will you want her to feel guilty for turning it down? What if it gets mice-eaten or water-stained in a few years?

Sell it or donate it, and someone could be making happy memories with it right now instead. Or you could make a decorative pillow for your bed from the dress. Whatever you do, ensure that the dress is treated with the respect it deserves, which doesn't mean leaving it in your basement for decades to come.

Your kids' belongings. If you're keeping your kids' baby clothes, homework assignments, toys, and books for them to enjoy looking at later or to give to their own kids a few decades from now, you may want to rethink your plan.

There's no guarantee that they'll ever get more than a moment of mild enjoyment from looking at this stuff. They may want to provide their own kids with *new* treasured possessions, rather than musty toys and books that have been sitting in a cardboard box for most of their lives.

Designate one bin or tote for each of your children. Clearly label it and then pick a few items that will carry the most sentimental value over the years—one or two items of baby clothing, a special blanket or rattle, some early art masterpieces and stellar school reports—to place in this "memory box." Then part with the rest.

Bulk consumer goods. If you've been storing giant jars of pickles or eight dozen rolls of toilet paper from the bulk-goods store, and your stockpile is

Annie Leonard, the founder of the Story of Stuff Project, travels a lot. On a trip to Nepal, she bought a beautiful pair of earrings that immediately became a treasured possession.

"They were so pretty! They were just $2 in Nepal, but when I wore them, people complimented them all the time. So when I went back, I bought 10 pairs, each with a different color stone in them. But all of a sudden, I didn't care about them as much. When I had one pair, I treasured them. When I had 10 pairs, they got lost, I didn't know where they went, and I stopped paying attention to them."

It's a basic principle in the field of decluttering: When you have a massive trove of similar items, you're not going to value each one very much. I see this all the time. When homes are cluttered with many similar items, the significance of any specific item diminishes dramatically. We're all familiar with the expression "quality, not quantity," and there's an aspect of that here. More is seldom better. And in my experience, "more" usually dulls the senses to the beauty and uniqueness that makes things special.

So make your home a place where you value quality rather than quantity. Keeping fewer sentimental items will make them more special to you.

simply taking up too much room, it's time to shrink it down. If you're not going to use something in the next 3 to 6 months, but it's still good, pass it on to someone who will, whether friends or a food bank.

If an item is past its expiration date, throw it out. It's wise to look for a bargain, but piling up vast reserves of food and personal goods that attract vermin and go bad before you can use them isn't a practical use of your home's space. The zombie apocalypse isn't happening anytime soon, and I guarantee that if it does, you'll have bigger problems than finding toilet paper!

Final Task

If you haven't ushered all your malignant items out of your home in the past 6 weeks, go around and collect them. Take them out. Put them in the trash, haul them to Goodwill, give them away on Freecycle, or sell them on eBay.

If you've stayed on track with the program and completely decluttered each area of your home during each week, congratulations! Your home is now free of malignant items that make you feel unhappy when you look at them. You also got rid of all the benign clutter that was lingering around, taking up your space and wasting your time but offering nothing useful in return.

Everything that remains has a good reason to be in your home. It has value to you, and it's not exceeding the space you've provided for it. Your home now reflects the more clearheaded and physically streamlined person who lives in it.

If you fell behind and didn't finish some of the areas of your home during their allotted weeks, that's perfectly fine. Now's the time to go back and complete the job. It doesn't matter that it's taking you longer than 6 weeks. All that matters is that you finish.

But . . . wherever you are right now, your job isn't over. It's actually just starting.

Week Six
Mindset Adjustment

People often want *me* to give them permission to discard their sentimental items. This week, learn to give yourself this permission.

As you go forward, when you find yourself wanting to hold on to objects that have a special meaning, ask *why*. Doing so isn't necessarily a bad thing. But before you cling to material possessions, be sure you understand why you're doing it.

Your home is only so big, and it'll never be able to hold everything that you want. Your hands are only so big, too. If you're carrying too much stuff, you might not be able to pick up something new that your life offers you.

Week Six
Fitness Activities

Walking frequency: Go 5 days.

Duration: Take a 30-minute walk around your block, your neighborhood, the park, or on a treadmill if you have one. Walking in place while watching TV or listening to music works as well. As you walk, plan out your decluttering strategy for the day (or the following day if you're exercising in the evening).

In addition, perform these movements on 2 or 3 nonconsecutive days after your muscles are nice and warm from walking or decluttering. Use objects you found in your basement/attic/garage/shed, such as antifreeze bottles or detergent bottles, to do the following:

- ▸ 10 Walking Lunges with Glute Kickback (page 187)
- ▸ 10 Woodchoppers (page 191)
- ▸ 10 Biceps Curls (page 163)
- ▸ 10 Shoulder Raises (page 176)

Use your basement stairs to do

- ▸ 10 pushups
- ▸ 10 Triceps Dips (page 186)

In addition, take four to five breaks during cleaning to go up and down your basement stairs (or any other stairs you have) for 1 minute to get your heart rate up.

Congratulations! You've reached the end of the 6-week program. If you're like the test panelists who served as the guinea pigs for the *Cut the Clutter, Drop the Pounds* program, some of the rooms of your home may be barely recognizable and your body has slimmed down to a leaner, fitter version.

Savor your success. Celebrate your accomplishment with a special (healthy!) dinner or a day trip with your loved ones. But please don't use this as an opportunity to stop paying attention to your home and health. These 6 weeks were intended to be the *start* of a new phase in your life. You didn't just shake up your existence so you could go right back to your old habits. Those will just lead you back to the cluttered, unhealthy life that caused you so much pain.

Truthfully, you're not going to have an end point when it comes to staying mentally and physically fit while living in an uncluttered home. If you're alive, you're not finished.

It's time to turn your attention now to long-term maintenance. In some ways, preserving your improvements is easier. In other ways, it requires even more focus and dedication. After all, we all live in an environment that encourages obesity. And now your home has a lot more open space, which has a tendency to invite new clutter.

But you now have plenty of tools to protect yourself from all the clutter that wants to reinvade your home and body. In the final chapter, let's talk about how to put those tools to work and learn a few new habits that will help create an additional shield around you.

Chapter 15

HOW TO MAKE YOUR POSITIVE CHANGES LAST A LIFETIME

I fly frequently, both around America and on regular trips to Australia, which means I witness a fair amount of airline-related drama. Every plane's a stage, I suppose, and there are lots of ready players.

Recently, as I was boarding a cross-country flight, a traveler put on quite the performance for the rest of us fellow passengers. At the time I found it inconvenient and annoying, although it did end up providing a useful teaching point for this book!

This passenger was blocking the aisle and preventing the rest of us from reaching our seats. As she repeatedly tried to slam her oversize carry-on luggage into the overhead bin, she shouted at the top of her voice, "I CAN'T BELIEVE THEY MAKE THESE BINS SO SMALL." The overhead compartment wasn't the problem that day. The problem was her luggage—or, more specifically, the size of her luggage. She would have sounded much more reasonable if she'd shouted, "I CAN'T BELIEVE I THOUGHT SUCH AN INAPPROPRIATE PIECE OF LUGGAGE WOULD FIT IN THIS OVERHEAD COMPARTMENT!"

When we board a plane, we know that the space available for our stuff is not flexible. The plane is a metal container with rigid dimensions, with no magically expanding overhead bins to be found. It contains a preset amount of space, and everything—passengers, crew, luggage, cargo, and equipment—is all accounted for in the allocation of this available space. The visual tool in every airline boarding lounge demonstrating the size of carry-on luggage that will fit into the overhead bin is a testament to how much space has been set aside for your personal items: not much.

Your home is similar. Just like the overhead bin, you only have the space you have. It doesn't expand. It will only comfortably hold so much stuff, and now, at the end of this program, you know exactly how much stuff that is.

In fact, you also know how much each room, each bedside table, and each shelf will hold. You know what your home looks like when it's overstuffed, and you know what it looks like when it's holding a reasonable amount. I'm guessing that you're now far more aware of how you *feel* when your spaces are overloaded—that feeling of being overwhelmed and unable to breathe, paralyzed by the things you own, and unable to feel peace and calm in your own home.

If you don't honor and respect your space, you can never feel completely at home in it. Your body also works like this.

For your body to thrive, you must show it honor and respect, too. It functions best within certain obvious limits. It's only designed to use a set number of calories per day. Only so much food, alcohol, and sugary drinks will "fit" within these limits. Unlike a plane or a house, however, your body can expand. And that's what it'll do when you choose to ignore its limits, showing yourself little honor and respect by taking in too many calories or the wrong type of foods and drinks and not burning off enough through physical activity.

You've now gone through a momentous period in your life. You've developed a new relationship with your body and your home. You've picked up new habits and shed old ones. Hopefully, your mind feels freer and less burdened.

Still, you've only been doing this for 6 weeks. That's not a lot of time. If you fall back into your old habits or return to your old ways of thinking, your home can descend into chaos again—pretty quickly. Your pounds can also return, and in a few months, you could be heavier than you were when you bought this book.

Somewhere, that airline passenger might be repeating the same dramatic performance with her luggage every single time she boards another plane. Right now she might be flushed with outrage, feeling surprised all over again as she shoves the suitcase with all her weight (and starting yet another trip unhappy).

This doesn't have to happen to you. Once you acknowledge some basic truths, then live your life with those truths in mind, you can maintain all your improvements for the rest of this year and next year and the rest of your years.

The central truth, when it comes to keeping your home and body decluttered, is this: *You only have the space you have.*

The space available for your stuff is *not* flexible. Your home only has so much space. Your body can only take in a certain number of calories and still maintain its current weight. When you use these limits as a starting point, you can adjust your behaviors to live an uncluttered, healthy life within the space you have.

In this final chapter, I'd like to review a few more habits that will help you maintain the improvements you've made in your home. I'll also highlight some advice that scientists have discovered while studying people who have preserved their weight loss for years.

The New Realities That Will Maintain Your Clutter-Free Home

I've said many times that successful decluttering and organizing doesn't start with "the stuff." It's not about the stuff. So often we get caught up in the things we own—especially if they're so overwhelming that they cause heartache and stress—and forget that change comes first in the way we *think* about what we own. It starts with our mindset and our routines.

So be sure to incorporate these ideas into your daily life to maintain and build upon the successes you've already achieved. These methods of maintaining a clutter-free and organized home may actually seem *too* simple. But I can guarantee that the simpler the maintenance strategy, the greater the impact it will have as you move forward.

1. Never forget the vision you have for your life, your home, and your personal spaces. I've asked you to detail your vision for the space you're tackling each week. Your vision is the foundation for deciding what objects come into a space, what you put into your body, and how you spend your time. By constantly revisiting the question "What do I want *from* my life?" or "*from* my space?" or "*from* my body?" you will be sure to keep your focus on the things that help you create your best life.

2. "Later" does not exist. Now is the time to do the things you need to do.
As I tell people at every opportunity I have, *clutter is decisions delayed*. The moment you begin to procrastinate—"I'll put this in its proper place later" or "I'll throw this away later because I feel too guilty to get rid of it now" or "I'll make the bed later," or use any sentence that contains the word "later"—you have begun to lose the battle against your stuff.

Instead, make all your decisions in the present moment. As you've learned throughout this book, remaining aware of the present moment—which is the only time that truly exists—dramatically improves your ability to live the life you really want.

This "I'll get to it later" thinking is very easy to slip into. It's the path of least resistance. It convinces us that we're dealing with things, even though we're not. If the thought occurs to you that you need to put something in its proper place or throw it away, do it now. "Later" is the best friend of clutter. Don't make it your friend, too.

3. Finish what you start. On a similar note, if you realize you need to do a task, carry it out to its end right now. Don't do part of it and plan to finish the rest later. If you stop too soon, then resume later, the task will take more time. In the simplest terms, complete the cycle!

Your laundry provides a great example of what I'm talking about. Have you ever done this? You run the washer but don't get around to drying the laundry. Two days later, you find that the damp load of clothing has turned into a mildewed, smelly mess. You have to waste your time, detergent, and electricity rewashing it before you can dry it.

Or maybe you've snacked on a bowl of salsa with chips, then set the bowl in the sink. The salsa remnants form a hard crust overnight, and you have to scrape it out before you put it into the dishwasher. Add up enough of these extra demands, and you've lost a substantial chunk of time you could have applied elsewhere. That's one of the benefits I hope you discovered from the *Cut the Clutter, Drop the Pounds* program. Yes, living a decluttered lifestyle does take a few extra moments here and several minutes there throughout the day. But often, these moments save you from getting mired in a lengthier hassle later. Like Leah, the test panelist you met in Chapter 12, discovered: A well-run and streamlined household frees up time you can put to better use.

No matter the task, complete the cycle. If you start a load of clothes, put them in the dryer when they're washed. When your clothes are dry, fold them and put them away instead of allowing wrinkles to set in while they linger in a pile.

When you use a dish, rinse it off and put it in the dishwasher right away. When you empty the container of milk, immediately jot it down on your shopping list. When you finish the toilet paper, replace the roll. When your car is running low on gas, fill it at the next station you see. When you bring the mail into the house, throw out the junk, open everything, and put items that need attention in the tray on your desk.

If you open something, close it. If you get something out, put it away. If you move something, put it back where it belongs. If you borrow something, return it. Regardless of the task, the key to maintaining an organized space is the same: Finish the cycle!

4. Honor and respect the physical limits of your space. I began this chapter with an emphasis on the limits of your space, but it's worth repeating here. This program has taught you to designate a space for the things you have, with a place for everything and everything in its place.

Thus, you should have a clear idea of how many items each space within your home will hold: How many shirts will hang in your closet; how many containers of berries you can fit into the produce drawer of your refrigerator; how many pairs of socks will go in your dresser and still allow the drawer to close; how many books will fit on your bookshelves; and how many bins of holiday decorations will reasonably fit in your garage while still providing room for your car.

By working within the limits that your home places on you, the things you own and the spaces that you have will stay tidy, uncluttered, and organized.

5. One in, one out. Maintaining the limits you've established is easier when you follow the simple technique of removing an item from your home for every item of a similar kind that you bring in.

A new one comes in, an old one *must* go out. When you come home from a back-to-school shopping trip, your kids have to get rid of as many clothes as they add to their closet. When you bring home new shoes, an old pair must go. When you buy a new can of beans, you have to eat or get rid of the can that was already in your cupboard. This technique maintains a balance in your home so that it never again becomes overstuffed. Practice the one in, one out technique until it becomes a natural part of the way your family operates.

6. Routines create order. I'm guessing that during the past 6 weeks, you've fallen into a pattern of exercising at a certain time, tackling your decluttering tasks in a certain order, shopping for healthy food at designated times, and preparing meals in certain ways.

By creating this daily rhythm of activity, you shifted into routines that support your healthier choices and more mindful living. Keep preparing your weekly meal plans at the same time each week, exercising at the same time each day, and dealing with your mail in a similar fashion each time you bring it into the house.

Decide now when you'll regularly clean and organize each room in your home so it doesn't fall into griminess or chaos for long. Now is also a good time to mark in your calendar when you'll reassess how your maintenance is going, whether 3 months, 6 months, or a year from now. Walk through your home, being mindful of what you see. Is each room still honoring your vision? Has your vision changed? Have circumstances in your household changed that require you to work harder in certain areas? By noting this commitment in your calendar, you acknowledge the importance of checking in on yourself and your home.

7. Perfection is never a reasonable goal. Listen carefully: I don't expect you or your home to be perfect! In fact, I believe that perfection is the enemy of an orderly, uncluttered home. When you strive for perfection, you remain constantly disappointed because the goals you set are simply unattainable, and so you are constantly falling short of where you think you should be.

Life is messy and it often gets tough, so expect a little failure here and there. It's not a bad thing if it causes you to reassess your progress, look at where you fell short, and recommit to a happier, healthier life. Being organized doesn't mean rigidly demanding a picture-perfect home. Organization is about creating the life and the home you want: happy, fun, warm, welcoming, and most importantly of all, a reflection of who you are as a person.

8. Turn clutter into kindness by continually collecting items for donation. In that spirit, keep a few small hampers around your home and toss in items the moment you realize you no longer want or need them. I'd recommend putting a hamper in your clothes closet and one in your entryway closet.

When you finish a paperback book, toss it in. When you realize your son's pants are too short, toss them in. When the kids no longer play with a toy, in it goes. Make a monthly appointment on your calendar—here's another routine!—to take the contents of your hampers to your nearest donation center. If you haven't collected enough to bother making a trip when donation day rolls around, survey your home and toss in more items, then load the car and make a trip that will turn your clutter into kindness for someone who's more needy.

9. Create decluttering traditions. As I noted earlier in the book, our society has all sorts of traditions that entail packing more stuff into our homes:

Christmas, Hanukkah, graduations, anniversaries, and so forth. But we don't have many rituals for shedding our possessions, aside from spring cleaning (which hardly anyone actually does).

As you now also know, living like the rest of society will lead your house to grow overstuffed again. So be different. Set up a family tradition to weed through your possessions several times a year, for a full 2 hours on each occasion. Pick dates that you'll remember, such as:

▸ When your quarterly taxes are due

▸ The week before each family member's birthday

▸ Midway through every school vacation (summer, spring, winter)

10. Think before you buy. For the rest of your life, being mindful of what you're doing and what you're buying *must* be an element of every shopping trip. The items that you buy should meet the following criteria before you hand over your money or credit card. They should:

▸ Contribute to the vision you have for your home and the life you want.

▸ Satisfy a need you have. That's a *true* need, not a momentary sense of boredom, sadness, or worry. A true need means "I dropped two plates last week and must replace them in order to serve dinner," not "If I buy these retro plates, my hipster friends might appreciate my cleverness when I have them over for dinner someday."

▸ Offer a real value. In your judgment, the thing you're about to buy should appear durable and should perform the function you need from it. Most important, if a low price is its only redeeming quality, you shouldn't buy it.

▸ Be the result of a well-thought-out decision, especially if it's expensive. In my experience, people have a particularly hard time parting with costly things that they bought in a spontaneous moment. That's usually the backstory behind the unused elliptical machine and the designer clothes with tags still on them.

▸ Work right now. New shoes must fit you today. Don't anticipate that they'll stretch out enough to become comfortable. Don't buy something if outside factors must fall into place before you can use it.

11. Lose your sense of guilt about gifts. People keep their homes filled with things they never wanted because they don't want to run the slightest risk of hurting a gift giver's feelings. Your commitment with gifts stops the moment after you say, "Thank you so much, this is so thoughtful of you."

Again, if a gift comes wrapped in obligation and tied with a ribbon of guilt, it's not really a gift at all. It's a punishment. It's a weight that someone expects you to carry. Learn to pass this stuff along to someone else.

Take it to Goodwill. Sell it online. Set aside a shelf in a closet or your garage for items that you'll "re-gift" to others. Before doing any of these things, check the item carefully to make sure it doesn't contain a card addressed to you.

If the gift giver confronts you later, be honest: "I loved it, but we have so much stuff in our house, I had to pass it on to someone who could use it."

The Changes That Will Help Make Fat Stay Away

Losing a substantial amount of weight is quite the accomplishment. But keeping it off for a long time? That's something of a rarity, many researchers have noted. Even the American College of Sports Medicine (ACSM) commented, "It is generally accepted that most individuals can lose weight but cannot maintain weight loss."

Researchers aren't exactly sure how many people who lose weight keep it off long-term. One reason is because studies tend to use different numbers to define weight loss, as well as different lengths of time that determine "long-term."

But it's safe to say that the majority of people who shed pounds for their 20th class reunion don't maintain their new weight to their 30th.

▸ A study that included more than 14,000 Americans found that about 1 in 6 adults who have ever been overweight or obese has lost at least 10 percent of the weight and kept it off long-term. The researchers noted that these numbers—which they found heartening—were more optimistic than previous studies had found. Also, they defined "long-term" as at least a year. I'm hoping you keep yours off much longer than that.

▸ An earlier study found that people who went through weight loss programs had gained back an average of about 77 percent of the lost weight after 5 years.

However, you can find lots more encouragement when you shift your focus to the people who *do* keep off the weight for many years, even if they are in the minority.

In 1994, a club of sorts began for people who were maintaining their weight loss, called the National Weight Control Registry. Much of what we know about keeping weight from returning for years comes from this group. To join, adults must lose at least 30 pounds and keep it off for at least a year. (I truly hope and expect that, if you incorporate this program's changes into your daily life and routines, you'll go on to maintain the weight loss for more than a year.)

Researchers studying the registry participants and other weight loss successes have found that the following habits appear useful—or even necessary— if you want to keep off the pounds you worked so hard to shed.

1. Move frequently and often. According to the ACSM, getting roughly 200 to 300 minutes of physical activity weekly may help you maintain your weight loss. While not enough studies are available to show *exactly* how much you need, research does suggest that following a "more is better" outlook is helpful, according to the ACSM.

A study of nearly 2,900 men and women in the registry supports the importance of physical activity. Over a 10-year period, these folks started with an average of 69 pounds lost and ended with 51 pounds still gone. However, those who did less exercise regained more weight.

Doing 300 minutes of physical activity each week—in other words, 5 hours—is a substantial endeavor. If you have a full-time job, kids, or both, this is likely going to account for a large percentage of your free time. Keeping your body moving for this long, and this often, will require some scheduling, planning, and dedication.

I highly recommend that you:

▶ Make exercise a priority. If your vision of your body is that it will remain fit, healthy, and able to function at a high level, then exercise is one of the habits that you must do regularly to achieve your vision. To create the time, cut out an activity that *doesn't* move you toward your vision (for example, television). According to the National Weight Control Registry, 90 percent of its participants exercise an average of about an hour a day. Also, 62 percent watch less than 10 hours of TV weekly.

▶ Accept it. Staying active appears to be mandatory if you want to keep off the weight. Struggling against this rule wastes your time and energy.

▶ Learn to love it. I came to enjoy physical activity relatively late in life. For a long time, I looked at exercise as something I had to suffer through. Now I get a lot of enjoyment from it. Find activities that you like to do. If you haven't found any yet, keep looking. Avoid doing the same type of exercise over and over, since this can lead to injury and burnout. Always set new goals for yourself and celebrate your improvements.

2. Weigh yourself. A Japanese study that followed 90 middle-aged people after they went through a yearlong weight loss program found that the participants who kept off weight were more likely to weigh themselves. The study of people in the National Weight Control Registry found that those who weighed themselves less frequently had more weight regain.

Yet another research project—which reviewed the results of 12 earlier studies that included more than 16,000 people—found that in 11 studies, those who weighed themselves weekly or daily lost more weight or maintained more of their weight loss. The researchers didn't know exactly how often you need to step on the scales, but they suggested that doing it weekly seems to be a reasonable schedule.

Three-fourths of the participants in the registry weigh themselves at least once a week. Weighing yourself every week is a sign that you're continually mindful of your weight. Though you're not overly focused on every day-to-day fluctuation, you're able to detect any weight gain before it becomes substantial. This weekly ritual also holds you accountable to your maintenance plan. Every 7 days, you have a reminder that you accomplished a powerful achievement and you're working to keep it going.

3. Keep an eye (and your mind) on what you're eating. You lost weight by moving more and being mindful of what you ate. We've already covered the importance of continued exercise. You also need to stay aware of what you're eating in order to enjoy long-term success.

That's the finding of a study that tracked 110 obese women for 3½ years after they went through a weight loss program. Those who kept an eye on their food and calorie intake—as measured by a questionnaire—were more likely to remain "successful" weight loss maintainers.

So keep eating lots of fruits, vegetables, lean meats, and whole grains. Limit junk food and heavily processed items. Remove any soda from your diet. Stay aware of the size of the portions on your plate and stop eating when you feel satisfied, even if you're not finished. Focus your mind fully on your food and turn off other distractions while you're eating.

Remember: New physical activity and eating habits led to your weight loss. You can't return to your old ways and expect to keep your new weight.

4. Plan ahead. The women in the study mentioned above who kept off their weight were also more likely to plan their meals ahead of time. This makes perfect sense to me. When you keep your kitchen stocked with nutritious options and you think about what you'd like to eat at future meals, you set yourself up for success.

This keeps you from reaching for the easiest option—such as fast food or takeout—when you're hungry and don't have anything at home to eat. Taking time to plan out your meals might also serve a function similar to weighing yourself: It reminds you that you're taking deliberate steps to protect the investment you made in your health when you lost that weight.

5. Keep going. The study that followed participants in the National Weight Control Registry for 10 years found that people who'd kept their weight off for longer tended to *continue* keeping it off. Perhaps this is a matter of becoming more comfortable with your health habits as time goes by. Staying active, keeping an eye on your weight, and making smart food choices may become easier with more practice.

As your unhealthy old habits grow smaller in the rear-view mirror, hopefully the memories of the good feelings they gave you grow fainter and fainter.

Nanette Cooley, 54

POUNDS LOST: 20.6

AMOUNT OF CLUTTER REMOVED: 12 to 15 bags

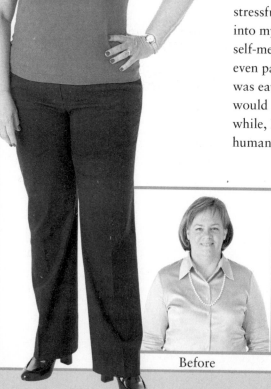

Before

Nanette knows where her journey into clutter began: in her childhood home. "I grew up in the house that my grandparents built when they were first married," she explains. "There were three generations of us in this house, and a lot of antiques, dishes, furniture, and *stuff* had accumulated over the years. When my mother passed away, I inherited it."

It's also no mystery how she put on extra pounds. "I would come home from work after a stressful day, and I'd throw things into my mouth," she says. "I was self-medicating with food and not even paying attention to what I was eating. Whatever I could find would go into my mouth. After a while, I almost felt like I was a human garbage can!"

She definitely learned how to conquer both challenges. Nanette had the distinction of losing the most weight of all the women in the program—and she had the second-biggest weight loss overall. Not only did she lose 3 inches from her waist and nearly 3 inches from her hips, she also shed almost 10 percent of her body weight!

"Before, I wasn't able to stick to a plan. I wasn't able to stick to my goals. I would get frustrated. There were always personal issues coming up, and I would have stress and anxiety," she says. But this time, "I did everything in my power to position myself where I would not fail with the program. I maintained the exercise program and the mindfulness and tried to stick to the eating program. I just resigned myself to the fact that *I would not fail with this*."

She sorted through the possessions that two generations of her family had left in her care. "The program gave me permission to donate those things, to get rid of those things, to let it go without feeling guilty about it."

She set aside another day just to wrestle her closet into control. "My wardrobe closet was a disaster. I had probably two or three sizes of clothing, shoes I've collected over the years, and stuff I didn't want out in my visual space, so I'd throw it in there to get it out of sight," she says. "I spent the whole day cleaning that closet, and it was a *transforming* experience."

We spoke after the program was finished, but Nanette was still seeing improvements from all her new habits. "Now before I put something into my mouth, I think, 'Is this something important to me? Is it something I need? Is it something that's going to nourish me in the proper way?' I had a stressful day at work just the other day, and there was candy and junk around. I said, 'I'd love to have one of those candy bars. But no, that is not going to do me any good. It's not going to help serve my purpose,'" she says.

"I'm most grateful that I set up some great behavioral patterns. I'm continuing with the program and I've lost even more weight."

AFTERWORD

When I work with *over*cluttered, *under*happy clients, the time we spend together is frequently very emotional. Sometimes they cry in frustration. Sometimes they grow tense as they reflexively cling to the contents of their homes. Sometimes they argue with their spouses.

But their feelings tend to turn positive as they see the improvements they're making. As they walk around the rooms that are no longer cramped, I see the freedom in their faces. As they haul out bag after bag of trash and items for donation, it's as if all this weight were physically coming off their shoulders.

If we stay in contact afterward, I frequently hear about how they've found new happiness and direction in their lives, which had gotten buried under all their clutter. My clients begin to see how the clutter in their home affects every other element in their life—especially their weight and overall well-being. For me, it comes down to a simple principle that I repeat over and over: You simply cannot make your best choices or your healthiest choices in a cluttered, messy, disorganized home.

I can't tell you how meaningful it was for me to work so closely with the volunteers who signed up to go through this program, then carefully track their progress over time. Not only did I watch their weight fall and their clutter levels subside, I received real-time updates on all their joys and discoveries.

I hope you'll share your own successes from this program with me and the other readers of this book through social media. Believe me, I will be celebrating with you, whether you've just lost the clutter and the weight, or you're maintaining your progress for yet another year.

At the end, I'd like to turn things over to Melissa H., one of the test panelists, who can say it far more eloquently than I:

I have to say that these past 6 weeks went really fast. But 6 weeks was long enough to start some new habits. As for the diet, I can honestly say I started making better choices. As for the exercises, I did struggle with finding time to declutter and do the exercises at the same time. But I am consciously making an effort to walk and MOVE more! As for the decluttering, I was not able to declutter my entire house in 6 weeks, but just getting started has motivated me to keep going. Keep putting one foot in front of the other. This book is not just about the 6 weeks in the plan, it's about what we learned over the 6 weeks that helps us each and every day for the rest of our lives.

ACKNOWLEDGMENTS

So many people have helped to take this book from a vague idea to the object that you're holding in your hand. It's impossible to thank them all.

To my life partner and husband, Ken—always there, always encouraging, always on my side. This book is as much his as mine.

To my family and friends—I'm guessing that it's often not easy living with or spending time with the "organizing guy." I just wish that after all this time you'd all realize it's really not necessary to close the doors to your spare rooms every time I visit! Thank you for the support, the good humor, and the constant encouragement.

To Nancy Fitzgerald, then at Rodale, who made the first call. It was her enthusiasm and belief in this project that started the ball rolling, and her initial guidance was invaluable.

To a wonderful wordsmith Eric Metcalf—this is our first collaboration and I hope not our last. It's a huge pleasure to work with someone as skilled, smart, and unflappable as Eric. His ability to whip a paragraph into shape, to locate the best piece of research, or to find just the right scholar to chat with is incredible.

To the brave and wonderful people who volunteered as test panelists to trial the 6-week *Cut the Clutter, Drop the Pounds* program:

Megan Billowitch, Amy Blythe, Margie Cherry, Nanette Cooley, Kristen Downey, Jan Eickmeier, Elizabeth Erwin, Brenda Hanna, Linda Hayes, Melissa Heckman, Dayl Klinger, Melissa Leo, Maria Luci, Robin Musselman, Maria Ramroop, Marcia Rehrig, Tiffany Rehrig-Schaeffer, Joe Shigo, Suzanne Smith, Julie Stewart, Marcia Teeno, and Leah Zerbe.

Thank you not just for your enthusiastic involvement but also for your honesty, perseverance, and humor. This was an adventure for us all, and your part in it all was critical in shaping the early direction of the program and what has found its way into this book.

Thanks also to the skilled scholars, researchers, and authors who so generously shared of their knowledge and experience:

Jeanne Arnold, PhD; Edie Goldbacher, PhD; Annie Leonard; Kristin Neff, PhD; James Roberts, PhD; Jenny Taitz, PsyD; Kiara Timpano, PhD; David Tolin, PhD; Diana Winston; and Peter Whybrow, MD.

To the wonderful exercise physiologist Liz Davis, BA, MS, for her assistance with the exercise program and the photos that help us all to maintain good form when getting into shape!

To my collaborators and contributors at Rodale—my editor Marisa Vigilante, Katie Kackenmeister, and the Rodale sales and marketing teams including Anne Egan, Brent Gallenberger, Emily Weber Eagen, and Lori Magilton. This book is our first project together and already I know that I have one of the best teams in the business working with me.

Finally, to all of you who have enthusiastically supported my work these many years—we all know that what we own can bring us great happiness or a crushing sense of paralysis. It's been through your willingness to share your stories, to tell honestly of your struggles, and to allow me into your homes and lives that I've been able to help chart a course that I believe will enable us all to live richer, fuller lives.

INDEX

Underscored page references indicate sidebars and tables. **Boldface** references indicate photographs and illustrations.

failure to discuss, <u>264</u>
improved, after
    organizing home
    office, 265
stress about, 263–64,
    <u>264</u>
Finishing projects, for
    maintaining
    clutter-free home,
    310–11
Fitness activities. *See*
    Exercise(s)
Flat surfaces. *See also*
    Horizontal surfaces
clearing, in living room,
    285–86
Floor, bedroom, clearing,
    234–35
Focus, survey for
    measuring, 43–44
Food
    disallowed in bedroom,
        228, 231
    memories of, 203–4
    prepared, in refrigerator,
        <u>203</u>
Food attitudes, examining,
    204
Food choices
    analyzing, 201
    poor, clutter causing, 25
Food preparation items
    necessary, 212
    types to discard, 208,
        213
Food shopping, <u>199</u>
Freebie snacks, <u>154–55</u>
Freezer, 209–10, <u>210</u>
Fruits, as snacks, <u>150–51</u>
Functional fitness plan. *See
    also* Exercise(s)
    development of, xv,
        79–80
    purpose of, 81
    results from, 80, **80**
Furniture
    living room, malignant,
        284
    rearranging, 236, 288
Future
    saving items for, 20–21,
        29
    worrying about, 53

G

GAD-7, for measuring
    anxiety, <u>40–41</u>
Games, as family activity,
    287, 288
Garage. *See* Storage areas
Generalized anxiety
    disorder, 28
Generalized Anxiety
    Disorder 7-Item
    (GAD-7) Scale,
    <u>40–41</u>
Ghrelin, increasing
    appetite, 225
Gift cards, <u>264</u>, <u>270</u>
Gifts
    emotions attached to,
        12–13, 294
    guilt about discarding,
        16–17, 313–14
    wrong reason for
        keeping, <u>301</u>
Glassware, 213
Goldbacher, Edie, 45, 46
"Good enough"
    philosophy, vs.
    perfection, 273
Greed-reduction classes,
    57–58, 63
Guilt
    about discarding gifts,
        16–17, 313–14
    after emotional eating,
        46
    as reason for keeping
        items, 6, 57, 237,
        296

H

Hampers, for collecting
    donations, 312
Hanna, Brenda
    on benefits of
        mindfulness, <u>56</u>
    success story of, <u>88–89</u>,
        88
Happiness, 10, 21, 64–66
Hayes, Linda, success story
    of, <u>290–91</u>, **290**
Health problems, chronic,
    from sleep
    deprivation, 226

Heirlooms, reluctance to
    get rid of, 301–2
Hoarding and hoarding
    disorder
    ADHD with, 28, 32
    anxiety with, 27–28, 32
    clutter vs., 15, 25,
        26–27, <u>26</u>
    continuum of, <u>26</u>
    depression with, 28, 32
    obesity linked to, 23,
        24–27
    prevalence of, ix
    survey scores indicating,
        38, 39, 78
    traits for diagnosis of, 39
Hobby area, in dining
    room, 215
Home
    embarrassment from, vii
    factors influencing state
        of, 34
    limited space in, 309
        airplane analogy
            about, 307–8
    respecting, 311
    rating condition of, xi
Home office
    clutter in, negative effects
        of, 7, 263–64
    decluttering tasks, <u>265</u>
        cleaning off horizontal
            surfaces in zones,
            271
        creating a vision,
            265–66, <u>266</u>
        dealing with
            malignant items,
            275
        establishing zones,
            267–70
        organizing file
            cabinets and
            storage spots, 271,
            273
        organizing Zone 3,
            274–75
        sorting out malignant
            items, 266–67
    limits in, <u>268</u>
    supplies for, 268–69, 270
    systems in, <u>268</u>
    virtual clutter in, <u>272</u>

Weight gain. *See
  also* Obesity;
  Overweight
causes of
  aging, 26, 157
  sleep deprivation, 225
  failure to notice, viii–ix,
    157
Weight loss
  benefits of, 296
  commitment for, 158
  from decluttering, xiv,
    79, 159–60
  difficulty of, 73, 82
  maintenance of (*see*
    Maintenance, of
    weight loss)
  managing expectations
    for, 83–84
  new clothing after, 254
  potential for, xiii
  recommended physical
    activity for, 158

success stories (*see
  Clutter Chronicles*)
temporary vs. lasting,
  33–34
time frame for, 73
unrealistic goals for,
  246–47
Whybrow, Peter, 8, 9
Winston, Diana, 55,
  57–58, <u>59</u>, <u>61</u>,
  63, 64
"Wish clothes," problem
  with keeping,
  245–47
Woodchoppers, 191, **191**,
  305
Work
  average time spent on,
    viii
  reduced calorie burning
    from, 279–80
  sitting at, 279
Workout videos, 287

Work supplies, disallowed
  in bedroom,
  228–29, 231

Y

Yoga, 159, 160. *See also*
  Exercise(s)

Z

Zerbe, Leah, success story
  of, <u>276–77</u>, **276**
Zones
  dividing rooms into, 209
  home office, 267–70
  kitchen, 212
  storage area, 300–303